PTM

The Power Trial Method

PTM

The Power Trial Method

David J.F. Gross ▪ Charles F. Webber

The National Institute for Trial Advocacy (NITA)

© 2003 by THE NATIONAL INSTITUTE FOR TRIAL ADVOCACY, INC

Anthony J. Bocchino,
NITA Editor in Chief
Temple University Beasley School of Law

Zelda Harris,
NITA Associate Editor
University of Arizona College of Law

Gross, David J.F. and Charles F. Webber, *The Power Trial Method* (NITA, 2003)

ISBN 155681-770-3

Library of Congress Cataloging-in-Publication-Data

Gross, David J. F., 1963-
    The power trial method : PTM / David J.F. Gross, Charles F. Webber.
        p. cm.
    Includes index.
    ISBN 1-55681-770-3 (alk. paper)
    1. Trial practice--United States. 2. Jury--United States. I. Title: PTM. II. Webber,
Charles F., 1965- III. Title.

KF8915.G76 2003
347.73'52--dc22   2003068641

Preface

We are a couple of trial lawyers who love to talk about trials. We constantly talk to more experienced trial lawyers, younger lawyers, and each other about what works and what doesn't work at trial. We learned a great deal from these people. From these discussions, we developed a full-day seminar on "How to Win Your Next Civil Jury Trial," a series of law school lectures, and an intensive in-house trial practice program at our law firm. This book is an extension of these activities. It is an effort to write down what we have learned so far and to share it with others. We do this with the recognition that we have a lot more to learn.

The book is called the *Power Trial Method* (or *PTM*) for two reasons.

First, it's a great name. Who wouldn't want to learn something called the Power Trial Method? Other names have been considered (one of our partners suggested the "Adequate Trial Method," also known as "ATM"), but none of the other names had that special ring to it.

Second, we really believe that too many trial lawyers lose sight of the simple and obvious fact that, as we like to yell out at seminars, "It's a JURY trial!" Too many trial lawyers believe it's *my case*, and *my* witness, and *my* trial. They are wrong. The *jury* has the power to decide whether you win or lose. (The judge plays a role as referee and can certainly take the case away from you, but the judge is *not* back in the jury room making the decision.) Once you see that the jury has the primary power, then you need to think about how to tap into that power on behalf of your client. This book teaches you how to do that.

The book covers the basics of civil jury trials (most of which would apply to criminal trials as well) and provides the same type of advice one would hear from any experienced trial lawyer or, for that matter, any good book on trial practice (of which there are many). But the book discusses these approaches and methods through the PTM lens and strives to make learning about trials fun and fast. And this latter point is probably what distinguishes our seminars and this book from others: There are very few, if any, trial practice books or materials that can be described as fun or a quick read.

We would like to thank Jerry Snider, one of the best trial lawyers in America, for teaching each of us how to try a case the right way. There are many other lawyers (both inside and outside our firm) who have also guided us along the way, but if we start naming names we might leave someone out.

We would also like to thank everyone who assisted in creating this book. Jack Fribley approved the project and provided constant support. Colleen Sheffler (with support from Jeff Johnson) of the Minnesota State Bar Association's Division of Continuing Legal Education guided us through our trial practice seminars and offered many helpful suggestions. Several colleagues were instrumental in editing earlier drafts of the manuscript, including John Connelly, Tamera Durst, Debbie Ellingboe, Margaret Flesher, Brian Freeman, Jim Hartnett, Colleen Sheffler, and Karen Wilson. Kim Curtis designed the cover pages and assisted in the overall design of the book. Anita Pelzer designed and implemented the text and graphics (with assistance from Cheryl Fautch). Our Legal Administrative Assistants, GloryAnna Hegeholz and Jerri Lou Holmgren, also helped along the way.

Finally, we would like to give special thanks to our loving families (Teresa, Chelsea, Hayley, and Isabelle Gross and Denise, Daniel, and Michael Webber) for their wonderful support.

David J.F. Gross

Charles F. Webber

Faegre & Benson LLP

About the Authors

David J.F. Gross is a graduate of Harvard Law School, *magna cum laude*, a former law clerk to the Honorable Levin H. Campbell of the United States Court of Appeals for the First Circuit in Boston, Massachusetts, and a former Trial Attorney for the Civil Division of the United States Department of Justice in Washington, D.C. One of Faegre & Benson's lead trial lawyers, Gross was lead trial counsel for Wyeth in *Wyeth v. Natural Biologics*, a successful trade secret trial involving the billion-dollar drug Premarin®. He teaches Basic and Advanced Patent Litigation at the University of Minnesota Law School.

Charles F. Webber is a graduate of the University of Chicago Law School, Order of the Coif, and a former law clerk to the Honorable Frank H. Easterbrook of the United States Court of Appeals for the Seventh Circuit in Chicago, Illinois. He has won civil trials involving securities, commercial warranties, conversion, civil rights, legal malpractice, and other areas. He was lead trial counsel and obtained a complete defense verdict in the prominent whistleblower case, *Chadwell v. Koch Refining Co.*

Summary of Contents

Contents

Chapter 1

Where's the Power?

The PTM method begins with a simple question: Where is the power in the courtroom at trial? Who really has the power to decide whether you win or lose? In this chapter, you'll learn:

▲ why you should focus on power in the courtroom

▲ who has the power to decide whether you win or lose

▲ how that power is used in most cases

Introduction

This book addresses a wide variety of trial skills, including how to connect with the jury (chapter 2), develop themes (chapter 3), prepare for trial (chapter 4), present your opening statement (chapter 5), examine witnesses (chapter 6), introduce evidence (chapter 7), use demonstrative exhibits (chapter 8), make objections (chapter 9), deal with experts (chapter 10), handle jury instructions (chapter 11), give your closing argument (chapter 12), and conclude your trial (chapter 13). Before turning to these topics, however, we will consider the threshold issue of assessing who has the power to decide who wins at trial.

Who Has the Power?

Who will declare the winner in your next trial?

There are three power sources at trial. The jurors are the principal power source, as they have the ability to decide whether you win or lose in almost every case. Trial judges are another important power source. They can short-circuit or nullify the jury's power by entering a directed verdict. The appeals courts are a third power source. They have the power to overturn the jury's or judge's decision and declare a new winner.

Who has more power: the jury, the trial judge, or the appeals courts? This question is a bit more complicated than it sounds. To arrive at an answer, it may help to work backwards from appeal to post-trial to trial.

Power Sources

The Jury

The Trial Judge

Appeals Courts

Appeals Courts

The appeals courts have the final say in deciding who should win at trial, so at first blush you would think that they have the most power. But they are limited in several respects.

They cannot exercise their power—and decide who wins or loses—unless an appeal is brought. Appeals are not brought in many cases because parties often settle after trial or agree to comply with a judgment. When appeals are brought, the scope of review in many areas of law (some more than others) is quite narrow.

Don't hang your hat on the appeals courts.

Guidelines and rules also apply to appellate briefs. Lawyers cannot raise every issue on appeal but instead must choose only a few potential winners. This means that much of what occurs at trial, and affects who wins or loses, is not brought to the attention of the appeals courts, making them powerless when it comes to those issues.

These limitations and others suggest that in most areas of the law appeals courts are not the principal power source at trial.

Trial Judges

Trial judges have the ultimate say about who wins or loses at trial, and they have the advantage of listening to the evidence at trial and entertaining motions before, during, and after trial. While they are limited by rules and traditions that narrow the scope of review of a jury verdict, they can shape the record—and decide who wins or loses—much more deliberately than can the appeals courts. This leaves judges with an enormous amount of power.

Trial judges can also influence the jury by making evidentiary and other legal rulings. And the judge can influence the jury by sending the jury non-verbal and verbal messages about who should win or lose. Juries respect judges and usually follow the judge's lead. If the judge is showing favoritism of any kind, it will affect the jury.

The jury has the initial power to decide who wins:

Jury Verdict

ABC Company, Plaintiff

v.

XYZ Company, Defendant

We, the Jury find for the

___✔___ Plaintiff

_____ Defendant

But the trial judge and the appeals courts have the power to trump the jury's decision:

Jury Verdict

ABC Company, Plaintiff

v.

XYZ Company, Defendant

We, the jury find for the

 Plaintiff

 Defendant

Accordingly, and as a matter of abstract theory, trial judges may have the most power of the three groups at trial. Whether they choose to exercise that power, however, is a separate question. (See below.)

The Jury

If given a chance by the trial judge, the jury decides who wins or loses at trial, though this decision is subject to review by the trial judge and the appeals courts. How extensive is this power?

It depends.

If the judge plays a minimal gate-keeping role during trial and gives the jury wide latitude in making its decision, then the jury is the true power source at trial. The jury will hear the evidence, listen to the arguments, and then decide who wins or loses. The verdict will be final. And that will end the matter.

Judges have a mountain of discretion to use at trial.

Conversely, if the judge does everything possible to keep power away from the jury (both during and after trial), then the jury is a minimal power source at trial. The jury will hear only certain evidence (and may not hear other important evidence), will listen to only certain arguments, and will make a preliminary decision on who wins or loses that will be subject to close scrutiny by the assertive trial judge, who will make the final decision.

In such circumstances, the trial judge may choose to reverse the jury verdict and pick a new winner. This is the reality of trial practice.

How is Power Used At Trial?

Because the jury's power depends on the extent to which the judge exercises her power, the real issue at trial is not "Who has the power?" but "Who is exercising the power?"

In most cases, the trial judge will give the primary power to decide who wins or loses to the jury. In doing so, the trial judge will choose not to play a major gate-keeping role and not to overturn the jury's verdict. It is this delegation of power that usually makes juries the principal decision-maker at trial.

PTM

Chapter 2

The PTM Approach to a Jury Trial

When you enter the courtroom and begin a trial, you need to consider how power is used in that courtroom, and then do everything you can to tap into those power sources. In this chapter, you'll learn:

▲ how to assess the trial judge's use of power

▲ how to persuade the jury to use its power

▲ what it means to be a PTM trial lawyer

Assessing Power in the Courtroom

As you prepare for trial, a threshold issue is the extent to which the trial judge will assert herself both during and after trial. To what extent will she use her power in the courtroom? This issue can be broken down into three simple questions about the trial judge:

▲ How does the judge run her courtroom?

▲ What are the judge's tendencies on objections and the questioning of witnesses?

▲ To what extent will the judge direct a verdict or throw out a jury verdict?

As you begin to answer these questions, you will be more prepared for, and better able to react to, the power sources at trial.

Tap Into the Jury's Power

Since in most cases the jury will decide whether your client wins or loses, you will need to focus on the jury and develop an approach to tapping into the jury's power. To do so, ask yourself the following questions:

1. Do I view trial through my own eyes?

2. Do I act like someone else at trial?

These are difficult, but important, questions.

3. Am I nervous and intimidated at trial?

4. Do I look unorganized at trial?

5. Do I fear the unknown at trial?

6. Am I acting like a jerk?

If you answer "yes" to any of these questions, you are not respecting the jury's power and, as a result, you are travelling down the road to failure at trial. The PTM approach lets you take full advantage of the jury's power so you can present your best case in the proper environment.

1. View the trial through the jury's eyes

Who has the power to choose the winner and loser at trial? A small group of citizens who probably have never met each other before the case, never served on a jury, never gone to law school, never sat quietly and listened to someone ask people questions for an entire day (let alone several days), and never understood concepts such as causation, burden shifting, foundation, hearsay, and other legal concepts you did not understand yourself until law school or beyond.

Welcome to our jury system.

So how do you tap into the power held by the group of citizens who will decide your client's fate? You need to place yourself in the position of the jurors and view the trial through their eyes.

This will be a challenge for you. As a trial lawyer, your greatest asset—and your greatest liability—is your knowledge of the law and the facts of your case. It's a great asset because you could not win your trial without knowing the legal rules and the specific facts of your case. It's a tremendous liability because the jury does not share your knowledge, and thus you need to set all that knowledge aside to see your case through the jury's eyes.

Once you set that knowledge aside, think about how you would act if you were on the jury for your trial. Forget your legal training for a minute and try to figure out how you would act if you were a real person. You know you would try to pay attention to the testimony and evidence, and you would certainly try to achieve a just result. But how else would you act?

Shortcuts

"If I were a juror in my trial, I would have trouble understanding the complexity of my case, and I would look for reasonable shortcuts to help me decide complex issues."

If your case has any complexity to it, you would have a difficult time resolving that complexity without taking some major shortcuts. Why? Consider the following thought experiment:

You have just been transported to an advanced chemistry class at a major university. A complex equation is on the chalkboard, and two professors are debating whether the equation is correct. One of the professors says that the equation is correct. She describes the underlying chemical theories in great detail and says, convincingly, that the equation is right. The other professor says that the equation is all wrong. She also describes the underlying chemical theories in great detail and says, convincingly, that the equation is wrong.

The professors turn to you, someone who has no background (let's assume) in chemistry, let alone advanced chemistry, and they ask you to determine who is right and who is wrong. You are not allowed to look at any textbooks or to ask any questions. You must decide solely on the basis of what you heard and what you saw on the chalkboard.

How would you vote? What more would you need to know? The background of each professor? They are both from prestigious universities and have published textbooks on chemistry. The demeanor of each professor? Each appears generally trustworthy. The financial incentive of each professor? One professor will win money if she's right and the other will lose money if she's wrong. Again, how would you vote?

The truth is that you would have no idea how to decide this problem. You don't know anything about chemistry (if you do, select another field for your thought experiment), and you simply cannot assess who is right and who is wrong.

If you can't decide who's right, what do you think a jury would do?

Yet as a juror, you need to decide issues that are just as complex as the above example, even though you lack the expertise and ability to do so. So how do you do it?

Juries use reasonable shortcuts to decide complex issues, and your job as a PTM trial lawyer is to figure out and use the best shortcuts so that the jury can support your client's case. Coming back to our chemistry class example, suppose one of the professors had written a memorandum admitting that the other professor was right. Even if the professor later tried to explain that memo away, you might rely on the memo—and not the merits—to decide who is right. This example shows you the power of admissions by a party opponent, as such admissions are a shortcut the jury uses to decide a complex issue.

Another shortcut involves a credibility assessment. If one of the professors appeared to be lying about a collateral fact—such as whether she received a kickback on textbooks used in her classroom—you might discount her entire testimony on the merits for that reason alone.

The various shortcuts available to a jury are of infinite variety, yet they always involve simple issues, such as whether an expert witness appears evasive, whether the witness has the proper credentials, whether a company has improper motives for bringing a lawsuit, whether a company has destroyed or lost key documents, and even whether a lawyer has proven what she said she was going to prove.

You win or lose trials often on the basis of these shortcuts. Experienced trial lawyers know this. Inexperienced trial lawyers do not.

Have you made a list of shortcuts for your next trial?

Lack of Control

"If I were a juror in my trial, I would be frustrated by my lack of control, and I would react negatively to anyone who seemed to take advantage of my lack of control."

Whether they wanted to serve on a jury or not, whether they viewed jury service as an honor or as a burden (or both), every juror is frustrated by the immediate loss of control that comes with sitting on a jury.

Before they enter a courtroom, potential jurors must sit in a crowded room with little or no food and wait—and wait—to be called to a courtroom. By the time they see you, they may already be tired or cranky.

When they are finally selected for a trial, they then must adhere to a strict set of rules governing their conduct. They arrive each day at a time set by the judge. They typically sit in an assigned seat. They take a break at a time set by the judge. Other people —the lawyers and the judge—decide the order of witnesses and the questions that will be asked of those witnesses. Other people decide what exhibits to give the jury. Sometimes the jury doesn't even get to see the exhibits, even though seemingly everyone else in the room gets to see them. The jury has no say over any of these matters.

And it gets worse. Sometimes the lawyers and the judge discuss things quietly at the side of the bench, and the judge orders the jury not to listen. Sometimes the judge abruptly excuses the jury for a long or short break while the lawyers and the judge talk about some unknown issue or problem. And sometimes a trial that was supposed to last three days lasts almost three weeks.

How would you feel if you were treated like that?

Jurors resent constant side bars and other interruptions.

Suppose someone sent you to a continuing legal education seminar, and you learned at the seminar that you could not pick the subject matter of the seminar, that you could not pick the speakers, that you could not arrive late, that you could not leave the room for a break unless it was an "official" break, that you could not ask any questions, that there would be times where you would have to sit quietly while the seminar instructors talked amongst themselves, that you might be sent outside on a whim for short or long periods, and that the seminar might take three days or it might take three weeks.

You would not attend that seminar. Or if you did, you would leave the seminar almost immediately. You would never subject yourself to that kind of experience.

Yet that is what we demand that jurors do.

Distractions

"If I were a juror in my trial, I would sometimes feel distracted by the events of my own life."

What kind of attention span do you have? If you were asked to sit and listen to other people talk for about seven hours a day on a subject in which you had little or no interest, do you think you would listen carefully for the entire day?

Of course not.

Jurors can't focus on every single question and every single answer at trial. They are distracted by the issues in their own lives—and they will think about those issues throughout the trial day. The sooner you accept this fact, the better job you'll do at trial.

Because jurors are distracted by their own lives, you need to do everything you can to keep the trial: (1) interesting (jurors will

Rules for Jurors

▲ No talking at all during trial

▲ No talking about the case with each other during breaks

▲ No talking about the case with your family at night

▲ No questions of witnesses

▲ No questions of lawyers

▲ No say in what happens at trial

▲ No say in the order of witnesses

▲ No say in the subject matter of the trial

▲ No asking for clarification or explanation

▲ No eating

▲ No drinking

▲ No sleeping

▲ No unauthorized breaks

▲ No phone calls

▲ No working or reading during trial

▲ No tardiness

be less distracted if they enjoy the trial); (2) uncomplicated (this permits the jurors to follow the trial even if they are not hanging on to every word); and (3) fast-paced (the jurors may favor your side if they think you are trying to help them get back to their lives as soon as possible). On the other hand, you risk losing the jury if you make the trial boring, complicated, and slow-paced.

Connections

Most trial lawyers move too slowly with their case. Pick up the pace!

"If I were a juror in my trial, I would look for connections between what is happening at trial and what is happening in my own life."

When jurors watch television, read the paper, and interact with others, they form a set of experiences and beliefs that shapes how they understand and view the world. These experiences and beliefs influence how they react to the testimony and arguments at trial. If they recognize connections between their own lives and the evidence and arguments at trial, they will have no trouble deciding who should win and who should lose. If they see no such connections, then they will have a lot of trouble making that decision.

Your job as a PTM trial lawyer is to connect with the jury's experiences and beliefs as you present your arguments and evidence. You need to shape your case with these connections in mind. This means that you should not focus exclusively on the merits of your case. Instead, you should focus on how the jury is going to connect with your case and, in doing so, rule in your favor.

2. Be your persuasive self

The most common mistake made by beginning trial lawyers is to try to act like someone else at trial. This never works, since it is difficult to pretend to be someone else for longer than a few minutes, especially under stressful conditions. The result is often failure and disappointment.

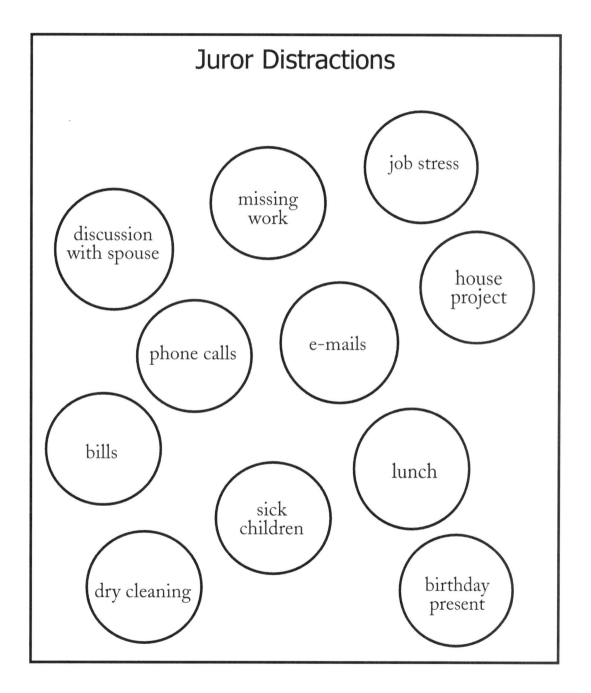

Juror Distractions

Dynamic Trial Lawyer Myth

Why are trial lawyers hesitant to be themselves at trial? The answer lies in what is called the *dynamic trial lawyer myth*. People who have not tried many cases often believe that the best trial lawyers are dynamic and overpowering. These dynamic trial lawyers speak with expression, raise their voices, run around the courtroom, move close to the faces of witnesses, and otherwise do things that seem "dynamic" and "exciting" to the layperson.

The dynamic trial lawyer, at least in his or her caricature form, doesn't usually exist in the real world. Trial lawyers have different levels of charisma, ranging from a little to a lot, but even the ones who have a lot of charisma do not maintain it at a high volume throughout the entire trial. No one wants to be near someone who is that forceful and overbearing. Do you?

What most lawyers fail to realize is that many of the leading trial lawyers in America are easygoing and soft spoken at trial. They seem calm and relaxed during trial and ask questions in a friendly and dignified manner. They have an aura of respect as they move about the courtroom. And as a result, they are not dynamic in the same way that fake trial lawyers on television or in the movies are "dynamic."

The best trial lawyers win so many cases because jurors view them as able and trustworthy, and jurors use the trustworthiness of the trial lawyer as another "shortcut" to deciding who should win or lose. If they trust the lawyer, then they feel comfortable believing what the lawyer is telling them.

Forget what you see on television or at the movies. Who do you trust in your own life?

Think about your own life. If you need someone to watch your children, your pets, your money, your car, or anything else, or if you want to buy a car, a house, a boat, or some other major item, to whom do you turn? The most dynamic person you know? The loudest person? The most aggressive person?

No.

You turn to someone you feel you can trust, and that person is probably not very dynamic or loud or aggressive. The person is simply trustworthy.

It follows that if you are a trustworthy person, you have the potential to be an effective trial lawyer. If you are not trustworthy, you will have a tough time at trial. The key is to be yourself. Since people trust you outside of trial when they see that you are true to yourself, they will trust you inside the courtroom if they see the same thing.

Not Just Any Self

Being yourself at trial is only the beginning. You need to focus on how to be your *persuasive* self at trial. You present your persuasive qualities at trial (your persuasive self) because—as you might imagine—you are trying to persuade the jury to rule in your favor.

There is no formula for persuasion when it comes to effective trial advocacy. You should base your persuasive approach on how you act when you are trying to be persuasive in every day life. How do you persuade your friends to go on a trip with you, persuade your family to support you in one of your pet projects, or persuade a salesperson to accept a return without a receipt? What mannerisms do you use? What's your tone? What type of arguments do you make? How do you stand when you talk in such circumstances? What type of eye contact do you use?

As you begin to answer these questions, you will figure out how you should act at trial, as whatever works for you outside of trial should also work for you inside the courtroom.

If it works for you in real life, it should work at trial as well.

3. Show confidence

There is only one attitude that you can have as you prepare for your trial. You must be convinced, based on the applicable law and likely evidence at trial, that you can win. If you do not have this attitude, it is virtually guaranteed that you will lose. Indeed, if you cannot convince yourself that you should win, how can you ever hope to convince a jury of strangers that you should win?

You also must be convinced that you know what you are doing and have the ability to prepare and try the case. If you do not believe that you are competent to handle the trial, the client will not have much confidence in you and, more importantly, the jury might think you are lost or confused. This is bad.

Accordingly, when you think about your case, when you talk about your case, and when you walk into the courtroom to begin the first day of your trial, you should do so with the attitude that you can win and that you know how to handle every aspect of a jury trial. You are not hesitant or tentative with your adversary, the judge, potential witnesses, or the jury.

Attitude is everything.

It is important to remember that your adversary, the judge, your client, and the jury will not necessarily know how experienced you are or whether you know what you are doing. If you act with confidence, even when you are dead wrong, you might be able to escape some otherwise sticky situations. In addition, the jury will respect you if you act as if you are in control even when you are wrong, and it may not respect you if you act like you are out of control even when you are right.

4. Be organized

Jurors like to see an organized trial lawyer, as they believe such a lawyer is less likely to waste their precious time at trial or otherwise mess things up. You should follow the guidelines in chapter 4 regarding trial preparation and do everything in your power to keep a clean and organized table.

5. Embrace problems, surprises, and mistakes

Ask experienced trial lawyers whether things tend to go wrong at most trials and they will uniformly tell you "absolutely." No matter how carefully you prepare for trial, something unexpected always happens.

What could go wrong? All these and more:

▲ Your witness fails to show up.

▲ Your star witness changes his mind (or worse, changes *sides*).

▲ A critical box of exhibits disappears.

▲ The opposing expert gives a new opinion at trial.

▲ The judge sustains every objection made by your opponent.

▲ The judge permits your opponent to call four new witnesses.

▲ The judge denies your motion in limine and overrules your key objections.

▲ Your expert witness forgets her opinion.

▲ Your technology fails.

▲ Your pants split during opening statement.

▲ Your co-counsel gets hit by a car.

▲ You lose your trial notebook.

▲ Your client can't stop laughing in court.

▲ You trip and fall on your face.

One of these events, or something similar, will occur at your next trial. Your reaction to the event is what matters: Do you take it too seriously and allow it to ruin your entire trial? Or do view it with some humor (if possible) and do your best to recover?

When you're knocked down at trial, don't just lie there in a pool of self-pity. Get back up and start fighting for your client. That's what any experienced trial lawyer will tell you.

6. Don't be a jerk

It shouldn't be necessary to include this point, but don't be a jerk before, during, or after trial. Treat opposing counsel, court personnel, your co-workers, the judge, and everyone else with respect. Don't snap at members of your staff or anyone else who is trying to help you. And don't let the dark side of your personality take over and turn you into a mean-spirited person. Stress is not an excuse for bad behavior. It is a reason to try harder to show good behavior.

Adopt a zero-tolerance jerk policy.

PTM

Chapter 3

Understanding the Theme Thing

What does it mean to have a theme for trial? Why do you need a theme? Should you have one theme or many themes? In this chapter, you'll learn:

▲ how to create a one-sentence description of your case

▲ how to make fairness points

▲ how to react to your opponent's themes

"If you can't write your movie idea on the back of a business card, you ain't got a movie."

—*Samuel Goldwyn*
Metro Goldwyn Mayer

Sam Goldwyn might have made a good trial lawyer. To paraphrase Sam: If you can't write your trial theme on the back of a business card, you ain't got a trial theme.

But exactly what is a "theme"? Is it simply a gimmick? Does it have any substance to it? Are you supposed to have one theme or many themes? Should the theme be obvious or subtle? Are you supposed to identify your theme to the court and to your opponent prior to trial? Do you tell the jury that you have a theme? In short, exactly what is this "theme thing"?

The first thing you should know about themes is that they come in all shapes and sizes and serve all kinds of different purposes for trial. There is no right way to select a theme and there is no wrong way to use a theme.

Instead of struggling with the concept of a theme, you should try to accomplish two basic objectives as you prepare and begin your trial. First, you should tell the jury what your case is about in one sentence. Second, you should develop a series of fairness points designed to show why it is fair for your client to win and unfair for your client to lose.

Can you describe your case in one sentence?

Say It in One Sentence

As you present your case to the jury, you need to simplify all your arguments and all your facts into a single sentence. If you cannot define the case and focus the main question for the jury, your opponent will do so. And one thing you want to avoid is your opponent defining the central question in the case for the jury. This is not good.

This one-sentence test is a good way for you to force yourself to streamline the issues in the case, and it is an excellent way for you to introduce the case to the jury. You can begin your opening statement with "this is a case about . . ." You can also end your opening statement by repeating your one-sentence description of the case, and you can return to this sentence at the beginning and end of your closing argument. If this sentence, standing alone, is persuasive to the typical juror, then you will increase your chances of winning by using the sentence in this manner at opening statement and closing argument. If you get it right, the jury will enter the jury room with your one-sentence description in mind, and jurors will repeat your sentence during the course of deliberations in order to help you win your case.

Rather than forcing yourself to come up with a theme, force yourself to describe why you should win and what the case is about in a single sentence. The sentence does not have to be a short sentence. In fact, you can cheat a little by adding some clauses and conjunctions to the sentence. Of course, the shorter the better, but sometimes it is difficult to describe a complex case in a short sentence.

What's Your PJR?

Whether your description of the case works depends on only one factor: How will the jury react to the sentence? We refer to this factor as the Possible Juror Reaction, or "PJR." You should consider the PJR for various one-sentence descriptions of your case and choose the description that has the best PJR. You do this by sharing the description with your friends, family, and colleagues and listening to their reaction. If you find that you are criticizing their reaction ("That's not what I meant" or "You didn't hear what I said"), then you need to develop a more effective description.

Listen to feedback on your theme.

To illustrate this process, consider the following examples of one-sentence descriptions of cases followed by one view of the PJR.

1. "This is a case in which a company that builds homes actually admitted that a house it had built had a major construction defect, but then the company refused to do anything to fix the defect."

PJR: *Wow. If someone built a house for me and my family and it had a big problem like some kind of construction defect, I'd be really upset. I would get really angry if they admitted there was a problem but then didn't do anything about it. I know this kind of thing has happened before—these builders sometimes have a problem and then don't fix it.*

Note that the one-sentence description is a general description of the case and thus doesn't name the parties or delve into the particular facts. In the example, the sentence does not explain how the company admitted there was a major construction defect, describe the nature of the defect, or discuss how or why the company refused to fix the defect.

Bad Example

This is a case in which the XYZ Construction Company, which is a builder of homes, built a house for my client, the Wallace family, and when it built the home it failed to provide the three feet of padding in the base unit of the extended porch as required by the state code, and the failure to provide this padding created a series of structural integrity issues which we believe constitute a major construction defect and after the Wallace family complained to XYZ, the company sent a letter to them admitting that XYZ had not provided the proper padding and that this was a major defect but then the project was placed on hold by one of XYZ's engineers because XYZ experienced a surge of complaints in another neighborhood and so it focused on that neighborhood and ignored my clients.

PJR: *I didn't quite follow that. What exactly happened here?*

There is nothing wrong with telling the jury the facts of your case. But don't pack all the facts into your one-sentence description at the beginning of your opening statement. Doing so makes the jury work too hard too early in the process.

2.   "This case involves a man who got himself fired from his job so that he could sue the company and try to make money through a lawsuit rather than through good, honest work."

PJR: *I always thought it was unfair when people tried to get themselves fired just to make some money. I never did that and it really bugs me when people do that. I remember a guy at work who brought that ridiculous lawsuit against the company I work for. That was a big joke.*

How to Introduce Your Theme

This is a case about _____

This case involves _____

In this case _____

We are going to show you that_____

You will see that _____

The evidence will show that _____

We will prove that _____

This case concerns _____

During the trial, you'll learn that _____

[No introduction] _____

3. "In this case, a group of business people took a gamble and lost, and now they want to go back in time and change their bet."

PJR: These business people are always trying to have it both ways. If they made an investment and it didn't go well, then they should have to accept the consequences just like everybody else.

Do you agree with the PJR for each point? How would you describe it?

4. "We are going to show that a supplier sold our company some wood which worked fine in our product for about a year, and then the supplier changed the way it made the wood, and our company experienced $1,000,000 worth of problems in the field."

PJR: If it ain't broke, don't fix it. This product was working fine until the supplier made some kind of change to the wood. Sounds to me like the change must have caused the problems.

5. "You'll see that the defendant admits that its product falls within our patent in every respect but one, and further admits that the one thing it did to avoid falling within the patent is a minor and insignificant change."

PJR: This sounds like the company is violating the patent but trying to get around it on some technicality.

There is no such thing as a case that is too complicated to describe in one sentence. In every case, you should be able to boil it down to a single sentence. In addition, there will be cases in which you do not necessarily want to describe your case in one sentence to the jury. But even in those cases, you should be able to describe your case in one sentence to yourself, your client, and your witnesses. Sometimes the jury will come up with the sentence itself if you present evidence and argument which strongly suggests the sentence without ever saying it in so many words. But why make the jury come up with the sentence? Give them yours!

One important note about evidence: You'll need to decide the extent to which you want to base your theme on undisputed facts (the more conservative approach) or disputed facts (the more aggressive approach). Remember that the PJR will change dramatically if you fail to prove your theme with credible evidence.

Fairness Points

In addition to summarizing your message in one sentence, you should make "fairness points" to the jury during the trial. These points do not necessarily have to relate to each other, and they do not have to flow from your one-sentence description of the case. Rather, they are simply points about your case that you want to make sure the jury understands.

These fairness points are not dependent on the particular instructions given by the court or the particular elements of your claims. One of the most common mistakes made by inexperienced trial lawyers is to place too much emphasis on the legal elements of their claims and the proof required to satisfy those elements. It goes without saying that you will lose your case if you cannot prove the legal elements that make up your claims. In every case, therefore, you need to create some sort of matrix in which you connect the evidence you want to offer with the legal elements of all your claims or defenses. But juries do not necessarily go into jury rooms with legal elements on their minds. They think in terms of basic fairness, not five-pronged legal tests. So give them what they want: a sense of fairness.

To understand how best to arrive at your fairness points for trial, you should set aside the legal elements of your claims or defenses for a moment and ask yourself these questions: Why is it fair for my client to win? Why would it be unfair for the other side to win? The answers to these questions have little to do with the elements of the claims or the instructions to the jury. The answers instead have everything to do with ordinary life experiences and ordinary conversations.

Experienced trial lawyers focus on fairness points to win their trials.

Another way to think about fairness points is to ask whether there is something good about your client that you can share with the jury. List everything you can imagine that shows that your client is a good person or company and your client has engaged in good behavior. Then ask whether there is something not so good about the other side. Finally, think about whether something about the relationship between the parties suggests that it would be unfair for you to lose.

Testing One-Sentence Descriptions

Not So Creative:

To your spouse: "Here's my theme for trial: _____.
                 Is it any good?"

A Bit More Creative:

To your hairstylist: "There's this guy who _____.
                      What do you think?"

A Little Over the Top:

On an elevator: "Hey everyone. What do you think about _____?
                   Anyone?"

Here are examples of the types of points you might want to make at your trial, either explicitly or implicitly, followed by the PJR.

Do you see a different PJR for these points? Why?

1.   The defendant made over $1,000,000 in profits in his business dealings, and we are only asking that he return $100,000 to the plaintiff.

PJR: *The defendant is still going to make a lot of money if he gives the plaintiff what he's asking for. It's not going to be a big deal for him.*

2.   The defendant has meticulous records for everything he ever did in his life, but he cannot show you a single piece of paper relating to the transactions in this case.

PJR: *It seems a little fishy that the only transactions without supporting documents are for the one time the defendant is sued. Something seems wrong here.*

3.   The only thing the defendant does is make this one product, and the entire future of the company depends on the success of that product.

PJR: *I wouldn't want to do anything to completely shut down the defendant company. That would be pretty harsh. I hope we can resolve this case without destroying the company.*

4.   Our company has been around for over eighty years, and no one has ever suggested _____ until this case.

PJR: *The company's history seems pretty clean. It doesn't seem like the type of company that would engage in that type of behavior.*

5.   While my client worked seven days a week to help this company, the owners of the company, who are now suing my client, worked short hours and took long vacations.

Watch for these points at your next trial.

PJR: *I can't stand it when people get rich without working for their money. I don't want to give them any more money. They'll be fine without any damages.*

6.   My client is a surgeon who does one thing and one thing only: She saves lives every single day.

PJR: *I like that doctor. She really tries to help people. She is a life-saver. I'm not going to hurt her career in this case.*

7. My clients are hardworking people with families.

PJR: *I like hardworking people with families. They should get more of a break in life.*

8. A judgment against my clients would ruin their business and force them to fire over fifty people.

PJR: *I wouldn't want to be responsible for fifty people losing their jobs.*

9. All the executives at the defendant company will tell you that they are ashamed at how the company acted in this case.

PJR: *If the higher-ups at the company think something is wrong with this deal, then something must be wrong.*

10. A judgment against the defendant will be like a drop of water on a windshield: The company won't even notice it.

PJR: *I'll sleep fine tonight if I rule against the defendant. It's no big deal.*

Be careful. Some of the above points might be improper if they are made explicitly in open court; indeed, some of these points may be the subject of motions in limine (see discussion below). Use good judgment and find a proper purpose before suggesting or implying any of these or similar points.

The above list contains points that might work in some cases and might not work in others. The list and the PJRs are designed to jump-start your thought process. Everyone's list will vary depending on the circumstances of his or her case. Even experienced trial lawyers, moreover, will disagree on the PJR for each item on the list.

Don't forget that merits still matter in a jury trial.

Do not forget about the elements at issue in your case. You will spend a great majority of your time in preparation for trial by focusing on the merits. If you are missing an element, either the judge or jury will most likely rule against you. The merits will dominate the presentation of evidence at trial. But your one-sentence description and your fairness points will, in the end, help turn the jury in your favor. A jury rarely reasons, "I know it will be extremely unfair for this side to win, but we think that side should win anyway."

In short, you have to keep your eye on two things: The legal requirements and the simple jury themes. If you can translate the former into the latter and combine them both at trial, your odds of success improve dramatically.

Reacting to Your Opponent's Themes

Let's suppose you have followed the PTM approach and, as part of that approach, you've developed an effective one-sentence description and strong list of fairness points. You show up for trial, and as soon as your opponent opens her mouth, she hits you with two or three devastating fairness points and a knock-out description of her case. Without any response, you are limited to complaining that your opponent has "pulled a fast one" on you by her aggressive use of trial themes. And the more complaining you do, the worse you feel.

One of the most difficult decisions is whether to try to prevent opposing counsel from making certain fairness points.

To avoid a strategic ambush at trial, put yourself in the position of your opponent. Try to describe your opponent's case in one sentence and make a list of all the fairness points available to your opponent. This will not be as easy as you think. You may believe your opponent has no case—none at all—and the only fair result is for your client to win and your opponent to lose. Guess what? You're wrong. Any experienced trial lawyer will know how to sum up their case in a persuasive sentence and how to fight you with a long list of fairness points. You need to do so as well.

Once you have thought about things, you then need to develop a strategy for responding to your opponent's possible themes. You may need to change your one-sentence description to accommodate your opponent's description, and you may need to add or drop some of your fairness points.

You also may need to file motions in limine to prevent your opponent from making certain fairness points, such as mentioning your client's net worth at trial. But watch out: You may have done a better job at coming up with fairness points against your client than your opponent did, and you might not want to give your opponent any new ideas for how to win at trial.

Chapter 4

Mastering Trial Preparation and Set up

Most of the anxiety about trials is based on the sense that you are forgetting something. Would it help if you had a list of things to do? In this chapter, you'll learn:

▲ basic tasks involved in trial preparation

▲ what written materials you need to prepare for most trials

▲ how to set up a courtroom for trial

Stop Panicking and Start Preparing for Trial

Someone just asked you to handle a trial. What do you do now? As soon as you learn that you're going to trial, begin working on the items discussed below.

The Sample Civil Trial Rules in the Appendix will give you some good ideas for trial preparation and proper conduct at trial.

Trial Date

You should know your trial date, including whether that date is a "trial ready" date (be prepared to begin trial) a "date certain" (you're going to trial), or a "show up and wait" date (you spend the morning trying to find a judge).

Deadlines

Know your deadlines, including those for exchanging information with your opponent and filing pretrial submissions. Write these deadlines down and ask someone (such as your assistant) to make sure you don't miss any.

Special Rules for Trials

Does your state or federal court have any special rules for trial practice? Ask around. Go to the law library. Call the clerk's office. Do whatever you can to track down and read any special rules for trials.

Courthouse and Courtroom

This item often causes unnecessary stress on the first day of trial. Write down the address of the courthouse and the courtroom number for your trial. Learn directions to the courthouse.

Judge

Learn as much as you can about your trial judge's background and her general approach to jury trials. Consider the following:

▲ Read a biography of your judge from a local directory of judges.

▲ Ask your friends and colleagues about their experiences with the judge at trial.

▲ Call the judge's calendar or administrative clerk and talk to the clerk about the practices of the judge at trial.

▲ If the judge has a pretrial conference, ask the judge about her rules for trial lawyers.

Through the above sources, you should try to learn whether the judge is formal or informal, strict or permissive, and other things that will help guide you at trial.

If you've clerked for a judge, you understand the important role they sometimes play in deciding legal issues.

Judge's Law Clerk

Know the name of the judge's law clerk, who may or may not play a major role in deciding important legal issues at trial.

Co-counsel

Learn who (if anyone) is trying the case with you. Talk to them right away and coordinate your tasks. This is true for co-counsel representing the same party and, to a lesser extent, co-counsel representing a different party on the same side of the dispute.

Opposing Counsel

Learn who you are trying the case against. Without spending too much time on this item, learn some background information on your opponent. Call him or her and try to work together on the orderly exchange of information.

Sample Questions About Your Trial Judge

1. How strict is the judge on the manner of making an objection?

2. Should you ask permission to approach a witness?

3. Does the judge want a binder of potential exhibits?

4. How and when does the judge handle objections to deposition testimony?

5. Where should you put your easel and oversized exhibits?

6. Can you leave your things in the courtroom at night and/or on weekends?

7. Does the judge prefer briefs on issues that arise during trial?

8. Can you stand and walk around during examinations?

9. Can you (or must you) use a lectern during trial?

10. Can you (or must you) pre-mark exhibits?

11. Does the judge draft a set of jury instructions before the charging conference, or does she choose from the parties' proposed instructions?

12. Who goes first for voir dire of potential jurors?

13. Does the judge allow lawyers to question the jurors during voir dire?

Court Reporter and Administrative Clerk

Know the name of the judge's court reporter (who will create the trial transcript) and administrative clerk (who will handle the exhibits at trial).

Case Files

Gather and review the pleadings, correspondence, legal research, and other files for the case.

Hotel and Office Space

Think about where you want to work each night during the trial and with whom you'll be working. If necessary, make hotel and office arrangements.

Trials can be miserable if you forget to warn your family about your schedule.

Family Coverage

Talk to your spouse and other family members about your trial. Let them know when you think you'll go to trial and how long you think it will last. If you need child care, make the necessary arrangements.

Technology

Develop a plan for using technology in the courtroom. In addition to your basic demonstratives (chapter 8), do you want to put exhibits on an overhead projector? What about a video projector (ELMO)? Do you want to use PowerPoint slides? VCR? DVD? Other types of technology?

Clothes

Figure out what you want to wear during trial and set the clothes aside.

Trial Consultants

If you're using a trial consultant for any purpose (technology, jury research, etc.), coordinate all relevant tasks with the consultant.

Leave These Clothes and Jewelry At Home

Really big and expensive watches

Anything orange

Your "lucky" diamond pinky ring

White socks

ANYTHING CORDUROY

Earrings the size of hubcaps

Hats

Tuxedoes, gowns, or other formal wear

Eminem T-Shirt

Leather ties

Athletic shoes

Paralegal

If applicable, meet with your paralegal and go over this entire list. No matter how busy you think you are, a fifteen-minute organizational meeting with your paralegal can save you a lot of time in preparing for trial.

Support Staff

Know which support staff members (if any) are assisting you. Work with them.

Trial Witnesses

Call your witnesses and tell them the trial date and their expected date of testimony. Tell your witnesses to bring some work or a good book with them to the courtroom so that they will have something to do while they are waiting. Apologize in advance for any delay, and assure them that there probably will be some delay as the wheels of justice grind slowly. If you have adequately forewarned your witnesses and told them to bring some work or reading materials with them, they will endure any delays with much more patience.

You will win or lose your next trial based on your witnesses. Treat them well.

Write your witnesses a letter with the same information you provided in your phone call. If necessary, arrange for subpoenas to be issued to your witnesses, and don't forget to pay any applicable witness fees in advance. Begin a pattern of continued communication with your witnesses. Don't let them slip away.

Gather and review any witness statements or depositions. Begin preparing outlines of direct and cross-examinations (chapter 6). Most important, try to reduce the number of witnesses you will call at trial. Witnesses are unpredictable; you should call them only if you need them and for no other reason.

Exhibits

Select the exhibits you intend to use for trial and make enough copies for use by all parties, a witness, and the judge. Begin work right away on your demonstrative exhibits (chapter 8).

Look through deposition transcripts, summary judgment papers, and other important materials to find the best exhibits for trial.

Talk to your opponent about exhibits:

▲ When will you show each other charts, graphs, and other demonstrative exhibits? Two weeks before trial? Two days before trial? Two hours? Your position will depend on how you compare the value in surprising your opponent with your exhibits versus the cost of preparing for trial without seeing her exhibits.

▲ Try to stipulate to authenticity and even admissibility with respect to non-controversial exhibits.

▲ Agree on a numbering system for the exhibits.

Trial Notebook

Put together a trial notebook with the following items:

▲ principal pleadings

▲ pertinent orders

▲ your pretrial papers

▲ opponent's pretrial papers

▲ voir dire questions

▲ opening statement outline

▲ witness outlines

▲ deposition transcripts

▲ "pocket memos" (briefs on possible issues that might arise during trial)

▲ legal research

▲ reduced-sized demonstrative exhibits

▲ closing argument outline

▲ notes

Trial Box

Throw together a "trial box" with whatever items you need, such as the following:

▲ rules of evidence

▲ pens and paper

A good trial box can reduce unnecessary stress.

▲ document flags or "stickies"

▲ stapler

▲ binder clips

▲ extra folders

▲ highlighters

▲ markers

▲ three-hole punch

▲ paper clips

▲ cell phone

▲ aspirin

Transcripts

Consider whether you want a transcript of your opponent's opening statement (you probably do), selected testimony, or anything else from the trial. Talk to the court reporter in advance and ask whether your plan is feasible.

Appeal

Think about any appeal issues that may arise before, during, or after trial. Develop a strategy for creating a record for whatever issues you can anticipate.

Client

Don't skip over appeal issues. An entire book could be (and has been) written on this subject.

Talk to your client about the trial and appeal process (many clients don't understand how trials actually proceed). Tell your client the budget for the trial to avoid any surprises when it's over. Review your core trial strategy and discuss your client's position on settlement. Make sure your client knows what results are possible and what results are probable. Don't sugar-coat anything. And don't let your client bully you into creating unrealistic expectations.

Pretrial Submissions

Pretrial submissions are typically defined in the court's pretrial order and include the following items. The format of the examples may not necessarily suit all judges or jurisdictions. You should review the rules and practices of your jurisdiction and of your judge to determine the proper style or format.

1. Exhibit list

You may not have decided exactly what exhibits you will and will not introduce during the trial. List all exhibits that you *may* want to introduce at trial. The exhibit list should contain the exhibit number and a brief description of the document.

You'll probably want to list the exhibits in the order you plan to use them at trial. What if you are not sure of the order? Most judges (there are some exceptions) will permit you to introduce exhibits out of order and will not object to you limiting the number of exhibits introduced at trial.

2. Witness list

List all witnesses you *may* want to call at trial. In many jurisdictions, you need only list the names of the witnesses. Other jurisdictions require their address and/or phone number. Still others require a brief statement of the subject matter of their testimony. Check the applicable rules and court orders before submitting your list.

Witnesses, unlike exhibits, need not be pre-numbered. You do not have to list the witnesses in the order in which you will call them at trial.

3. Jury instructions

List all instructions you want the judge to consider, including instructions on issues that your opponent needs to prove. The format will vary from court to court. (For more information on jury instructions, see chapter 11.)

4. Special verdict form

Almost every trial involves a special verdict form of some variety. The special verdict form is simply a list of questions that the jury must answer—usually "yes" or "no"—followed by one or more questions on the amount of damages that the jury awards. The special verdict form usually tracks each element of the case that the plaintiff must prove.

The cardinal rule of special verdict forms is that simpler and shorter is better. Very few judges will send an eleven-page, fifty-three-question special verdict form to the jury (unless you have a nine-week trial with seventeen substantive issues). Some of the best special verdict forms ask only two questions: one on liability and one on damages.

The special verdict form may be the most important pretrial paper in your case. Get it right.

The special verdict form is, in a sense, the most important pretrial document you will be submitting, for it is the only one that the jury actually fills out and gives to the judge at the end of the trial. It represents the jury's answers to the questions that you will have been debating throughout the entire trial. You need to make sure that you are asking the right questions and that you are asking the questions in a simple and understandable fashion.

The only disadvantage to using a special verdict form is that jurors' answers to the questions are sometimes contradictory. Try to eliminate the possibility that questions might be answered in a way that is inconsistent. This is another reason to keep the form short. A lengthy special verdict form only increases the odds of getting inconsistent answers.

Bobby Freeman, Plaintiff

v.

Officer Jacky Curtis, Defendant

Special Verdict Form

(1) Did Officer Curtis act reasonably in light of all of the circumstances that he faced on January 1, 1999?

Yes_____   No _____

(2) What amount of money (if any) will adequately and fairly compensate Bobby Freeman for any injuries that he may have suffered on January 1, 1999?

$_____

Questions That Might be Too Slanted

1. Was the Defendant negligent in drinking beer, driving over the speed limit, and running through a stop sign before slamming into the Plaintiff?

___ Yes, of course.

___ No, we didn't watch the trial.

2. How much money should Defendant pay Plaintiff when we all know that Defendant has millions and millions of dollars available and wouldn't even notice a five or ten-million dollar verdict?

___ $5,000,000

___ $10,000,000

5. Motions in limine

The admission or exclusion of a key piece of evidence can sometimes affect the outcome of a trial. A motion in limine asks the judge to admit or exclude such evidence.

Whether to file a motion in limine requires some strategic thinking. The advantage of making a motion in limine before trial is that you can get answers to important evidentiary questions, which may help you decide to include or exclude certain witnesses, include or exclude certain exhibits, or choose one trial strategy or another.

The disadvantage is that the motion tips off your opponent to the specific pieces of evidence that concern you the most. This can be especially damaging if you move to exclude evidence that your opponent was not even *aware of* before making the motion in limine.

You can avoid a bad loss at trial with a good motion in limine.

Motions in limine are not required. You can always make your objections at trial as the evidence is offered. You should save motions in limine only for those pieces of evidence that are important to your case (either in a positive or a negative sense) and only when a determination of admissibility will have an impact on your trial tactics.

It is quite common for the judge who hears the motion to defer any ruling until trial so that she can see how the evidence at trial develops and learn more about the case before doing so.

6. Trial memorandum

A trial memorandum describes the basic facts and legal issues in your case. It should start with a basic summary of the facts. It should then discuss the applicable legal principles, including any important cases. If your case is straightforward, you need not go into great detail on the law, as the judge will probably already have a sense of the general legal principles that apply. If the case is more unique or complicated, a longer discussion of the law might be necessary.

Oops!

COUNSEL: And your honor, we move to exclude any testimony about my client's past criminal convictions, including the three perjury convictions. They are not relevant in this case and are also unfairly prejudicial.

OPPOSING COUNSEL: Wow. I had no idea. Can I see the documentation?

COUNSEL: Uh, sure. Here you are.

OPPOSING COUNSEL: Your honor, these are clearly relevant to credibility. Under the rules of evidence, I can impeach the witness with these certified copies of convictions.

COURT: That's right. Motion denied.

Writing a trial memorandum takes some judgment. You want to tell the judge why you should win the case, but you have to remember that you will be telling your opponent at the same time. If there are some issues or tactics that you think your opponent does not know about, don't place them in the trial memorandum.

Setting Up the Courtroom

You need to keep five points in mind when setting up a courtroom for trial. Each point helps you respect the power of the jury in your trial. The courtroom is the stage and the jury is the audience. The courtroom set up must serve the *jurors'* needs.

1. Arrive early

Go to the courtroom early—early in the morning on the first day of trial, or better yet a day or two before trial starts—to examine the courtroom environment. Consider:

Whatever you do, don't write a sloppy, error-filled trial brief.

▲ What parts of the room can the jury see?

▲ What parts of the room will the jury have trouble seeing?

▲ Where are the light switches (especially useful if you are going to be showing images projected on a screen)?

▲ What door do the jurors come through when they come into the courtroom (so that you don't set up large exhibits in their path)?

▲ Where can you hide your large exhibits (to the extent you want to hide them)?

▲ What does it feel like to be in the courtroom?

▲ How is the lighting?

▲ How is the sound?

▲ Where will you plug in your technological aids?

Trial Memorandum Balancing Act

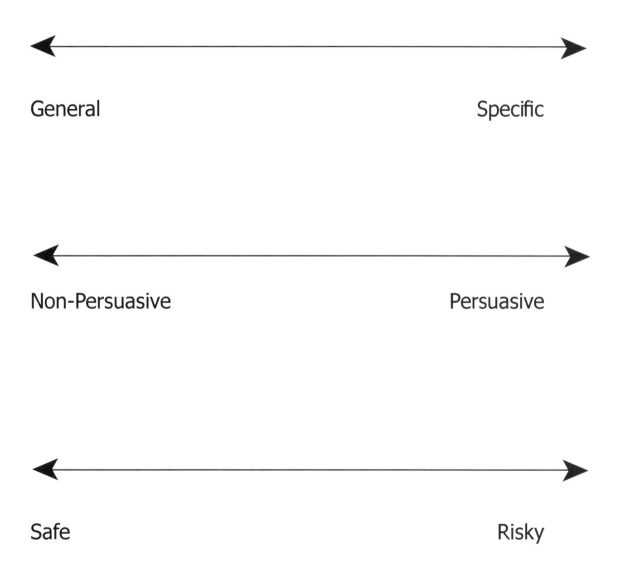

General   Specific

Non-Persuasive   Persuasive

Safe   Risky

Trial lawyers have strong, though divergent, views on how to choose the right table for trial.

2. Select a table

Which table do you want at trial? The table closest to the jury helps you to "bond" with the jurors, though it also places you and your client in a fishbowl of sorts. You have to be extra careful that you are conducting yourself professionally and respectfully when you are sitting closest to the jury.

3. See things through the jury's eyes

Set up the courtroom based on what the jury can see. The greatest demonstrative exhibits and the greatest technology in the world are not going to help you if the jury cannot see them.

You must put things as close to the jury as you can without blocking entrances and exits and paths where the judge, clerk, or jurors will walk. You should sit in the jury box and see if you can read the charts or exhibits that you will be displaying. Ideally, you will set up your screens and exhibits where the judge, the jury, and your opponent can see them.

But what happens if the courtroom is small and you cannot set up so that everyone can see things? Many people mistakenly give the judge preference in this situation. But remember who the primary decision-maker is in your case: the jury (chapter 1). It is more important that the jury be able to see things than the judge or your opponent.

4. Test all equipment

It is vital to make sure that everything you are going to use in your trial presentation—whether it is a simple overhead projector and screen or a more complicated computer-generated presentation using DVD technology—works perfectly in the courtroom before you even stand up for trial on the first day.

5. Have a plan B

If you are really nervous, you might want to have a plan C as well.

Be prepared for the total failure of your primary technology on the first morning of trial. If you are using a laptop computer with a PowerPoint presentation, bring a set of transparencies as a backup. If you've arranged a delivery of enlarged exhibits, bring a reduced-size set in case the messenger delivers the blowups to the wrong courthouse.

Your Nightmare Comes True

COUNSEL:	Let's begin with the video. Ahem, let's see. Give me a second. Uh oh.
COURT:	What's the problem, counsel?
COUNSEL:	My video player has lost power.
COURT:	Do you have the information on hard copies?
COUNSEL:	No, your honor.
COURT:	Ask your next question.
COUNSEL:	All right, your honor. Had we shown the jury a video, what would they have seen?
OPPOSING COUNSEL:	Objection, your honor.
COURT:	Sustained.
COUNSEL:	Nothing further.
COURT:	Call your next witness.

PTM

Chapter 5

What You Need to Know About Openings

Your opening statement is the principal vehicle for introducing the jury to your case. Are you ready to give your
opening? In this chapter, you'll learn:

▲ the rules for opening statement

▲ organizing ideas for your opening statement

▲ strategic issues for every opening

Can We Talk?

Jurors listen to opening statements to see who should win the case. Are you ready to tell them?

Most lawyers, if they could make a wish, would prefer to dispense with calling witnesses, introducing exhibits, and putting evidence into the record, and just speak directly to the jury. It would be so much quicker. And the story would be told in a much more coherent fashion, not in the piecemeal and sometimes disjointed question and answer, witness-by-witness format.

The opening statement permits you to tell your story to the jury in the way you want to tell it. It is also your first chance to start bonding with the jury. It will be the jury's first impression of you (apart from what occurs at jury selection), and we all know the importance of first impressions.

What Works

1. Keep it simple

The content of your opening statement should be simple and streamlined. You want to give the jury an overview of your case. Tell them a story. Make it interesting. And always remember that jurors are people and not lawyers. They could not care less about legal terms and concepts. They just want a compelling story.

Compare the following two snippets from opening statements and ask which one you would rather hear if you were a juror with no legal training:

Bad Example

Ladies and gentlemen, this case arises under Section 10(b) of the Securities Exchange Act of 1934, which forbids the making of any false or misleading statements in a prospectus or other interstate communication in connection with the purchase or sale of a security. The plaintiffs were purchasers and holders of convertible debentures. They allege in this case that the defendants, jointly and severally, made various fraudulent and misleading statements to them in connection with their purchase of the convertible debentures. These false statements concerned the value of the company's accounts receivables and inventory, whose value was grossly inflated in various balance sheets and other financial statements that were given to my clients. We will be able to prove materiality and justifiable reliance in this case, and will ask you to award substantial damages to the plaintiffs for their injuries.

Good Example

Ladies and gentlemen, this case is about a couple of very simple principles that we all know and that we all understand. Some of these principles we learned as children. And they are just as true today as they were when we learned them years ago. Perhaps the most important principle in this case is tell the truth, and do not lie to people or mislead them. During this trial, we are going to show you that the defendants broke that basic rule. The defendants in this case are ABC Corporation, its president, and its vice president. We are going to show you that ABC Corporation, its president, and its vice president, made false statements to people about the financial health of ABC Corporation. The evidence will show that the defendants said things that made people believe the corporation was a lot healthier than it really was. My clients, Jane Doe and John Roe, are two of the people who heard those statements. They trusted the defendants. When the defendants said the company was doing well, my clients believed them and decided to invest in the company by buying some convertible debentures of the company. And I will tell you in a minute what convertible debentures are. My clients paid a lot of money to buy the convertible debentures. And they did it based on the promise that ABC Corporation was doing well. But you will learn in this trial that the promise turned out not to be true. The evidence will show ABC Corporation was not doing well at all. The value of the company went down, and so did the value of the plaintiffs' convertible debentures. All they want in this lawsuit is the money that they lost because the defendants broke a simple rule. They did not tell the truth about the company.

This latter statement, unlike the first, tells the story in simple terms. It identifies the theme of the case right up front. It also identifies the plaintiffs and defendants—a very basic, but often overlooked piece of information for an opening statement. The statement is relatively informal; there is no legalese or $10 words. And when there is a technical term—"convertible debentures"—the lawyer promises to define that term later in the opening statement.

2. But not too simple

Simplifying the opening statement does not mean dumbing it down. You need not pretend that you are addressing a group of third graders. But you probably should assume that you are addressing a group of reasonably intelligent high school graduates. There is no need to insult their intelligence, but you should take the time to make sure that everything you say can be understood by every juror. Certainly do not be condescending.

Jurors resent condescending speeches by condescending lawyers. Wouldn't you?

If you are explaining a concept that you think most of the jurors understand already, but you just want to make sure, tell them that. Say something like: "Most of you probably already understand this, but I want to just take a minute to make sure that we are all on the same page at the very beginning before we get on with the story."

3. Introduce your themes

As discussed in chapter 3, use your opening statement to communicate your themes, including your one-sentence description of the case and your various fairness points. If you do nothing else during your opening statement, you at least want the jurors to understand your one-sentence description of the case such that they could repeat it back to you if asked.

4. Organize your presentation

How should you tell the story? That depends on the case, as always. Eight times out of ten, you will tell the story chronologically—the most familiar, easy to follow format.

Good Example

This is a case about a company that refused to stand behind its products in the face of overwhelming evidence that it was not making those products properly. In 1994, the WoodGuy Company started selling wood to my client, Acme Manufacturing. Acme used the wood in its products for two years without any problem. But then Acme started getting complaints from its customers about the wood products that Acme was making out of wood that it bought from WoodGuy. Acme did an immediate investigation of the problem, and discovered that sometime in 1995, WoodGuy changed the way that it manufactured the wood that it sold to Acme, and that this change in manufacturing caused problems with the wood. Acme told WoodGuy in December of 1996 that its investigation revealed a problem with WoodGuy's manufacturing methods, and asked for WoodGuy's help in resolving the problems. In January of 1997, WoodGuy sent Acme a letter insisting that there was nothing wrong with its manufacturing methods and that all of the problems that Acme was encountering were its own fault. Acme wrote to WoodGuy in February of 1997 asking WoodGuy again to help resolve the problems with the wood products. The next month, WoodGuy wrote back to Acme again insisting that there was no problem with its manufacturing methods. Acme had to start this lawsuit in order to recover the damage that was caused when Acme's customers started returning products that were defective and Acme had to give those customers refunds.

Bad Example

The evidence in this case will show that my client, Acme Manufacturing, lost a lot of money when it had to replace products that its customers returned to it because the products weren't made properly. Acme spent a lot of time trying to figure out what the problem was with the products. It did that investigation after it had ordered the products for about two years with no problems. Acme actually started purchasing the products in 1994. The products being various kinds of wood from WoodGuy. When the problems came to light, Acme wrote to WoodGuy and asked for their help in resolving the problems. This was after an investigation that Acme did that showed that WoodGuy wasn't manufacturing the wood right, and that the wood was starting to crack and deteriorate early. Acme wrote several more letters to WoodGuy after that first letter that I mentioned, but to no avail.

Were you able to understand that last snippet without reading it twice? It is slightly out of chronological order, but the difference is significant.

There may be times, however, in which you may not want to tell a story chronologically.

Good Example

On January 1, 1999, three-year-old Jane Doe was severely burned by scalding hot water in the bathtub in her parents' apartment at the Golden Hills Apartments. The burns were so severe that Jane will have to undergo years of painful skin graft operations. The evidence in the case will show that she has endured a lot of pain and suffering, and her parents have had to spend a lot of money on medical bills to treat Jane's injuries. And those medical bills are growing even today. We all know that accidents happen. But it turns out that this was no innocent accident. You will hear evidence during this trial that what happened to Jane Doe was virtually inevitable. You will hear that in the days leading up to Jane being scalded, the maintenance workers at the Golden Hills Apartments were repeatedly told about problems with the water heater in the basement of the apartment building. And they never fixed those problems. You will learn that what happened to Jane could very easily have been avoided.

Sometimes a flashback method is the most interesting and compelling way to tell the story. Or sometimes another method works. It depends on the story you want to tell and how you want to tell it.

5. Use a touch of drama

Since an opening statement is supposed to be an overview and not argument, it is challenging to work much drama into the opening statement. Challenging, but certainly not an impossible task. As with closing arguments, the very best opening statements are ones that please both the left and right sides of the brain by combining an effective presentation of the facts with some emotion and enough fairness points to convince the jurors that not only *should* they be on your side, they actually *want* to be on your side.

6. Focus on evidence

You are not permitted to argue your case during the opening statement—hence the name "opening statement" rather than "opening argument." Remember that there has been no evidence presented at the time you make your opening statement, so there is no basis for you to make any sort of an argument at that time. The most you can do during your opening statement is to give the jury a preview of what you believe the evidence *will be*.

It is easy to keep your opening statement on the straight and narrow and not have it veer into the forbidden zone of argument. Four magic words will help: "the evidence will show." By prefacing your factual statements from time to time with those words, you are making it clear to everyone (especially the judge, who is the one who rules on objections to your opening statement) that you are not arguing, but are merely informing the jury what you believe the evidence will be during the trial. And that is what an opening statement is for. It may seem odd that four magic words can spell the difference between impermissible argument and permissible statement, but that's how it is done and that is how you need to do it if you want to at least *look* like you know what you are doing.

Judges will give you more leeway if you emphasize what the evidence will show.

Don't become too carried away with "the evidence will show." You need not start every sentence with the phrase; the key is to use the phrase just enough to remind everyone from time to time that you are making an opening statement and not arguing.

Note also that using the phrase "the evidence will show" does not always immunize one from any objection. If you routinely spice your opening statement with statements like "The evidence will show that my opponent is a big fat liar," or "The evidence will show that no sane person would believe the stupid story that the defendant will try to sell to you," no amount of saying "the evidence will show" is going to save you from an objection that you are being argumentative.

How to Say "the evidence will show"

"We will show"

"You will learn during trial"

"You will see from the evidence"

"We will show you"

"It will be clear from the evidence"

"We will prove to you"

Should I Object?

The only objection typically raised during opening statement is that the lawyer is being argumentative. You can raise this objection if your opponent is habitually stating things as fact without the obligatory "the evidence will show," though this usually is a mere technicality and is easily repaired. A more appropriate time to raise the objection is when your opponent starts to veer over the line into outright advocacy or starts to make particularly incendiary statements of fact.

How much argument is too much argument is a difficult judgment call. Most judges will permit some outright argument in the opening statement but will not permit counsel to take it too far. How far is "too far" depends on the particular judge hearing the case.

If opposing counsel starts to claim that certain of your witnesses are not going to be truthful or starts to level allegations of moral turpitude or other scandal against your witnesses, your opponent is engaging in improper argument and you should object as soon as you can stand and get the words out of your mouth. At the other end of the spectrum, your opponent's recitation of undisputed facts or facts that do not damage you is not objectionable, even if your opponent never says, "the evidence will show." There is obviously a wide area in between those two extremes, and it takes many trials before you will develop the educated ear necessary to distinguish proper opening statement from improper argument.

In general, you should tell yourself *not* to object during your opponent's opening argument. Objections interrupt the flow of your opponent's opening, and while that might sound like a good idea at first blush, it can easily irritate the jurors, who simply want to hear what the case is about without enduring constant interruption. In addition, there is a good chance your objection will be overruled and the jury will think that you are interfering with your opponent's opening.

Object only when you believe it's necessary and only when you think the judge will sustain your objection.

One objection that you most certainly should not make during your opponent's opening is the objection that counsel has misstated the evidence. There has been no evidence in the case yet, so there is nothing for counsel to misstate. What you should do instead is make careful note of what your opponent promises the evidence will be. As we discuss below, if she cannot deliver on that promise, you can score points in closing argument.

What do you do if your opponent objects and the judge sustains the objection? Don't argue, don't whine, and don't lose your composure. Simply tell the jurors that you're only giving them an overview of what you expect the evidence to show and that they should base their decision only on the actual evidence.

Strategic Considerations

1. Don't make promises you can't keep

You can lose a trial by over-promising in opening statement.

If you are unsure how the evidence will come into trial, telling the jury what the evidence "will show" may constitute something of a gamble. Among the biggest mistakes in opening statements are unkept promises. As we discuss in chapter 12, if you promise to deliver certain evidence to the jury and don't make good on that promise, you'll probably hear about it in your opponent's closing argument:

> Ladies and gentlemen, Mr. Hawkins promised you in his opening statement that he would prove that three of my clients inspected the bicycle before Mr. Doe got on to ride it and that they knew that the bicycle was defective, but they let Mr. Doe get on and ride it anyway. Well, you have just sat through three days of trial and you heard nothing of the sort. Never—not once—did anyone in this trial say what Mr. Hawkins claimed in his opening statement. And folks, that is just indicative of Mr. Hawkins' whole case. He simply has not been able to prove what he said he was going to prove, and he cannot prove what he needs to prove to recover in this case.

Do not make an evidentiary claim in opening statement unless you are reasonably certain that you will be able to prove that claim with evidence. And the more important the piece of evidence, the more certain that you will want to be that you can get the evidence in.

What if you are not sure that you can get the killer piece of evidence into the record? What if the evidence is subject to an objection that could go either way at trial? This is a difficult judgment call. It is probably better to leave the point out of your opening statement if the fact truly is a killer fact that the jury will probably remember and expect you to prove. If you succeed and get the fact into evidence, then your closing argument just got 90 percent better. If you don't succeed, at least you haven't promised something that you could not deliver.

Don't risk losing your case by mentioning evidence that might be excluded from trial.

2. Consider how much you want to disclose

Do you tell the *whole* story during your opening statement? Generally, you want to tell the jury about everything that you are going to present. But remember that while you are telling the jury, you are also telling your opponent what you will prove. If you have some surprise fact that your opponent does not know about (which is fairly rare), some spin on a fact that your opponent may not be prepared for (more common), or there is some other aspect of your case that you would like to hold back from your opponent for the time being, then you may want to leave the fact out of your opening statement.

3. Consider addressing the weak points in your case

Should you reveal the weak parts of your case to the jury during opening statement and, if so, to what extent? If there is a bad fact about your client or your case that you know is going to come out, most lawyers advocate telling that to the jury in opening statement. While you may be uncomfortable highlighting the bad parts of your case in opening statement, there are two good reasons to do so:

▲ It increases your credibility with the jurors. They will feel like you are giving them the truth rather than a sales pitch.

▲ Revealing the bad parts of your case during opening statement allows you to immediately defuse the bad information by explaining it in your own way.

Good Example

As I have already explained, you will learn during this case that Mr. Anderson is a hardworking man who never missed a day at work at the Acme Company and was never disciplined by the Acme Company or involved in any misbehavior at the company. But you will also learn during the trial that Mr. Anderson has a criminal record. He will take the stand and explain it to you, and he makes no excuses for it. Nine years ago, while he was in college, he was arrested for shoplifting. Mr. Anderson will testify that the shoplifting arose out of a fraternity prank. Mr. Anderson returned the merchandise that he had taken, and he pled guilty to the shoplifting charge. He paid a $500 fine and did forty hours of community service. Mr. Anderson knew that what he did was wrong, he immediately pled guilty, and took his punishment. He is not proud of what he did ten years ago, but the important part is that it was ten years ago. You will hear that Mr. Anderson has had no brushes with the law—not even a parking ticket—since that mistake he made ten years ago.

The strategy of disclosing adverse information during your opening statement is complicated when you are not certain whether the adverse information will come out at trial or not. Obviously, if the jury is never going to hear the bad information, then you do not want to tell it during your opening argument.

Bad Example

Ladies and gentlemen, I want to tell you one thing right here and right now. When the police questioned my client, they asked him if he was willing to take a lie detector test. He said that he would be willing to do that. He took the test, and he failed it. He then asked to retake the test, with a polygrapher of his own choosing. The police allowed him to do so. He took the test, and failed it again. He then asked for a second opinion and the chance to take the test with yet another polygrapher of his own choosing. He failed that test too, but, in his defense, his failure the third time around was not as pronounced as his failure in the first two tests. I just want to clear that up right now, so there's no question about how my client did on his lie detector tests.

Delivery

1. Be your persuasive self

There are as many ways of delivering an opening statement as there are opening statements. You have your own style or oratory, your own way of telling a story—your own "persuasive self" (chapter 2). Use your own style, and no one else's, because juries often have a sense of when a lawyer is putting on airs or acting in a manner that is not consistent with his or her personality.

A lawyer who is loud, boisterous and even bombastic during opening statement and closing argument, but who is soft-spoken and meek during the rest of the trial, is going to hit the jury as a bit of a psycho. The closer your courtroom personality is to your real life personality, the less likely it will appear that you are simply acting during the trial.

2. Be relaxed

Your style in opening statement should be as relaxed as possible. You will be very tense if it is your first time in front of this jury (perhaps your first time in front of *any* jury). Here is where acting skills must take over. If you can act relaxed even though you are quite nervous, you will have won half the battle.

3. Don't read

Do not read your opening statement to the jury from a prepared script. It shows a lack of confidence and is likely to bore the jury. A brief outline of topics that you want to cover in opening is just fine, as the jury won't hold it against you if you refer to notes from time to time. But don't just read a speech to the jury.

You might be surprised at how many lawyers read their openings and bore the jury to near tears.

4. Move around a bit

Where do you stand when delivering your opening statement? (By the way, you will be standing during your opening. *Never* sit.) It depends on the court you are in. Some courts require you to stand behind a lectern whenever you address the jury, the court, or a witness. Other courts let you do as you please.

Generally, if you're allowed the freedom to move about during your opening statement, you should use it and not tie yourself to a lectern or to counsel table. A little movement every now and again keeps the jurors interested in what you are saying.

Even if the judge requires you to speak behind a lectern, you can still incorporate some movement into your presentation. Perhaps you can step to the side of the lectern while resting your arm on it, or make some (appropriate) hand gestures from time to time. Make sure the movement is not distracting, however. If you have a tendency to pace back and forth when you talk, either concentrate on restraining that urge or use a lectern to limit your movements somewhat. Jurors like *some* movement, but they don't want you racing back and forth in front of them at a breakneck speed.

Chapter 6

The Genuine Way to Fake an Effective Examination

It takes years to develop an effective method for asking witnesses questions on direct and cross-examination. But it doesn't take years to make it look like you know what you are doing. In this chapter, you'll learn:

▲ what makes an exam a "cross" or a "direct"

▲ how to present an effective direct examination

▲ how to cross-examine a witness without looking foolish

Which is Which?

When are you conducting a true "direct" exam and when are you conducting a "cross" exam? At trial, the judge will most likely refer to the first lawyer's examination of a witness as the "direct" exam and the second lawyer's examination as the "cross" exam. When the first lawyer returns for more questions, the judge will call this "re-direct" and, in those few cases when the second lawyer returns for more questions, the judge will label this "re-cross." (It usually stops there—don't expect a chance at "re-re-direct.") But for purposes of knowing how to prepare an examination at trial, you should separate your examinations by whether the witness is non-adversarial or adversarial. This will help ensure that you don't make any obvious mistakes in your approach.

You should always know whether you are conducting a cross or a direct exam.

When we talk about direct examination, we mean the examination of a non-adversarial witness in which you are required to ask non-leading questions. This obviously includes your client, your client's relatives and friends, and other people who would be willing to talk to you outside the courtroom environment or, if they were not willing to talk to you, would also refuse to talk to the other side as well.

When we talk about cross-examination, we mean the examination of an adversarial witness in which you are permitted to ask leading questions. This obviously includes your opponent, your opponent's relatives and friends, and other people who would refuse to give you the time of day outside the courtroom and would be happy to assist the other side in preparing for their examination at trial.

When is a Direct Exam a Cross-Exam (and Vice Versa)?

One of the best ways to move your case forward—particularly if you represent the plaintiff—may be to call an adversarial witness as a witness at trial. For example, you might call the defendant as your second witness (after you call the plaintiff, of course, since you probably don't want to make the defendant the most important witness at trial). When you call an adversarial witness, this is labeled an "adverse direct examination" or a "cross under the rules." Even though it has this label, you should think about it as you would any other cross-examination and follow the cross-examination method discussed later in this chapter.

Similarly, if the other side calls your client as a witness, your examination will be labeled a "cross-examination" (or possibly a "friendly" cross-examination). Even though it has the cross-examination label, you should view this exam as the equivalent of a direct exam and follow the direct examination method discussed in this chapter. Don't think that you can lead your witness simply because you are the second lawyer to ask the witness questions and, more importantly, don't pass up the opportunity to introduce your witness to the jury under your terms and from your perspective.

Make sure you prepare your client for a surprise "adverse direct" by the other side at trial.

Voir Dire for Adversity?

If the other side calls a witness friendly to their side, and starts asking leading questions of their friendly witness, you may object on the grounds that the witness is not sufficiently "adverse" to permit leading questions. (The simple objection is "Leading.") If the witness's adversity is not obvious, and the judge permits leading questions, and you care about leading questions by the other side with this particular witness, you may want to ask the judge to voir dire the witness for adversity.

Q. Brief voir dire on the issue of adversity, Your Honor?

Court: Proceed.

Q. Ms. Witness, did you meet with opposing counsel to prepare for this trial?

A. Sure.

Q. Did you discuss some topics of your examination?

A. Yeah.

Q. Did you refuse to cooperate with opposing counsel in any way?

A. No.

Q. Your Honor, this witness is not adverse to [the other side], and I object to counsel's use of leading questions.

Court: Sustained. Counsel will not lead the witness.

How to Conduct Direct Exams

Many lawyers note that you "win your trial on direct." This is because the direct examination is the principal vehicle for introducing your evidence at trial. And, as discussed below, there's a right way and a wrong way to conduct your direct exams.

1. Watch the talk show hosts

There are a few talk show hosts (such as Larry King or Brian Lamb) who seem to understand that the *guest* is the true star of the show. Next time you watch one of these shows, pay attention to how little these hosts actually say during the show. Their questions are short and open-ended. The hosts listen to the answers. They care about the guest. And they keep things moving from topic to topic.

You should present your direct examinations just like your witness is on one of these talk shows. The witness is the star. Your questions are short and open-ended. You listen to the answers and appear to care about the witness's testimony. And you keep things moving. Just like Larry King or Brian Lamb.

If you don't think you could host a talk show, then you'll have trouble creating effective direct exams for trial. Keep trying until you feel comfortable in that role.

"What Happened Next?"

What is an open-ended question? It is first and foremost non-leading. A leading question is one that suggests the answer. "And then you went to the store, right?" is a leading question. "Where did you go next?" is not a leading question.

Conducting a direct examination without leading questions is difficult, especially if your witness is not too savvy and needs a little help to stay on track. It is permissible to use leading questions to change topics or to help a witness avoid a particular area that the judge may have ruled is off-limits during the trial, but other than that, you are generally expected to operate through non-leading questions.

"What happened next?", "What did you do then?", "And then what did she say?" are all non-leading questions. They are also open-ended questions. If you have a witness who tells the story well and has confidence, you should ask a lot of open-ended

Signs That Your Witness May Be Somewhat Adverse

❑ He won't return your phone calls prior to trial.

❑ He returns your phone calls only so he can swear at you and hang up.

❑ He asks for a list of your questions, which he gives to opposing counsel with a note: "hope this helps."

❑ He asks whether you can "match" the money he's getting from the other side for testifying.

❑ He keeps referring to your client as "the pinhead."

❑ He tells you "I hope you lose and I hope your client dies."

❑ His address and phone are the same as your opponent's.

❑ He is your opponent.

questions. You play the role of facilitator, prompting them every so often to discuss another topic, but you let them tell the story. That is the ideal direct examination.

Judges Vary

Jurors appreciate open-ended questions on direct examination. They like to focus on how the witness, and not the lawyer, presents your side of the story.

Judges have different ideas on what constitutes an impermissible leading question on direct examination. Some judges will require you to ask truly open-ended questions throughout your exam unless the question is for background purposes. Other judges will let you go very far toward suggesting an answer as long as you give the witnesses at least two options ("Would you say that you were under duress from the constant yelling by defendant or would you say you were not under such duress?").

Regardless of how much leeway provided by your trial judge, jurors always prefer non-leading questions. Strive to ask such questions unless you have a good reason not to do so.

Just Fade Away

You really know that your direct exam is working when the jurors focus on your witness and ignore you and your questions. The jurors want to establish connections between what's happening at trial and what's happening in their own life (chapter 2), and they can make such connections by bonding with your witnesses on direct examination.

Stay in the background as much as you can. Simply guide the story instead of pushing it in most cases. The exception is when you have a witness who is prone to going off track. In those cases, you need to take a firmer hand in directing the story.

2. Know your story

Because direct examinations are the primary way of telling your story at trial, you should make sure you have a story to tell. The structure of your opening statement or closing argument can often be a good guide to what you need to establish in your direct examination.

Great Questions During a Direct Exam

Why?

Who was there?

What happened next?

Please continue.

Can you explain?

What happened?

Where was this?

What did you hear?

Describe what happened

What else did you see?

And then?

Tell us what happened

When did this happen?

WHAT DID YOU SEE?

DID YOU HEAR ANYTHING ELSE?

Then what happened?

Was anyone else there?

Did you see anything else?

TAKE US THROUGH THE INCIDENT

Who else was there!

What else did you hear?

How did you do that!

What did you say?

A Not so Great Question During Direct Exam

Am I right that Curly reached into his bag and took out a big watermelon, that he then threw the watermelon at you, that you ducked, that when you turned around you saw the watermelon hit Larry in the face, and that you then pointed at Moe and yelled "He did it!"?

Once you know your story, decide what witnesses you will need to establish all of the facts that you have put in your opening statement or closing argument. If you really want to be thorough, you can break your opening statement or closing argument into each sentence and decide what witness or witnesses will establish the facts set forth in each of the sentences.

In doing this, you should always have one eye on the law books. Make sure you will have testimony or evidence to support each of the elements of the claims or defenses you are trying to establish at trial. If you fail to do this, you are subject to having a directed verdict entered against you for failure to introduce evidence sufficient to support your case.

This exercise will help you avoid breaking any promises made during opening statement. You don't want to forget to prove any large or small details from your opening statement.

Keep your other eye on your themes (chapter 3). Try to use each of your witnesses to endorse or support at least one of your themes of the case. Do not be afraid of being repetitious when it comes to your main themes. If the jury has heard your main theme so often that they have it memorized, you have done an excellent job.

3. Outline your direct exams

Once you have determined the facts that you want to tell the jury and the witnesses you will use to tell those facts, you should then prepare an outline for each witness. The outline will guide you to a fast-paced, effective examination at trial.

Experienced trial lawyers might have a one-page outline for six hours of direct examination. The outline consists mainly of general topics to cover. The lawyer is experienced enough to ask all the background and substantive questions necessary to develop that particular topic. There is no shame, however, for less experienced lawyers to have a longer outline—sometimes even writing out each question in advance. This procedure can be useful; it helps you think through the entire direct examination in advance—a sort of dress rehearsal for the main event.

Having an outline should not be a millstone around your neck, though. The key to a successful examination and cross-examination is listening to the witness's answer and following up with an appropriate question. This requires being flexible, not tied to a prepared outline. If you are tied too closely to an outline, you will miss some golden opportunities to develop testimony that should be developed.

Bad Example

Q.   Sir, please tell the jury your educational background.

A.   I attended the University of Minnesota from 1987 to 1992. I then left the University to join Mother Theresa in fighting poverty and hunger in Calcutta.

Q.   Are you married, sir?

4. Does practice make too perfect?

Some lawyers like to rehearse the direct examination questions with the witnesses. A little bit of role-playing to prepare the witness for trial is a good thing, and you should certainly review the general areas of testimony and the exhibits that you'll use with the witness.

But you want your witnesses to appear spontaneous on the stand. Let them be themselves. You can try to smooth over the rough edges in their personalities prior to trial, but you are not going to be able to change their personality. Over-rehearsal often leads to answers that look like they were rehearsed. And if the whole presentation looks like it was rehearsed, the jurors are going to believe it much less then they would if it appeared spontaneous.

Make it look like you are having a conversation with the witness. If your witness misunderstands one of your questions, do not worry. Politely point out that he or she misunderstood what you were asking, and ask the question again. The more the direct examination seems to be a natural, spontaneous conversation between you and the witness, the more credibility the jury will give it.

Many trial lawyers are uncomfortable with less than perfect direct exams. But the alternative (perfect exams) is much, much, worse.

5. Avoid personality changes

It is important to let the witness be himself on direct examination because you know the witness is going to be himself on cross-examination, where he will probably not be prepared for the questions that will be asked. You do not want to have a witness display one type of demeanor during direct examination but then completely change personality during the cross-examination. The jury is likely to believe that the direct examination was just a rehearsed act.

Witnesses have foibles, just like every other human being. Juries understand this. It is fair for you to try and correct some of the more egregious foibles, but you cannot and should not correct them all.

When you are doing your direct examination, you should have at your side your outline for that witness and also all the exhibits you will need during that witness's testimony. Jurors resent lawyers who spend time fumbling around and shuffling through papers in search of the exhibit. Have all of the exhibits pulled out in advance so that your direct examination can proceed smoothly and efficiently.

Do not think that you have to tell the whole story through every witness in the case. Each witness probably knows a different piece of the story; sometimes there is not a single witness who knows the whole story. Get from each witness what she knows. Once she has made her contribution to the story, stop and move on to the next witness.

Staying focused on the main points helps keep your case moving at a fast pace. The jury appreciates this.

Pay attention to, and always keep in mind, the major points of the story that you are trying to tell. That will help you redirect a witness who has gone astray, and will help you develop the major themes of your case as you go forward.

How to Conduct Cross-Examinations

The best cross-examination is one in which you appear to have some very simple points which you want the witness to concede. Since your points are simple, there is no reason for you to expend too much energy to establish those points. The more relaxed you are, the more it will appear that you are completely in control and moving your case forward. If you're not too ambitious, you'll gain some ground on cross-examination, or at least *appear* to gain some ground.

1. Watch your tone

Your tone on cross-examination should be polite, friendly, and relaxed. You should avoid any semblance of combativeness, frustration or hostility. Do not rub your fingers through your hair in frustration, roll your eyes, or look sternly at the witness.

When you think of cross-exams, you probably think of the movie version, known as the "killer" cross. This is where the lawyer yells at the witness ("I want the truth") or otherwise dominates the witness into submission. There's no such thing as a "killer" cross in real trials—or if there is such a thing, it doesn't happen often enough to justify making it your goal in any particular trial.

To illustrate why it's not a great idea, consider the Possible Juror Reaction ("PJR") while you cross-examine the defendant in a breach of contract case:

Q. [You smirk at the witness.] I want to ask you about your performance under section 10 of the contract, Ms. Witness.

A. Sure.

PJR: *Why is the lawyer smirking? The witness seems pretty nice.*

Q. You never once supplied the tuna fish by the first of the month, as required by the contract, true?

A. Well, we were always having problems with—

Q. Ms. Witness, you're not answering my question. Listen closely.

PJR: *This lawyer is a jerk. I'd hate it if I was interrupted like that. My spouse sometimes does that and it drives me crazy. What's the lawyer's problem?*

Q. It is true that you never once supplied the tuna fish by the first of the month, as required by the contract, yes or no?

A. We did our best but we never made that deadline.

Q. [Sarcastic tone.] We did our best but we never made that deadline?

A. That's right.

PJR: *Wow. How boring. Why is the lawyer repeating the witness's answer with that tone? That's why I hate lawyers. I can't stand that kind of behavior.*

For now, you should erase any thoughts about "killing" or otherwise "dominating" a witness like they do in the movies. It won't work.

As you get more comfortable in cross-examining witnesses, it will appear more and more as if you are conversing with, rather than interrogating, the witness. Remember that the jury is used to participating in conversations but is not used to listening to disjointed questions followed by brief answers. You should thus strive to talk with the witness as if you were in an informal setting outside the courtroom. This is not to suggest that you should be overly friendly with the witness or call the witness by his or her first name. You should continue to be respectful and polite, while at the same time showing that you are capable of having a simple conversation with the witness.

2. You'll ask leading questions, right?

The core of each question on cross-examination should be a statement which you are making to the jury, such as "You were driving the truck." There are a million ways to make this statement; ten of the most common are set forth on the chart on the next page.

Experienced trial lawyers will sometimes depart from the rule that you should lead the witness on cross. But you should follow the rule in your first several trials until you develop a better sense of judgment at trial.

3. Organize your lines

A "line" of cross is a point you want to make with the witness. You establish the point implicitly by a series of short, leading questions. Many times you will avoid asking the ultimate question, which would make your point explicitly, because you don't want to risk an outright denial by the witness of your main point.

Here's a sample line of cross showing that a witness was driving recklessly:

Q. You were driving the truck, right?

A. Yes.

Q. You were driving about five miles over the speed limit, correct?

A. I believe so.

Q. You were talking on your cell phone while you drove, right?

A. Yes.

How to Lead Your Witness

1. You would agree with me that _____?

2. _____, right?

3. Isn't it true that _____?

4. _____, true?

5. It's fair to say that _____?

6. _____, correct?

7. You agree that _____?

8. _____, fair?

9. It's a fact that _____?

10. [State the fact] _____?

Q. It's fair to say that you swerved the truck over the center line at least three times?

A. That's true.

You would then argue during closing that the witness was driving recklessly since he was speeding, talking on a cell phone, and swerving over the center line. This is more effective than asking the witness "Do you agree with me that you were driving recklessly" and having him deny that fact.

Don't try to hit a "home run" by asking the witness to agree with your main point—save it for closing argument.

Write it Down

To organize your lines of cross-examination, take a notebook page and list the main point (or line) at the top of the page. Then list your supportive facts below the main point. Use a separate page for each line of cross. The above line would look like this:

YOU WERE DRIVING RECKLESSLY

▲ driving the truck

▲ going five miles over speed limit

▲ talking on the cell phone

▲ went over the center line at least three times

Avoid Bad Habits on Cross

saying "thank you"

nodding your head

repeating the answer

interrupting the witness

raising your voice

ACTING SURPRISED OR SHOCKED

checking things off on a notepad

taking long pauses

studying your notes

saying "okay," "exactly," "sure," or any similar word

walking around the courtroom for no reason

Use Transitions

If the judge and opposing counsel will permit you to do so (most will), you should introduce your main lines of cross-examination by making brief transitional statements. For example:

▲ Mr. Smith, I want to first ask you about exactly what you saw at the scene of the accident. [Begin question.]

▲ All right. Let's talk about your claim for damages. [Begin question.]

4. Get some rhythm

It's easier to get "yes" answers when your questions are short and truly capable of a "yes" answer.

You want to develop a rhythm in your questioning on cross-examination. The best way to create such a rhythm is by obtaining some form of a "yes" answer to every one of your questions. A cross-examination will appear effective if the witness appears to agree with everything you have to say.

What's at the Core?

The core of your question should be a statement you make to the jury. To use a simple example, suppose you want the witness to agree that the traffic light was red. The statement you want to make is obvious: "The traffic light was red." There are a variety of ways in which you can incorporate that statement in a question:

▲ You would agree with me that the *traffic light was red.*

▲ The *traffic light was red*, wasn't it?

▲ Isn't it true that the *traffic light was red?*

▲ The *traffic light was red*, true?

▲ The *traffic light was red*, correct?

▲ It is fair to say that the *traffic light was red*, right?

▲ You agree the *traffic light was red*, right?

If you are really in a rhythm with your questions, you may be able to make your statements to the witness and have the witness answer "yes" in response to each of the statements.

Here is an example of this format:

Q. You were driving the truck?

A. Yes.

Q. You were driving about five miles over the speed limit?

A. I believe so.

Q. You were talking on your cell phone while you drove?

A. Yes.

Q. You swerved the truck over the center line at least three times?

A. That's true.

Here's another example:

Q. I want to make sure I understand your testimony. The traffic light was red, right?

A. That's correct.

Q. It was sunny outside.

A. Yes.

Q. There was almost no wind.

A. That's right.

Q. And you could not see any other car as you approached the light?

A. Yes.

5. Emphasize important points

You may want to place more emphasis than usual on the particular statement that underlies your question. Do so only when you are certain that the witness will agree with the statement.

You're Positive, Right?

Be careful. Many witnesses will try to resist these types of questions. Use this approach only when you know it's going to work for you.

To continue the last example, suppose that the witness had testified at the deposition that the light was red and you were confident that the witness would agree with you that the light was red on cross-examination. Suppose further that you wanted to place great emphasis on the fact that the light was red. Here are some different ways to make your point:

▲ You are absolutely positive that that light at that intersection was red, correct?

▲ There is one thing we know. The traffic light was red, right?

▲ There is not a doubt in your mind that the traffic light was red, true?

▲ You know for an absolute fact that that traffic light on that day was red, right?

Confirm the Negative

Another way to place emphasis on a statement is to show that the witness agrees that your fact is true and that contradictory facts are not true.

Q. The light was red, right?

A. Yes.

Q. It wasn't green?

A. That's right.

Q. It wasn't yellow?

A. That's right.

Break it Down

You can also place emphasis on a statement by breaking the statement into separate points. To use a ridiculous example:

Q. There was a traffic light.

A. Yes.

Q. The traffic light had a color, right?

A. Sure.

Q. You saw that color didn't you?

A. Yes, I did.

Q. And you know what that color was, right?

A. Yeah, I do.

Q. It was red?

A. Yes.

Tell the Jury

Finally, one of the best ways to place emphasis on a statement is to have the witness speak directly to the jury when she reveals the fact that you believe is critical. For example:

Q. You were at the scene of the accident, right?

A. Yes.

Q. You saw the traffic light, right?

A. Yes, I did.

Q. And you were certain of what color the traffic light was, right?

A. Yes, I was.

Q. Tell the jury what color you saw.

A. (Turns to the jury) Red.

6. Impeach the witness without impeaching yourself

Impeachment is an effective form of cross-examination. To impeach a witness on cross-examination, you first need an impeaching document. The most common form of impeaching document is a deposition transcript, though the document could take many forms, including letters, statements, press releases or other documents in which the witness made a statement.

Here's the Deal

The impeaching document permits you to make an implicit deal with the witness: *If you agree with your prior statements, I will not read them to the jury.*

If you don't understand the terms of the deal, read this section again and again until you get it. Too many lawyers embarrass themselves by misunderstanding the implicit deal made with every witness.

Commit the terms of the implicit deal to memory and follow these terms during your cross-examination. Note that the deal is quite simple. The witness must agree with the statements the witness has already made. This does not mean that the witness must agree with similar statements, or with statements which are consistent with prior statements, but rather that the witness will agree with the exact same words used by the witness in a prior statement.

Use the Same Words

You need to remember to use the exact same words from the prior statement of the witness in your questioning. If you use different words, then you are breaking your implicit deal with the witness. For example, consider the following completely ineffective attempted impeachment:

Q. Ms. Halbert, you would agree that it was raining on the night of the accident, wouldn't you?

A. I'm not sure I'd say it was raining.

Q. Didn't you state in your affidavit that it was "drizzling"?

A. I sure did. That's what I mean, I didn't think it was raining. It was just drizzling.

In the above example, you may attempt to argue with the witness about whether "raining" is the same as "drizzling." There is no reason to become involved in such an argument, and the jury will not appreciate the time being wasted on this issue. What you should have done is realized that, according to the terms of the implicit deal, the witness must agree that it was "drizzling" on the night of the accident, and if she fails to agree you'll read her prior statement to the jury. The implicit deal was only about the word "drizzling." It did not cover any other word.

Accept the Limitations

You need to accept the limitations that come with using an impeaching document on cross-examination. To continue the above example, you should realize that the witness will either agree that it was drizzling outside or face direct impeachment. Either way, you will establish that according to this witness, it was drizzling outside. You may wish that the witness would agree that it was "raining," "pouring," or "wet outside." But if the witness did not use those words, you cannot use impeachment to force the witness to agree with those words.

Like it or not, you are stuck with the words used in the impeaching document.

Consider another example, based on an affidavit in which a witness swears it was "drizzling" outside:

Q. It was *drizzling* outside that night, wasn't it?

A. Yes, it was.

In this situation, the witness has lived up to the terms of your implicit deal. She agreed with the substance of her prior statement. You have no right to impeach the witness by reading the prior statement to the witness because there is nothing to impeach. Impeachment is possible only if the witness disagrees with the prior statement. (A separate issue is whether a prior statement constitutes an admission which can be used for purposes other than impeachment.)

Jumping the Gun

One of the most common mistakes made by beginning trial lawyers is to attempt to impeach a witness before the witness has disagreed with any prior statement. Consider the following example:

Q. Isn't it true that in your affidavit you stated that it was drizzling outside?

OPPOSING COUNSEL: Objection. Hearsay.

COURT: Sustained.

It is improper to read a prior statement, including deposition testimony, if the witness has not yet disagreed with the prior statement. If opposing counsel starts going down this road and quoting prior statements by the witness, you should object on grounds of improper impeachment. (Once again, we are setting aside the issue of admissions.)

Just Read It

This is one of the most common errors of beginning trial lawyers. They try to make too much out of an impeaching document.

When the witness disagrees with a prior statement, you are entitled to read that statement to the jury. You are not entitled to smile, to smirk, to sigh, to raise your voice, or to otherwise show disgust with the fact that the witness is disagreeing with the prior statement.

Do not give in to the temptation to be a jerk simply because the witness has disagreed with the prior statement. The jury will turn on you if it believes that you are making too much of the impeaching document. In fact, when you impeach the witness, you should show great respect for the witness and treat the witness with dignity. Do not gloat in any way. In addition, keep it short. When you are finished, move to a new question. Don't comment on the impeachment process.

Bing, Bang, Boom

The impeachment process is quite simple:

Q. It was drizzling that night, right?

A. No, it was not drizzling.

Q. On page 62, line 10 of your deposition, did I ask you this question: "What was the weather outside?" And did you give this answer: "It was drizzling outside." Did you give that testimony at your deposition?

A. Yes, I did.

That's it. The witness did not agree with the exact words of her prior statement, and therefore you read those words to the jury. You should now proceed with a completely new question. Resist the temptation to ask the witness to explain the apparent inconsistency between her testimony and her prior statement. The jury may view such questioning as too aggressive, or the witness might provide a reasonable explanation. You've made your point. Move on.

This is where judgment comes into play. You need to develop a feel for when to emphasize the impeaching document and when to take it down a notch.

Available Methods

There are many ways to use the impeaching document. You can approach the witness and read the testimony to the witness in the witness box. You can give the witness a separate copy of a deposition transcript and remain at table while you impeach the witness. Sometimes you can use an overhead or a video projector (*e.g.*, an ELMO) to read the testimony to the witness. The form you use will depend on the importance of the impeachment testimony and the leeway that the judge grants you. Regardless of the form that you use, however, you should maintain control of your cross-examination by *reading the testimony yourself* and simply asking the witness whether she gave that testimony.

Things Not to Say After Impeaching a Witness

Are you lying now or were you lying then?

Which is the truth?

That statement contradicts what you just said, right?

You're having trouble keeping your story straight, aren't you?

The truth hurts, doesn't it?

So first you said one thing, and now you are saying another?

One of those statements must be false, right?

I just impeached you, didn't I?

No Need to Explain

If you want to avoid permitting the witness an opportunity to explain purported inconsistencies in her testimony, you should use the exact same words from the prior statement (thereby preventing the witness from engaging in word games with you) and ask the witness solely whether she made the prior statement and *not* whether she still agrees with that statement or whether she can explain why she made a prior statement. All you want to know is whether the witness gave that testimony or made that prior statement, and nothing else.

If your question is clear, the witness will not have a lot of wiggle room. If, notwithstanding the clarity of your question, the witness tries to explain the inconsistency, you may say to the witness, "I apologize, but my question was simply: Did you or did you not give that testimony? And I understand your answer to be: You did give that testimony. Is that right?" The witness will usually say "yes" in response to that question.

PTM

Chapter 7

Some Ideas for Getting Documents Into Evidence

Beginning trial lawyers are often intimidated by the mechanics of getting exhibits into evidence. But it is not really such a difficult task. In this chapter, you'll learn:

▲ how to get documentary evidence admitted

▲ what are the "magic words"

▲ how to respond to objections

It's Not that Difficult

You have all your exhibits together and have premarked and prenumbered them (or completed whatever is required by your court's rules). You have them all neatly organized in folders and boxes. They are sitting next to you while you conduct the direct examination of your first witness. And now, four minutes into your direct examination, it is time to put in your first exhibit. How do you do it?

It is not all that hard.

1. Approach the witness—with the court's permission

Don't be tentative about asking to approach a witness. Speak with a strong voice and say "your honor, may I approach the witness?"

Begin by asking the judge for permission to approach the witness. This is a formality, but most trial judges require you to ask for permission before you get up and start walking up to witnesses. Some judges may tell you that you do not need to ask for permission; if so, just go ahead and walk up to the witness. But unless you get this issue hammered out with the trial judge in advance, make sure you ask for permission the first time you want to go up to a witness to hand him or her an exhibit. And unless the trial judge tells you that you do not need to, ask for permission each and every time you do so. Most judges insist on it (which is reason enough to do it), and it looks polite to the jury.

2. Have the witness identify the exhibit

Hand the witness the exhibit and say, "Mr. Doe, I am showing you Exhibit 1. Could you please tell the jury what Exhibit 1 is?" Here you are asking the witness to simply *identify* the document. The identification can be as simple as saying, "This is a letter that I wrote to Mrs. Jones on January 1, 1999."

3. Lay more foundation, if necessary

It is possible that you will have to lay some more foundation to get the exhibit into evidence. The process of "laying foundation" is nothing more than obtaining testimony from the witness to show that he or she really can identify the exhibit. For example, if the exhibit bears the witness's signature, you could ask the witness to confirm that his or her signature appears on the document. If the exhibit is a letter that the witness wrote, you can simply ask, "Did you write this letter?" and "Is that your signature that appears at the bottom of the letter?" If it is a contract that your witness has seen and read, but did not sign, you ask simply, "Have you seen this document before?"

4. Offer the exhibit

Once you have identified the exhibit and laid the necessary foundation, offer the exhibit. Before you ask another question, before you go another step, before you start to talk about the exhibit with the witness, offer the exhibit. This is very easy: "Your Honor, I offer Exhibit 24 into evidence" or simply "I offer Exhibit 24." Don't get caught up in the excitement of the trial and ask detailed questions of an exhibit that is not even admitted into evidence. Note that you should "offer" exhibits into evidence. Use the word "offer" and no other word.

Some judges will give you a hard time if you fail to use the word "offer" in seeking admission of evidence. Use it.

It also helps to build the record adequately if you offer exhibits into evidence immediately after a witness identifies them. Many lawyers—including seasoned trial lawyers—have forgotten to officially offer exhibits into evidence, which means they never become admitted into evidence and never become part of the record. *You have to offer the exhibit and have the judge admit it into evidence in order for it to become part of the record of the case.* If it's not part of the record, it's as if the exhibit never existed. If you train yourself to offer the exhibit automatically after it has been identified, you are less likely to forget to do it; it will just become a routine.

5. Deal with any objections

After you offer the exhibit, your opponent will say whether he or she objects to the admission of the evidence or has no objection. If your opponent says that he or she has no objection, wait for the judge to say that the evidence has been "admitted" or "received." Once the judge says that, it is official, the exhibit is now part of the record of the case, and you can continue with your questioning about the exhibit.

If your opponent objects to the evidence, what should you do? *Wait for the judge to rule on the objection.* Sit quietly until the judge rules. Don't offer any response unless the judge asks you to do so. If the objection is overruled, keep going with your next question. If the

"Offer" Exhibit 35. Don't say

❑ "I move exhibit 35 into evidence."

❑ "I move the admission of exhibit 35."

❑ "I move that exhibit 35 be admitted."

❑ "I ask the court to admit exhibit 35."

❑ "I'd like exhibit 35 to be in evidence."

❑ "Could we all agree exhibit 35 is in evidence?"

❑ "Any problem with exhibit 35 going into evidence?"

❑ "Exhibit 35 should be in evidence. True or false?"

❑ "What should we do about exhibit 35? Thoughts?"

❑ "I'm going to close my eyes. When I open them,
I want exhibit 35 to be in evidence."

objection is sustained, you will probably want to try to respond to the objection, either by asking the witness questions or by asking the judge for permission to address the merits of the objection.

Generally, you will be able to figure out from your opponent's objections and from the judge's ruling what you should do to try to overcome an objection. If you are confused, ask to approach and discuss it with the judge. That discussion will probably clue you in on how to fix the problem.

At some point, of course, you must simply give up on trying to obtain admission of an exhibit. If the judge has made it plain that the evidence is not coming in, you are going to look foolish to the jury in continuing to fight the battle. How long you keep up the fight depends, of course, on how important the evidence is to you. With exhibits that are not that important, you do not want to try the jury's patience fighting too long over them. But if the evidence is crucial to your case, you obviously want to fight harder to get it into evidence.

Remember, juries are generally not impressed by long-winded battles over the admissibility of exhibits. They do not understand the legal concepts being debated, and they generally just want to get on with the trial. Keep this in mind in deciding how long you will fight the good fight.

Calm down when the other side objects. You don't want the jury to think you're concerned.

Read this section in conjunction with chapter 9 (Six Objections You Should Know Something About).

A Few Substantive Ideas

It is not possible to cover all the ways in which you can respond to any objections, but some objections are more common than others and have a very common response (see also chapter 9).

1. Foundation

If the sustained objection is to "lack of foundation," you have not proven that the witness has reason to identify and vouch for the exhibit. You should ask some more questions that emphasize the witness's personal involvement with the exhibit. Did she create it? Write it? See it? Read it? Maintain it in her files? In general, the question is: "Where does this witness get off saying that this exhibit is what he says it is?" You should ask questions to draw out the answer to that general question.

2. Relevance

If the objection is to relevance, you should be prepared to explain to the judge why the exhibit is relevant to the case. If your explanation is going to be a long one, you might ask to approach the bench so that you can discuss the matter outside of the jury's hearing. Be prepared to explain the issues on which the exhibit is relevant, which may include how it ties in with other exhibits in the case.

If the relevance of the exhibit will become clear only once additional testimony and exhibits have gone in, you should explain that to the judge and ask the judge to admit the evidence conditionally. This is a bit of a strategic gamble for you, because if you are unable to establish the relevance of the document with later evidence, the judge will ultimately instruct the jury that it should disregard the exhibit that you are trying to offer. But if you are fairly sure that the relevance will all become clear later, you can ask the judge to admit the document conditioned on your ability to show the relevance through later testimony and exhibits. If the judge admits the document conditionally, *be sure to go back later (even after the jury has recessed) and ask the judge to definitively receive the evidence into the record.* Conditional admission of evidence is a loose end that you must tie up later.

3. Hearsay and the business records exception

If the objection is that the exhibit is hearsay, you need to know the hearsay rules in order to respond. That is easier said than done, but one of the most common ways to overcome a hearsay objection is to show that the document is subject to one of the many exceptions to the hearsay rule. And perhaps the most common of those exceptions is the "business records" exception (found in Fed. R. Evid. 803(6) and similar state evidence rules). Be familiar with the rule in any case that involves records generated in the ordinary course of a business. To obtain admission of documents under the business records exception, you have to ask the witness a set of basic foundation questions:

1. "Who created this document?"

2. "Was it his or her duty to gather information and create this document?"

3. "Is this document kept in the ordinary course of ABC Company's business?"

4. "Is it the regular practice of ABC Company to generate documents such as this one?"

If the witness is able to say "yes" to these questions, you should be able to obtain admission of the document into evidence. If your opponent renews the hearsay objection and it is sustained again, you will probably need to ask to approach the bench and discuss the matter with the judge to find out exactly what is wrong with the exhibit you are trying to introduce. Or, if it really doesn't matter much, move on to the next topic of your examination.

Chapter 8

The Best
Demonstrative Exhibits

One of the best ways to simplify your case for the jury is through the use of demonstrative exhibits. In this chapter, you'll learn:

▲ how to use a big pad of paper

▲ how to use charts and graphs

▲ how to use enlargements or "blow ups"

Keep it Basic

You should use demonstrative exhibits to reinforce *basic* points for the jury. If you think you need to reinforce *complicated* and *convoluted* points involving a great deal of data and information, don't use demonstrative exhibits. In fact, don't use anything at all, as the jury will not follow anything that is complicated or convoluted. So keep it simple.

The Big Pad of Paper

Don't rely on the courthouse to provide your big pad of paper. Bring your own and make sure it works.

Setting aside massive trials involving computers, videos, animation, and other expensive technology, there are three basic types of demonstrative exhibits about which you should be aware before you walk into your next jury trial: enlargements of existing documents, enlargements of special charts or graphs prepared for trial, and a big pad of paper. This latter category—the big pad of paper—is one that is overlooked by beginning trial lawyers but is potentially your best method of communicating with the jury.

A big pad of paper has several advantages over other types of demonstrative exhibits:

▲ *Little or no advance notice.* Since you are drawing on the pad of paper during trial, the exhibit does not exist prior to trial and you thus need not give the copy of the exhibit to the other side. (In most courts, you need only generally inform the other side of your intentions with this type of demonstrative exhibit.)

▲ *Flexible.* You can change your design of the exhibit minutes before you begin drawing on the paper.

▲ *Inexpensive.* It doesn't cost much to buy or borrow a big pad of paper. In fact, the courtroom might already have one.

▲ *Easy to use.* It doesn't take a lot of practice to learn how to write something down on a big pad of paper (though it takes a bit more practice than you might think).

Beginning trial lawyers put too much information on their demonstrative exhibits, including their pad of paper. Remember that the best demonstrative exhibit communicates a basic and simple point to the jury, *and nothing more*. Prepare your information on a piece of notebook paper, and then edit and re-edit that piece of paper until it has very few words on it.

Practicing on notebook paper helps you avoid wasting time.

You can use a big pad of paper throughout the trial, including opening statement, witness examinations, and closing argument.

Ideas For Opening Statement

1. Basic facts

One of the best ways to use a big pad of paper in your opening statement is to help the jury understand the most basic facts in the case, such as the names of the parties, the names of the trial counsel, or the names of certain key witnesses. To keep things moving during your opening statement, write down this type of information before trial—and consider showing it to the other side (just to be safe).

Gernon v. Snider Trucking Co.

Plaintiff : Jill Gernon
              (Attorney Steve Volling)

Defendant: Snider Trucking Co
                (Attorney Jim Fribley)

Snider Trucking Company
President Johnny Snider

Accounting   Manager Cameron Durst

Sales Manager   Lou Holmgren

    Sales Associates:

        Northwest Region: Mary Flesher

        Midwest Region: Jack Connelly

        Southern Region: John Hartnett

        Eastern Region: Jill Gernon
                        (Plaintiff)

Bad Example

Snider Trucking Company
3142 Wells Avenue
Dallas, Texas

President Johnny Snider (responsible for overall management of company; created company in 1977, principal witness at trial)

Sales Manager Lou Holmgren (responsible for overall sales; supervises sales associates; will testify about conversation with Defendant regarding sales commissions)

Accounting Manager Cameron Durst (kept all the records for sales commissions; will testify about Defendant's commission)

Sales Associates:

Northwest Region: Mary Flesher (responsible for sales in northwest part of country; will testify regarding sales activities)

Midwest Region: Jack Connelly (responsible for sales in midwest part of country; will testify regarding sales activities)

Southern Region: John Hartnett (responsible for sales in southern part of country; will testify regarding sales activities and his work with Plaintiff on the new sales plan)

Eastern Region: Jill Gernon (Plaintiff)

2. Non-argumentative concept or issue

A pad of paper also effectively illustrates a simple and noncontroversial concept, such as a standard formula, or an issue in dispute, such as a contract term. As long as you write down the concept or issue in an objective manner, you should not face an objection from opposing counsel during opening statement.

Sales Commission
at Snider Trucking Co:

First $50,000 in sales: 2%

Over $50,000 in sales: 3%

$$Profit = Revenue - Costs$$

3. Fairness points

A final way to use a pad of paper during opening statement is to make a fairness point (chapter 3) or any other kind of point that supports your theory of the case. The point should be simple and dramatic—it should catch the jurors' attention and influence how they view the remainder of the trial.

Be careful. Opposing counsel may object to this tactic as argumentative, and judges will differ on how they will rule on such an objection. You can increase your chances of success by making your point quickly and refraining from using the big pad of paper to make any additional fairness points during your opening. Even though you might make your fairness point quickly, your sheet of paper should remain in front of the jury as you continue to speak about other issues.

By the end of your opening statement, the jury will have heard you talk about your point, watched you draw it on a big sheet of paper, and continued to look at your piece of paper repeatedly for the remainder of your opening statement.

"The defendant is refusing to pay any money to my client. And I mean not one penny."

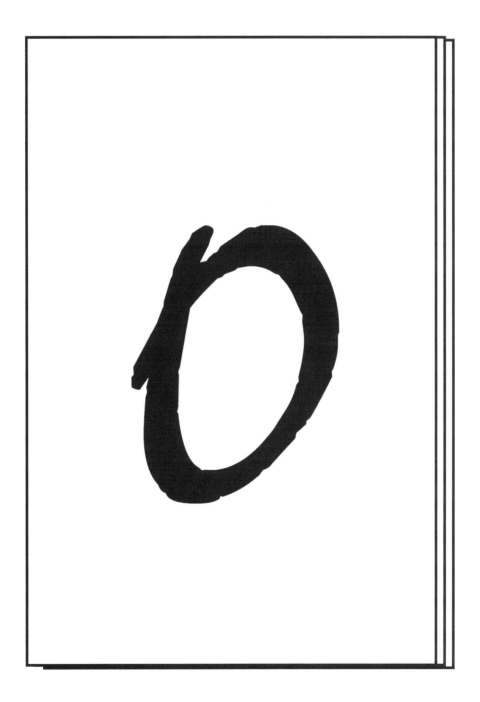

"No one ever complained about my client's sales activities while she worked at Snider Trucking Company. Not a single person."

"The plaintiff has already received $1,223,398.55 in sales commissions, and now she wants an additional $500,000."

$1,223,398.55

Ideas for Direct and Cross-exams

When using a big pad of paper with witnesses, you have a lot more latitude on cross-examination than on direct.

On direct, you can ask the witness to draw a simple diagram of a scene to assist the jury in understanding the basic facts of the case. (If details matter, then you may need to draft a more formal looking demonstrative exhibit to show the scene of the incident.) You can also return to the sheets used in your opening to convey basic (non-argumentative) information, such as the names of parties or witnesses. But avoid anything remotely argumentative during direct exams.

On cross, you can do all of the above and also make argumentative points with your adverse witness. In making such points, you are limited only by your own imagination and common sense.

For example, suppose you want to emphasize that an expert witness has testified for the defense in each of her twenty cases. (Let's pretend this is a highly significant fact in the context of your case.) One way to emphasize the point is by making a list of the numbers 1–20 and then ask the following questions:

Q. You said you testified as an expert 20 times, right?

A. Right.

Q. Am I right that you testified for the defendant in your first case?

A. Yes. (Write down "D" after number 1.)

Q. You testified for the defendant in your second case?

A. That's right. (Write down "D" after number 2.)

Q. In fact, you testified for the defendant in each and every one of your 20 cases, true?

A. That's correct. (Connect "D" with numbers 3–20.)

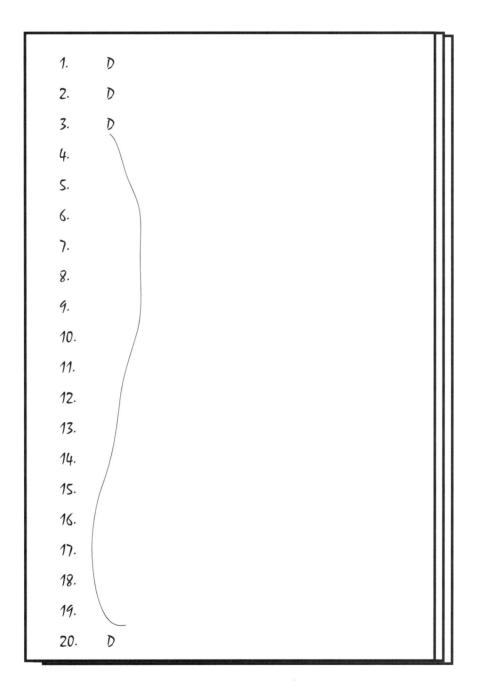

As another example, suppose you represent the defendant in a whistleblower case, and you want to emphasize that each of the three adverse actions taken by the defendant-employer against the plaintiff-employee was reasonable and not in retaliation for whistle blowing.

Q. You complained about the company's waste disposal practices in July, right?

A. Right. (Write down "July – waste disposal complaint.")

Q. Then the company gave you a written warning in August about your tardiness, correct.

A. Yes. (Write down "August – tardiness warning.")

Q. Then the company gave you a written warning in September about your failure to follow safety procedures?

A. That's right. (Write down "September – safety warning.")

Q. And the company gave you another written warning in October, again about tardiness?

A. That's correct. (Write down "October – tardiness warning.")

Q. You would agree that it was reasonable for the company to give you the written warning about your tardiness in August, wouldn't you?

A. I suppose so. (Write down "R" after August entry.)

Q. It was also reasonable for the company to give you the written warning in September about your safety violation, true?

A. I think so. (Write down "R" after September entry.)

Q. It was also reasonable for the company to give you the written warning about your tardiness in October, correct?

A. Yeah. (Write down "R" after October entry.)

July – waste disposal complaint

August – Tardiness Warning **R**

September – Safety Warning **R**

October – Tardiness Warning **R**

Ideas for Closing Argument

When you present your closing argument, you can use the big pad of paper to make all the points you made during trial, to organize your argument, and to summarize important testimony and documentary evidence. You might prepare the sheets before you begin your argument, particularly if you have more than a few words of text.

Don't Overdo It

By the end of the trial, you should have used only a few sheets of paper. You want the jury and the court to believe that the sheets of paper have assisted them in learning basic facts (such as names and dates) and fundamental points in your case. If you get too cute with your pad of paper, everyone in the courtroom will grow tired of you and your pad of paper.

You may use a pad of paper during your closing argument:

Defendant Was Negligent

- drank two beers that night
- drove over the speed limit
- ran the stop sign

Here's another example of using the pad of paper during closing argument:

Snider Trucking Owes
Plaintiff Extra Commissions:

- *"Company will pay all extra commissions earned during the applicable sales period."*

  (Sales Contract, Para. 10)
  "We should have paid those commissions."
  (Sales Mgr.)

- *"All extra commissions will be honored."*
  (August '01 Memo)

Big Charts and Graphs

A big chart or graph will have a dramatic effect on the jury. Like the big pad of paper, it should convey basic information or make a fundamental point. The best chart or graph is the one introduced during trial (whether in opening statement or direct examination), used more than once to make basic points with witnesses, and then used again during closing argument to win your case.

You need to spend a lot of time looking at different versions of the chart or graph before you make a final decision. Sometimes one color works better than another color. Sometimes a bar graph works better than a pie chart. It will depend on the facts of your case, but you need to spend the time to come up with the right chart or graph. If it lacks a "wow" effect, you should not use it to illustrate an important point in the case.

In addition, your chart or graph should be big. And when we say big, we mean *really big*. You want your chart or graph to stand out to the jury and become part of the courtroom. The jury should have no trouble reading the information on the demonstrative.

If you need to use several charts or graphs, then you should use an overhead or video projector (such as an ELMO) to illustrate your points. You should save your enlarged charts or graphs for your most important points.

It is a good idea to put your chart or graph on your exhibit list prior to trial and give it an exhibit number. This will increase the chances of it being entered into evidence at trial. If your chart assists the jury, the judge may permit you to introduce it into evidence. This will depend on the judge.

To illustrate the difference between a good chart and a bad one, suppose you want to show that your client brought in the highest net sales revenues (gross sales minus returns) of all the employees at Snider Trucking Company.

Bad Example

Sales Revenues By Employee

Employee	New Contracts	Renewed Contracts	Special Contracts
Flesher (gross)	$209,344	$135,993	$54,438
(less returns)	$2,477	$1,993	$563
Connelly (gross)	$322,890	$92,355	$30,020
(less returns)	$10,955	$800	$90
Hartnett (gross)	$210,451	$202,931	$11,821
(less returns)	$91,003	$15,905	$862
Plaintiff (gross)	$457,812	$490,268	$109,322
(less returns)	$31,483	$29,402	$13,337

Good Example

Net Sales Revenues By Employee

Plaintiff	**$983,180**
Flesher	$394,742
Connelly	$433,400
Hartnett	$317,433

Remember that the objective of a chart is to communicate a *fundamental* point ("Plaintiff brought in the highest net sales revenues") as opposed to a more complicated point ("There were three categories of sales, and when one examines each category of sales in terms of gross sales and returns one can see that Plaintiff had the highest sales revenues"). The same holds true for graphs.

Bad Example

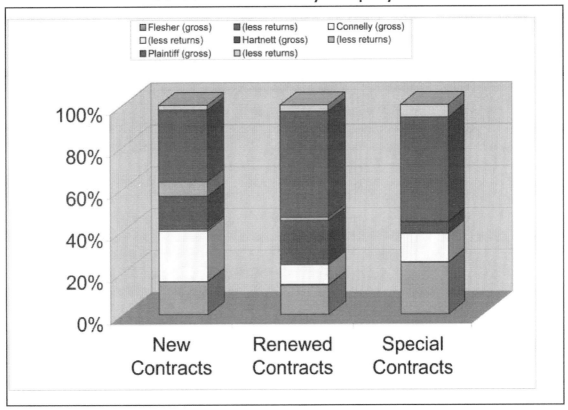

Good Example

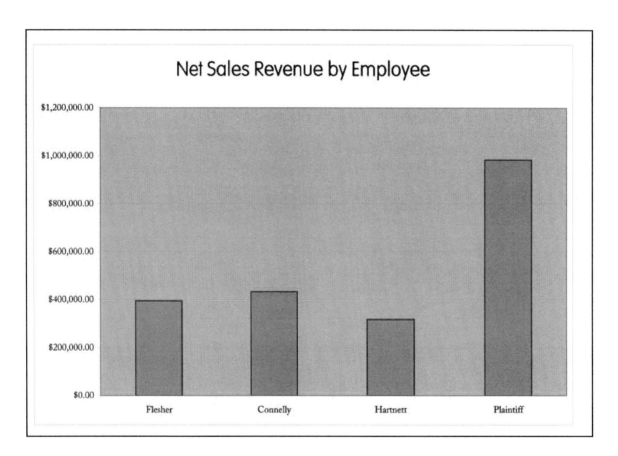

Whether you use a bar graph, a pie chart, or some other type of graph or chart depends on which graph or chart will have the biggest "wow" effect. Test several different versions and show them to others. The one with the best reaction is the one you should use at trial.

Enlarged Exhibits

Finally, you should consider enlarging one or two of the existing exhibits in the case for use as demonstrative exhibits. The best candidate will be a letter, note or memo that makes one of your fundamental points. Like the other types of demonstrative exhibits, you should make your exhibit big. It should be so big that a juror can read it without his or her glasses. And the jury should always know where the enlarged exhibit is in the courtroom. You may also want to highlight certain words in the enlarged exhibit, though you will need to get a jumbo highlighter to do so.

If the letter, note, or memo has too much text to constitute an effective demonstrative exhibit, draft an identical document and include only the important text (highlighted or underlined for effect). As long as you make it clear that you have deleted certain passages from the document, you can use the exhibit as you would any other demonstrative.

Compare the following two examples: an enlarged memo (with no editing) followed by one edited for effect.

Memorandum

August 10, 2001

To: All Sales Employees

From: Johnny Snider

Re: <u>Weekly Round Up</u>

This past week was a busy week for all of us. Two customers visited to suggest alternative ways to implement our national truck stop improvement program. One of the customers thought we should follow a more streamlined approach in which we phase in the improvements over a period of three years. The other thought we should follow most of the elements of our current program and give each customer the choice to accept the improvements if and when the customer desires such improvements. We'll keep working on this and let you know where things stand in a couple months.

We continue to have a problem with the trash in the cafeteria. Too many people are leaving their wrappers and other discarded items on the tables for others to clean up. This is unfair for all concerned and should be stopped.

Some of you have asked about the commission situation. All extra commissions will be honored.

Finally, I am still trying to figure out which computer system to select as part of our Information Technology Project. Please let me know your views on the use of laptops on the road and the need to access our e-mail system while working with customers. We are trying to balance the need for power with the desire to keep costs to a minimum. All thoughts will be appreciated.

Thanks again for the birthday present. I had always wanted a striped tie, and now I have one. I promise to wear it at the Christmas party this year!

Johnny Snider

Memorandum
August 10, 2001

To: All Sales Employees
From: Johnny Snider
Re: <u>Weekly Round Up</u>

* * *

Some of you have asked about the commission situation. All extra commissions will be honored.

* * *

Johnny Snider

Whether you are using a big sheet of paper, an enlarged chart or graph, or an enlarged exhibit, you should use the demonstrative exhibit throughout the trial to make your point. By the end of the trial, the jury should be familiar with your exhibit such that it has almost taken on the status of a witness. When the jurors go to the jury room for deliberations, you want them to talk about your exhibit and even joke about the fact that it played such a major role at trial.

Hey, That's My Exhibit!

You should always object when opposing counsel attempts to write on your exhibit. When you do so, inform the court that you intend to use the exhibit at other times during the trial and thus would appreciate it if counsel would not write on the exhibit. Conversely, if you do so in a calm and matter-of-fact manner, you may be able to write on opposing counsel's demonstrative exhibit during your cross-examination or closing argument. If the other side does not object as you begin writing, you are in the clear.

What About Their Demonstratives?

With respect to the other side's demonstrative exhibits, you should not appear defensive in your approach to those exhibits. Do not flip the exhibit over or otherwise try to hide it from the jury. Instead, take the opposite approach: Highlight the misleading characteristics of the exhibit as many times as you can during the trial. If you welcome the exhibit and appear to use the exhibit to further your own case, the other side may end up flipping the exhibit over or otherwise hiding its own exhibit.

The more you can show that the other side's principal demonstrative exhibit is the best reason for the jury to return a verdict in *your favor*, the more you will have taken control of the trial and increased your chances of winning. Of course, if you don't know what you are doing, you can create the opposite of your intended effect by showing the jury the obvious weaknesses in your case. If you do not have a silver bullet for the other side's demonstrative exhibit, then don't be as aggressive in your own use of the exhibits. Just ignore the exhibit without appearing to hide from it.

Chapter 9

Six Objections You Should Know Something About

The law of evidence doesn't have to be as convoluted as it appears at first glance. In reality, most trials involve only a few types of objections. In this chapter, you'll learn:

▲ how to make an objection at trial

▲ when to make an objection

▲ the six most common objections

"Objection"

Here's how to make an objection at trial:

1. Stand up

It is a good idea to stand when making an objection, though you would be surprised how many lawyers remain seated. Standing up shows respect for the judge and helps you maintain a presence with the jury. The only time you should remain seated is when the judge tells you to do so.

2. Keep it short

Don't make speeches when you object. Judges don't like speeches. Neither do jurors.

Keep your objection short and to the point. You can usually make your objection in two words, *e.g.*, "Objection, irrelevant." If you suspect the judge might not understand the objection, you can explain it in a short sentence. Precisely how you explain your objection is not important, just try to keep it brief. This is not the time for speeches.

If you need to explain your objection in any detail, or if you are concerned about the jury hearing your objection, then ask to approach the bench for a side bar. To do so, simply say "Objection, may I approach, Your Honor?" Of course, the jury can hear much of what occurs at a typical side bar. Keep this in mind and, if it is extremely sensitive, ask to address the judge outside the presence of the jury.

3. Stay positive

You should speak in a positive and firm tone when making your objection. Don't whine or complain. Jurors, like most people, associate whining and complaining with losing.

4. Don't react

You should show no reaction to the judge's ruling on your objection. This means no smiling or thanking the judge when your objection is sustained, and no pouting or looking frustrated when your objection is overruled. Just stand up, make your objection, get your ruling and sit down.

A Few Ways to Botch Your Next Objection

> Bang your knee on the table when standing and proclaim "Ouch." Just stand there for a few minutes until the pain goes away.

> Stand up and say "Abstraction."
> Then say "I mean Injection."
> Then sit down.

> Scream out "Objection, rule 40303, your honor." When the judge says "There's no such rule of evidence," look at the judge, shake your head, and say "That's exactly my point."

Do You or Don't You?

Beyond the "how" question about objections, there is the equally important question of "how often." There are many schools of thought here, ranging from those who advocate making almost no objections out of concern that the jury will see them as obstructionist, to those who think lawyers appear to be in control of the trial when they make objections which are consistently sustained.

Have a strategy for making objections at trial and then follow

A good approach for your first few trials (and beyond) is to *object when it is important and refrain from objecting when it does not really matter*. If you follow this rule of thumb, you may allow your opponent to ask an extensive amount of technically objectionable questions, but it will not make any difference in the outcome of the trial.

The Big Six

Six common objections are addressed below:

1. Irrelevant

Everyone understands the concept of relevancy, and thus we all know when our opponent is asking for irrelevant information from a witness. Unfortunately, however, both you and your opponent will nonetheless introduce a fair amount of irrelevant evidence at trial, and the judge will not necessarily sustain every relevancy objection even if the question is technically irrelevant.

You should therefore refrain from objecting every time you believe your opponent has asked an irrelevant question. Instead, use your relevancy objection to combat questions which are both irrelevant and in some way prejudicial to your case. If there is any evidence or testimony which would cause severe prejudice, you should bring a motion in limine prior to trial to exclude such evidence or testimony on Rule 403 grounds.

2. Argumentative

Whenever you think your opponent has crossed the line and is treating the witness with disrespect, you should consider making an objection that the question is argumentative. You should make the objection, however, only if you believe your witness needs your protection. If your witness is strong and can handle questions that appear unreasonable and unfair, or if you believe the jury is turning on your opponent because of the nature of her questions, you might want to sit back and watch while your opponent makes herself look bad by asking argumentative questions.

Here are some examples of questions and comments that judges might consider argumentative:

▲ "You seem to have trouble answering a simple question."

▲ "Just listen to my question."

▲ "Are you proud of what you did to my client?"

You can also use this objection when opposing counsel uses a threatening or loud tone of voice. Whether the judge will sustain an objection in such circumstances will depend on the amount of leeway your judge gives to lawyers on cross-examination.

Whenever opposing counsel seems to lose control and "cross the line," consider firmly objecting that counsel is being argumentative.

3. No foundation

An objection for lack of foundation is best used when opposing counsel seeks to push a witness into commenting on the evidence, speculating about the actions of others, or throwing out conclusions (typically about damages) without any basis. You should object on foundation grounds only when the witness is on the verge of providing damaging testimony without any basis or is being asked to guess. You should not object on foundation grounds simply because a foundation technically has not been laid.

What's the Basis?

A witness who has foundation for his or her testimony is someone who has a basis for making a statement. To understand the concept of foundation, we can use an over-simplified example. Suppose you wanted to ask a witness whether the traffic light was red, yellow, or green when the accident occurred. Your question would be straightforward: What color was the light when the accident occurred? In theory, one could object to the question for lack of foundation because counsel had not established that the witness had a specific basis for knowing the color of the traffic light. You could build a foundation with the following questions:

Q. Where were you when the accident occurred?

A. I was right there.

Q. Did you see the traffic light?

A. Yes I did.

Q. Could you see what color the light was when the accident occurred?

A. Yes.

Always ask yourself, "How does the witness know this fact?"

Remember that when opposing counsel makes a foundation objection, and the judge sustains the objection, you should develop a foundation by asking a series of questions which show that the witness had a basis for answering your original question. Once you finish that line of questioning, you can summarize the answer in a new pretext to the original question. You can say to the witness, "Based on what you saw, what color was the light?"

Voir Dire on Foundation

Conversely, if you want to establish that a witness has no foundation for testimony, one of the things you can do is ask permission from the judge to voir dire the witness. Your line of questioning should establish that there is no proper basis for the witness to answer the question. Here is an example:

OPPONENT: What was the weather outside last Saturday night?

COUNSEL: May I voir dire the witness, Your Honor?

THE COURT: Go ahead.

Q. You did not go outside your house last Saturday night, right?

A. That's right.

Q. And you did not see anyone outside of your windows last Saturday night, did you?

A. No I did not.

Q. And no one came inside the house who had been outside Saturday night, correct?

A. That's right, I was alone that night.

Q. And you spent the entire time that night in your basement watching movies, right?

A. Yeah, that's right.

Q. And you did not listen to any weather reports on the radio or television that night, did you?

A. No I just was watching my movies.

Q. And so am I correct that when you went to bed on Saturday night as you were falling asleep you did not know at that time what the weather was outside, right?

A. Yeah, I didn't know.

Q. Your honor, I object to lack of foundation.

Use Judgment

As the above example shows, you can think too much about the issue of foundation. Things can become quite theoretical once you enter the world of foundation. Try not to become preoccupied with this issue, and reserve any foundation objections for testimony about which you are truly concerned *and* about which you think the witness lacks any basis.

Here are some examples of questions which could draw foundation objections:

▲ "Why did Mr. Smith send you this letter?"

▲ "How much pain did your sister suffer?"

▲ "What was Ms. Jones thinking when she did that?"

You make this objection in three words: "Objection. No foundation."

If it appears the witness is guessing or fudging, and the issue matters to you, then you should make the foundation objection. Do not make this objection if opposing counsel will be able to lay a simple and effective foundation in response to your objection. Under those circumstances, you will appear to have wasted everyone's time by requiring opposing counsel to establish that the witness does have an obvious basis for the testimony.

What About Exhibits?

As noted in chapter 7, foundation objections will often arise in the area of documentary evidence. Typically, if a witness has not seen the particular exhibit prior to testifying, and is not familiar with the type of document at issue, then the witness may lack foundation for discussing the contents of the exhibit. For example, if opposing counsel seeks to introduce an invoice through a witness who is unfamiliar with that type of invoice and who did not receive that particular invoice, you could make a foundation objection. Of course, you should make this objection only if there is good reason for seeking to prevent the admission of documentary evidence.

For both testimony and documents, use the foundation objection sparingly. In fact, it is a good idea if prior to trial you and opposing counsel agree to withhold foundation objections (and any other objections) to various exhibits which are not particularly important.

It is almost never a good idea to require opposing counsel to spend extra time at trial laying a foundation for various exhibits of no consequence, because it is boring and the jurors will know that you're the one who forced them to endure the boredom. Focus on important exhibits and make sure that counsel has a proper foundation for introducing those exhibits and procuring testimony about the contents of those exhibits. In a typical trial, the number of such exhibits can be counted on one hand.

4. Hearsay

As you know, a document is hearsay if opposing counsel seeks to contend that the contents of the document (or statement) are true and if opposing counsel has not met one of the exceptions (typically the business record exception, see chapter 7). Under a strict definition and application of the hearsay rule, a wide variety of documents and statements could be withheld as evidence at trial.

In practice, however, parties usually introduce all kinds of documents and statements that could theoretically be considered hearsay. Each side introduces letters, memos, and other documents without worrying too much about whether the documents represent hearsay or whether particular exceptions are met. Accordingly, like other objections, you should reserve a hearsay objection for documents or statements you believe are damaging and constitute obvious hearsay.

Before you make your hearsay objection, prepare to address the relevant hearsay exceptions.

Witnesses Love Hearsay

Witnesses often overflow with hearsay testimony during a typical examination. They describe what others said to them, what they said to others, what others wrote in letters, and what they wrote to others in letters. Once again, you should not object to such testimony unless the testimony is particularly damaging.

For example, if the date on which a meeting occurred is irrelevant and meaningless, and opposing counsel asks a blatant hearsay question such as "Did Ms. Thomas tell you what date the meeting was held," you should refrain from making a hearsay objection.

Expert Witnesses and the Foundation Objection

The issue of foundation arises quite frequently with expert testimony, and thus you should ensure that your opponent's expert has a foundation for his testimony. If you have not seen a competent report from the expert or taken his deposition prior to trial, you should voir dire the opposing expert witness to learn the foundation of the opinion. In doing so, you will almost always be able to cast doubt on the foundation of the testimony. This is because the expert rarely will know everything and will rarely have studied the complete record of the case. Since you will almost always be able to show that the expert does not know some critical fact, you can almost always make some type of foundation objection. But you need to use your good judgment as to whether it is worth the time and trouble to go down this road. Judges give experts a lot of leeway, and do not demand perfection in their foundation.

Hearsay Tricks

In contrast, be wary of the skillful opponent who seeks to introduce damaging hearsay testimony through a witness. For example, suppose the date on which a meeting was held was critical, and the only basis on which the witness could testify about the date of the meeting was by giving hearsay testimony. The less skilled opponent would ask the following question:

Q.   Did you talk to Ms. Thomas?

A.   Yes.

Q.   Did Ms. Thomas tell you the date of the meeting?

A.   Yes.

Q.   What did she say?

COUNSEL: Objection. Hearsay.

COURT: Sustained.

A more skilled advocate will not be so obvious in seeking hearsay testimony. Opposing counsel will either ask the witness "When was the meeting held?" (thereby drawing a foundation objection) or will try the following good old-fashioned hearsay trick:

Q.   Did you talk with Ms. Thomas about the subject of the meeting?

A.   Yes.

Q.   What did you learn?

A.   It was held on May 5.

      [or]

Q.   What did you do after that?

A.   I wrote down the date May 5th.

Be ready for this trick by objecting as soon as you think the witness is going to blurt out the hearsay information.

5. Vague

If you have taken depositions, you have most likely come across the ubiquitous "vague" or "vague and ambiguous" objection. This objection clutters the record of many deposition transcripts. Many lawyers, particularly young lawyers, think they are effectively defending their witness at a deposition if they continually point out the vagueness of words such as "team," "business," and other words which in any other context would be perfectly understandable but which are magically transformed into incomprehensible terms at a deposition.

If you are one of these lawyers, you need to shake that habit before you walk into a courtroom for trial. It will be up to the witness to clarify the meaning of any ambiguous words. If the witness fails to do so, you will have an opportunity to clarify things on re-direct examination. But you cannot coach the witness or otherwise interfere with opposing counsel's direct examination by littering the record with vagueness objections. It will irritate the jury and judge—the main sources of power in the courtroom.

Deposition game-playing won't work at trial.

When to Object

The proper time to make an objection on vagueness grounds is when your witness appears to be genuinely confused by a question and the judge or the jury are similarly confused by the question. To save everyone's time, you can make a brief vagueness objection which the judge will most likely sustain or, in many cases, which opposing counsel will accept.

An objection on vagueness grounds is one of the few objections where it makes sense to give a little explanation of your objection. Begin the objection as you begin all objections—with the word "objection." Immediately follow the word "objection" with the phrase "vague as to . . ." or some similar statement. Here are some examples:

▲ Objection, vague as to time, Your Honor.

▲ Objection, vague. It is not clear which job counsel is referring to, Your Honor.

▲ Objection, vague. It is not clear which exhibit counsel is referring to, Your Honor.

Vague Objections Made in Deposition
(But Not Trial)

Q.   Did you manage anyone at the company?

COUNSEL: Object to form. The term "manage" is vague. What does that mean? The witness is not a baseball manager. He works for a normal company. Do you mean did he supervise anyone? Or do you mean something else? You have to rephrase you question.

Q.   Your objection is noted for the record. Are you able to answer the question?

COUNSEL: Object to form. The word "able" is vague. What do you mean is he "able" to answer the question? Is this some kind of test? The question makes no sense.

Q.   Your objection is noted for the record. Do you understand the original question?

COUNSEL: Object to form. The term "original" is vague. None of your questions have been "original." I mean, you're giving yourself too much credit, counsel. Try again.

Q.   I'd like to hear the witness try to answer the question.

COUNSEL: The witness may answer the question if she understood it. I think it is an impossibly vague question.

A.   I managed three people.

As with other objections, you should not make the vagueness objection simply because a question might be called vague if you think hard enough. Reserve your objection for times when it actually matters that the witness and the jury understand the particular words used in the question.

6. Asked and answered

Beginning trial lawyers often treat the "asked and answered" objection (or its related objection "repetitive" or "cumulative") as a technical objection. They listen for an exact question which has already been asked and answered and then spring to their feet with a technical objection. More experienced trial lawyers, however, treat this objection as a strategic one. This objection permits the trial lawyer to play a role in running the courtroom during trial.

If you yourself are moving too slowly at trial, set aside this objection. You don't deserve to criticize your opponent's pace if you are just as slow.

It is almost always good if the jury perceives you as someone who is trying to move the case along and opposing counsel as someone who is trying to drag things out. In an ideal trial, your direct examinations are short and to the point and your cross-examinations are even shorter. In contrast, your opposing counsel may show no concern for the length of direct examinations and may take even longer to labor through cross-examinations. After a few witnesses, the jury will see that you appear to know what you are doing and opposing counsel does not.

Let's Move On

The "asked and answered" objection is best used when opposing counsel has taken a long time with a witness (usually on cross-examination) and is attempting to cover the same area of testimony that had been covered hours earlier in the exam. If everyone in the courtroom, including the jury, appears tired and restless, you should wait for a few questions to go by and then state, "Objection, asked and answered. I believe we covered this ground this morning, Your Honor." You should make this objection with confidence and with a slight tone of impatience in your voice. If you do it right, the judge will agree with you and tell opposing counsel to "move on" or "let's wrap it up."

The "Asked and Answered" Blow Up

Q.   Did you ever read the contract, sir?

COUNSEL: Objection. Asked and answered. Counsel has
            already asked this question five times, Your Honor.

COURT: Overruled. Counsel has asked the question five
            times, *but the witness has not answered it yet*. Let's
            get an answer right now. Stop playing games.

A.   Yes, I read the contract.

COURT: Now that wasn't so hard, was it?

It does not matter if opposing counsel has asked the exact same question in the morning session. It matters only that opposing counsel appears to be delving into an area of questioning. Once the judge sustains your objection and admonishes opposing counsel, the jury will see you as the lawyer who's trying to keep the case moving toward a prompt resolution. This will put you in an excellent position, but be careful not to let it get to your head. You should not use this strategy too often during the course of the trial because the judge might not always agree with you. The more the judge disagrees with you, the more you appear to be trying to harass opposing counsel.

Finally, you know things are going really well when opposing counsel begins arguing with the judge after the judge sustains your objection. Once you hear counsel saying things like, "But Your Honor I didn't ask this particular question," or, "Your Honor, I don't believe I covered these questions this morning," everyone in the courtroom will begin to lose patience with your opponent.

Chapter 10

Dealing With Expert Witnesses

Professional expert witnesses can be intimidating, but they don't have to ruin your trial. In this chapter, you'll learn:

▲ what qualities describe an ideal expert witness

▲ how to teach the jury through your expert witness

▲ how to avoid humiliation on cross-examination

The Ideal Expert Witness

In no particular order, an ideal expert has the following characteristics:

▲ *Likeable.* People like her; you like her; other lawyers like her; her professional colleagues like her; everybody likes her.

▲ *Great Credentials.* She looks good on paper. She went to a good school (or schools), did well, joined the right professional organizations, obtained the right certifications, won some awards in her field, took on some leadership positions, and otherwise built an impressive resume.

▲ *Local Connections.* She is from the local area, went to school in the local area, or works in the local area.

▲ *Subject Matter Experience.* She has sufficient experience in the relevant area of expertise. She has studied the general subject matter and has worked on similar issues. As a result, she feels comfortable working in this area.

▲ *Litigation Experience (but not too much).* She has written expert reports in other cases and testified in deposition and at trial. She knows what information she will need to form her opinions, how to convey her opinions to the other side in a written report, how to respond to questions from the other side during depositions, and what works best at trial. But she doesn't testify for a living.

▲ *Service Oriented.* She gets things done on time and without complaint. She returns your phone calls and meets your deadlines.

▲ *Strong Teaching Skills.* She can teach difficult concepts and theories to lay people who have no interest in her field. She knows how to make a subject fun. You want to learn from her.

▲ *Credibility.* She doesn't lie or shade the truth. She tells you if you have a weak case and will refuse to testify for you if she thinks you are wrong.

▲ *Thoroughness.* She will conduct a thorough investigation of the facts relevant to her opinion. She won't ignore "bad facts" but will incorporate all facts into her opinion.

▲ *Supportive Opinion.* She has a strong opinion in support of your client's case. She is not going to waffle at deposition or trial in her core opinion.

Of course, in the real world, you will often use not-so-ideal experts to support your case at trial. In such cases, you will need to spend a fair amount of time with your expert working on some of these qualities (at least the ones that are capable of improvement).

Teaching the Jury on Direct Exam

The direct exam of an expert witness provides a great opportunity *for the expert* to explain to the jury why you should win and your opponent should lose. This is not your opportunity to talk to the jury or show how smart you are. You should fade into the background and let your wonderful expert do all the talking. This point is worth repeating. Let the expert talk to the jury without your interference. This may require a lot of work with your expert prior to trial, but it is well worth it.

This section assumes you have a good expert. If you don't, then think twice about following this approach.

Unlike testimony by fact witnesses, testimony by expert witnesses can be presented in a basic format that doesn't differ too much from case to case.

Each exam has six basic stages:

1. Introduction

2. Qualifications

3. Investigation

4. Opinions

5. Bases

6. Summary

These stages are shown below in a sample expert exam and commentary. The hypothetical case involves BIG FOOD, a national restaurant chain, suing Just Jukeboxes, a jukebox company, for breach of warranty. BIG FOOD claims it ordered and received one thousand defective jukeboxes from Just Jukeboxes. Your expert is testifying that the jukeboxes were defective because their internal wiring was unstable.

1. Introduction

Q. Ms. Engineer, please state your name.

A. Felicia Engineer.

Q. What's your job?

A. I'm the Chief Engineer at Very Important Engineering Firm, an engineering consulting firm.

Note that your expert introduced herself to the jury.

Q. Are you here to give us your opinion as to whether the Model 500 Jukeboxes received by BIG FOOD were defective?

A. Yes.

At the end of this phase, the jury knows the name of the expert, her job, and why she is on the witness stand. They should now have enough patience to listen to her background and qualifications. This last question is leading because you want to be careful how you phrase questions about her specific opinion.

2. Qualifications

Q. Please describe your background.

A. Sure. I'm from Local Town. I've lived here all my life. I have two daughters, aged 10 and 12, and I've been an engineer since 1985.

You just established the local connection. Now let's solidify the connection.

Q. Are you involved in the Local Town community?

A. Yes. I'm on the Local Town Planning Board, I'm a Girl Scout troop leader, and I sing in the Fall Pumpkin Festival each year.

The jury now really likes her. But don't overdo it. Move on to a new topic.

Q. Please tell the jury about your education.

A. I went to Local University and received a B.S. degree in Electrical Engineering in 1983 and a Masters in 1985.

Q. Did you receive any honors?

A. Yes. I was *magna cum laude.*

Q. Did you study stability theory in school?

A. Yes. I took three engineering courses that involved stability theory.

The case involves stability theory, and thus you should show the jury that your expert knows a lot about stability theory. If your expert had no experience in stability theory, you would need to make the question more general.

Q. What jobs have you had?

A. I worked for Really Big Company from 1985 to 1990. I started out working on micro-gadgets and then moved to macro-gadgets. I led the team that developed the fourth-generation product ABC, which is a component part used in various types of sound systems.

I then took a job at Super Fun Company, where I ran the product analysis group. I worked there until 1993, when I joined Can't-Think-of-Another-Stupid-Name-For-a-Fake-

Company in their product development and assessment division. I was the chief engineer in the division.

I joined the Very Important Consulting Firm in 1997, where I have been ever since. I consult with companies about their engineering problems and also work on cases like this one as an expert witness.

The expert has told the jury about her jobs in a friendly and casual manner. It didn't take too long, and you stayed out of the way. You let her talk and didn't break her job history into a series of irritating questions.

Q.   Have any of your jobs involved stability theory?

A.   Yes. I had to apply principles of stability theory in every project I worked on at Really Big Company and on many of the projects I worked on at Super Fun Company and Can't-Think-of-Another-Stupid-Name-For-a-Fake-Company. In my consulting work I often have to apply stability theory as well.

Q.   What professional organizations are you a member of?

A.   The American Society of Electrical Engineers, the Local Society of Electrical Engineers, and the Regional Society of Electrical Engineers.

Q.   Do you talk to others in your field about stability theory?

A.   Yes. At the annual convention of the professional organizations I just mentioned, I'll talk to other engineers about various theories, including stability theory. I also talk to my fellow consultants about projects, including projects involving stability theory.

Q.   Do you read the literature on stability theory?

A.   Yes. There are two major journals that publish articles on stability theory from time to time, and I subscribe to both journals.

Q.   Have you given any speeches on stability theory?

A.   Yes. I spoke on the subject three or four times at our firm and I spoke on the topic at a meeting of one of my professional organizations a few years ago.

Q.   Have you written about stability theory?

A.   Yes. I am the co-author of two papers on stability theory, both of which were published in the *Journal of Really Boring Articles for Electrical Engineers.*

By now, the jury understands that your expert knows a lot about stability theory. They are ready to hear about her investigation in this case.

3. Investigation

Q.   Did you conduct an investigation of the Model 500 Jukeboxes received by BIG FOOD from Just Jukeboxes?

A.   Yes.

Q.   What did you do?

A.   My staff and I visited BIG FOOD's warehouse and examined the jukeboxes. We first confirmed that the wiring for each of the jukeboxes was identical. We then brought three of the jukeboxes back to our office to take apart and examine. We conducted fifteen standard stability tests on each of the jukeboxes and recorded our testing and results in our lab notebooks.

      We also reviewed about ten thousand pages of design documents and other technical documents produced by Just Jukeboxes and relating to the wiring of the jukeboxes.

      I also read the depositions of the four engineers at Just Jukeboxes who worked on the design and manufacture of the jukeboxes, and I reviewed the literature on stability theory as it applied to wiring of stereo systems, music machines, and jukeboxes.

      I talked to my fellow engineers at my consulting firm about the technical issues and received their input and advice. I then wrote a report that described my findings and opinions.

That's it. You don't need to ask any more questions. The jury is now ready to hear her opinions.

4. Opinion

Q. Based on your years of experience and your investigation in this case, do you have an opinion as to whether the Model 500 Jukeboxes received by BIG FOOD were defective?

A. Yes.

Q. What is your opinion?

A. They were defective because they had unstable internal wires.

That was extremely easy, wasn't it? Just have the expert state her opinion in a sentence or two up front. Now comes the explanation.

5. Bases

Q. Please explain your opinion to the Jury.

A. Sure. I've brought some slides that explain my opinions. Could we put the first slide on the screen?

Q. Yes. Here it is. It has been marked as Exhibit 100.

If permitted by the Court, mark your demonstrative exhibits. This makes it easier to follow the transcript on appeal, and the judge may permit you to introduce your demonstrative exhibits (at least those that are not too argumentative) into evidence so the jurors can have them in the jury room during their deliberations.

A. It would help if I could use my pointer on the big screen. May I do so?

COURT: Go ahead.

[Witness steps down and stands in front of the jury near a big screen with a pointer of some kind.]

A. You'll see that this first slide shows three basic parts of an internal wiring system: the X wire, the Y wire, and the Z wire. These wires need to be stable in order to provide consistent sound for the jukebox. Now, what does it mean for the wires to be "stable?" To answer this question, we need to understand a few concepts of electrical engineering. May I use this big pad of paper to show these concepts?

COURT: You may.

The jurors feel like students in a classroom. This is fun.

A.   Let's start with a concept we all understand. Let me list three types of foods: high sugar junk food, high-caffeine coffee, and what I'll call "healthful food," which means simply vegetables, fruits, breads, meat, and other foods. If you eat a lot of high sugar food and high-caffeine coffee all day, and you never eat any other what I call "healthful food," what will happen? We all know what will happen. You get a big rush at some point during the day followed by a big crash.

Now let's go back to our three wires. The X wire and the Y wire bring high bursts of energy—just like high sugar food and high caffeine coffee. This type of energy is acceptable as long as the Z wire can counteract the X and Y wire with its own low level of sustained energy, just as it's okay for us to have some junk food and coffee as long as we eat some healthful food along the way. The wires are considered "stable" when all three wires are providing their own type of energy. But if the Z wire is not working properly, then you'll see high bursts of energy followed by big crashes.

Now let's see the next slide, which I think is Exhibit 101. [Lawyer puts next slide on the screen.] Now this next slide shows a magnified picture of the Z wire from one of the jukeboxes in the Model 500. It looks like a typical wire from this vantage point. But now let's blow it up for an even bigger perspective in the next slide.

Q.   Okay. It's Exhibit 102.

A.   You see how these strands are not intertwined with each other? This means that the Z wire cannot provide the type of sustained low energy needed to avoid crashes. It's like you just put someone on a diet of high sugar and high caffeine and cut out all healthful foods. They will have a lot of energy but a crash is inevitable.

Q.   I see.

You may have to throw in something like "I see" or "please continue" from time to time to avoid an objection on narrative grounds.

Q.   Now the way we test the relationship between the X, Y and Z wires is by something called "stability levels." [She goes to the pad of paper and write down key terms as she continues to explain her opinion.]

The jurors really feel like students now. They are having a good time.

6. Summary

Q.   Please summarize your opinion for the jury.

A.   Sure. It is my opinion that the Model 500 jukeboxes received by BIG FOOD from Just Jukeboxes were defective because they had unstable internal wires. As I explained, their Z wires didn't work properly and this resulted in unacceptably low stability levels, which caused the machines to be susceptible to crashes.

Q.   No further questions.

The jury now firmly believes the jukeboxes were defective.

Avoiding Humiliation on Cross-Examination

You don't want to lose ground on cross-examination of an expert.
Set low goals and, once you meet those goals, end your questioning.

When you prepare to cross-examine a professional expert witness, your principal goal should be to avoid abject humiliation. The brief way to do this is to remember that *the expert witness is smarter than you about her subject and you will likely lose if you try to prove that she is wrong.* Getting into a debate with an opposing expert will only allow her to explain and clarify her opinions, and you never want to *improve* the testimony of the opposing adverse expert witness by permitting the expert to clarify her opinions and explain why you are wrong and she is right.

The best way to avoid embarrassment is to ask only a few lines of questions and base those questions on the opposing adverse expert's written report, deposition testimony, other documents, or other uncontested facts. The questions should be limited in scope and susceptible only to a "yes" answer.

In your first few jury trials, never ask the opposing adverse expert to explain anything. Not once.

Remember that even if you believe she is wrong, and even if you believe she has made a critical logical flaw or failed to consider a critical factor, the jury may not see things your way. You can always show these flaws with your own expert witness, or in your closing argument, but it will be difficult, if not impossible, to do so with the adverse expert witness.

What Not to Do

The best way to understand how to avoid embarrassment on cross examination of an expert witness is to consider two of the most common bad examples: asking for an explanation and arguing with the expert.

1. Asking for an explanation

Let's suppose your expert has told you that the stability level of the internal wires of a jukebox can be adversely affected by placement near another major appliance. You want to make the point that you need to consider customer placement.

Q. Ms. Engineer, isn't it true that the stability level of the internal wires of a jukebox can be affected by where the customer places the jukebox at the restaurant?

A. No, I would not agree with that.

You are surprised at this answer. But no matter how surprised you are, do not ask the expert to explain his answer.

Q. Why not?

A. Well, when we talk about stability levels of the internal wires, we mean [continue to explain].

You just lost the flow of your cross examination, and the expert was able to take the floor and clarify her opinion and explain it to the jury.

2. Arguing with the expert

To continue the above Bad Example, you should not try to fight with the expert unless you have an undisputed fact in your hip pocket.

Q.   But isn't it true that placing a jukebox near a major appliance can adversely affect a stability level?

Now you are arguing with the expert. You'll lose the argument.

A.   No, that's not true.

Q.   Why do you say that?

You've just asked the expert to explain why you are wrong and she is right and why the jury should accept her opinions.

A.   We have to be careful about how we use the term stability level. In our field [continue to explain].

Have you had enough yet?

Ask Specific Questions

To avoid the above problems, ask the expert only questions that are so specific, and so focused on a particular fact, that the only proper answer is a specific and focused answer -- "yes" or "no." For this type of question to work, you need to be extremely specific and leave no wiggle room.

Q.   You have a degree in Electrical Engineering, correct?

This is a specific question. She either has that degree or she doesn't. The jury understands the question and expects a specific answer.

A.   Yes, I do.

You are now beginning to develop a rhythm. The expert is no explaining her opinions or making you look foolish. Keep asking specific questions.

Q. You don't have a degree in Industrial Engineering, right?

A. That's right.

You're on a roll.

Q. In fact, you never took even one course in industrial engineering, correct?

A. That's true.

It seems like you may be making a point. Whether you are or not, you are at least obtaining direct answers to specific questions rather than long answers that repeat the principles of the expert's direct exam.

Q. And you have never been certified by the Industrial Engineers Association's ISO Testing Program, right?

A. That's right.

Good flow.

Q. That testing program is what covers stability testing for machines like the Model 500?

A. Yes.

Q. There is no other testing program that would apply?

A. That's true.

Q. And under the ISO testing program you need to be an industrial engineer to conduct the test under the program?

A. I believe so.

Q. In fact, section 122 of the testing program states, "One must have a degree in industrial engineering and have received an ISO certification in order to conduct a test under this program." You are aware of that section, aren't you?

A.   Yes, I am.

Q.   And in this case, you conducted the stability tests with your assistant, John Tester, correct?

A.   Yes.

Q.   John Tester is an electrical engineer like you, right?

A.   Yes.

Q.   John Tester has not been certified under the ISO testing program, right?

A.   Right.

Q.   And no one in your office is certified under the ISO testing program, right?

A.   That's right.

Good. Now stop. You can argue the point to the jury in closing argument. Don't get greedy.

Obtain Specific Answers

If you ask specific factual questions, do your best to obtain specific answers. This rule does not apply to argumentative questions, but only to questions asking for simple facts. Let's repeat some of the questions above and show how you can obtain specific answers to those questions.

Q.   You have a degree in Electrical Engineering, correct?

A.   I took courses in many different areas of engineering.

The expert has failed to answer a specific factual question. The jury may not see this at first, but if the expert continues to refuse to answer such simple questions, the jury may start to turn on her.

Q. I understand, but I am correct that you have a degree in Electrical Engineering?

A. Yes.

You received a specific answer to your question.

Q. You don't have a degree in Industrial Engineering, right?

A. I took four courses in Industrial Engineering.

She's not answering your specific question. By now the jury may see that she has trouble admitting obvious facts.

Q. I understand you took classes in the subject, but you would agree that you don't have a degree in Industrial Engineering, wouldn't you.

A. I took the main courses in the subject.

Q. I am not asking you about your courses, but only about what degrees you received. And it is true that you didn't receive a degree in Industrial Engineering, correct?

A. That's true.

The jurors may realize that it is taking a long t me to obtain simple admissions from the expert. If this continues for awhile, they may start to dislike the expert because she is wasting everyone's time.

Q. And you have never been certified by the Industrial Engineers Association's ISO Testing Program, right?

A. I've read the ISO manual.

The jury may see a pattern developing. You are asking specific questions and the expert is being evasive. The jury will view the answers as evasive only if the jury views the question as simple and capable of a "yes" or "no" answer.

Q. You have never been certified by the Industrial Engineers Association's ISO Testing Program, right?

A.   I've reviewed the manual that provides the same information.

Q.   You are not certified, correct?

A.   I'm qualified.

Q.   I'm asking you only about certification. You would agree that you have not received a certification for the Industrial Engineers Association's ISO Testing Program, right?

A.   I haven't received an actual certification.

Q.   And since you haven't received an actual certification, you are not in fact certified, right?

A.   That's right.

If the expert keeps fighting with you about simple things, her credibility will diminish in the eyes of the jury. Continue asking specific questions capable of direct answers.

Beware of the Sham Expert

You may find yourself confronting a so-called "sham" expert—someone who is not really an expert in her field or who is an expert in an unrecognized field. In such circumstances, you should try to strike the expert as a witness before trial. The law varies from state to state, but state law throughout the country (and federal law) provide certain minimum requirements that a witness must meet before being qualified as an expert. Research these requirements and consider whether you can launch a pre-trial attack.

If you can't knock out the sham expert before trial, you need to follow the same rules for cross examining any other expert: Be cautious and avoid humiliation. Remember that the jury will not necessarily see the expert as a "sham." If you argue with the sham expert, or ask the sham expert to explain things, you'll most likely take a giant step backwards.

Chapter **11**

Understanding the Jury Instruction Process

For many lawyers, the process of drafting, debating, and deciding jury instructions for a particular case is one of the most uncomfortable parts of a trial. It needn't be. In this chapter, you'll learn:

▲ how to draft instructions in plain English

▲ some common objections to proposed instructions

▲ how to create your record for appeal

Instructions Matter

Many seasoned trial lawyers believe that jurors do not listen to instructions anyway, and that they decide the case based on the evidence and their own internal sense of who should win and who should lose. (See chapter 3.) While this may sometimes be true, many a jury will read the instructions very carefully, and decide the case based only on these instructions.

Spend time on your proposed jury instructions. They could win the case for you.

And at the very least, the jury will read the instructions to decide what to do in a close case or in a case where neither side has a particular claim on a jury's emotions. But the bottom line is the same in every case: You never want to lose a case that you could have won if your instructions had been better.

Follow the Law

At trial, the judge will almost certainly read some version of the following instruction to the jury:

> It is your duty to find the facts from all the evidence in the case. To the facts as you find them you must apply the law as I give it to you. You must follow the law as I give it to you, whether you agree with it or not.

Since the judge is reading the law to the jury, and the jury has to apply that law to the facts as they find them, it is obviously essential that the jurors *understand* the law that they will be asked to apply. A misstep here could prove devastating to the case, because if the jurors don't understand the law, they're likely to decide the case incorrectly. The challenge is how to draft the instructions so that they are both legally correct and understandable to the jury.

Speak English

People hate lawyers who talk like lawyers. And jurors undoubtedly hate receiving instructions on the law that look and sound as if they were written by lawyers *for* lawyers. You're *not* writing instructions for lawyers, you're writing them for a *lay jury*. It is important that the jury understand the instructions.

Yet it is amazing how many lawyers abjectly refuse to help the jury out in this task. They insist on proposing instructions that are written in dense legalese, understandable to virtually no one outside the field of law, and to precious few people inside the field. The jurors' first language is usually English, and it's certainly not Legalese. So make sure the jury instructions are written in plain English if you want the jury to understand them.

Get your mind out of law school and think like a normal citizen. If you were a juror, what type of instruction would you want at trial?

This sounds like a simple point, and it is. But people often overlook it. Consider the following instruction from the Third Edition of the *Minnesota Jury Instruction Guides—Civil* (or "JIGs," for short). This is an instruction on impeachment that until recently was given in virtually all civil trials in the State of Minnesota:

> In deciding the believability and weight to be given the testimony of a witness, you may consider:
>
> * * * *
>
> Evidence of a statement by or conduct of the witness on some prior occasion which is inconsistent with the witness' present testimony. This evidence may be considered by you only for the purpose of testing the believability and weight of the witness's testimony and for no other purpose. If, however, the statement was given under oath or the witness is a party or an agent of a party in the case, the evidence of the prior inconsistent statement or the conduct of a party or an agent of a party may be considered as evidence bearing on the issues in this case as well as for testing believability and weight.

What in the world does this mean? It is legally accurate, but that doesn't matter because almost nobody on the jury will understand it. Indeed, there are many lawyers who can't follow this instruction without moving their lips or reading it twice.

People are starting to understand that jury instructions should be in plain English, including (thank goodness) the drafters of various jury instruction guidelines. When it came time to update the civil JIGs for Minnesota, for example, the drafters decided it was time not only to update the law, but also to rewrite the instructions in plain English to the extent possible. The results are in the fourth edition of the JIGs, and they are very encouraging. Here is the JIG IV version of the impeachment instruction:

> You may consider what the witness did or said in the past, if it is not consistent with what he or she is saying now. If what was said in the past was not under oath, use it only to decide the truth or weight of what the witness is saying now. If it was under oath, or the witness is a party in this case, then use it to decide the issues in the case and the truth and weight of what the witness is saying now.

This is much better. It is still not entirely jury-friendly, but that's because the legal distinction it is explaining is a subtle and difficult one. The new instruction is much more simply worded, and manages to do the job with fewer words, to boot.

Remember: The most well-drafted jury instructions in the world will not make a whit of difference if the jury does not understand them. And it is absolutely crucial that you have this in mind as you draft your jury instructions.

Where Do I Start?

You should begin your search for jury instructions in the applicable pattern jury instructions that your jurisdiction has. There should be an instruction for many of the basic areas of law that you will encounter in a lawsuit. But the pattern instructions rarely cover all the things that you want to tell the jury about the governing law. For those other issues, you will have to rely on a statute or a case. You need to do some research and understand all of the nuances of the law that applies to your case in order to propose a good set of jury instructions.

Your state may not have JIGs (or may call them something else). Ask around and find out what applies to your case.

Make sure that you understand all of the elements of the plaintiff's case and all of the defenses to that case. Is there some nuance or exception that applies only when the facts are a certain way? If so, understand what the nuance or exception is and if there is any possibility that it applies in your case. You should end up with a list of the cases and statutes that state the various propositions of law most helpfully for your case. Start with those as the baseline.

Could You Translate That Please?

Now comes the difficult part. Your job is *not* to find the most concise, well-supported statement of the law that you can drag out of a statute or case. You have to go the next step: *translate that well-stated proposition of law into plain English so that a jury can understand it.*

One way to convert the instruction into English is to pretend that you have to explain the instruction to a reasonably intelligent family member who is not a lawyer. You have to use common words and phrases, and not legalese. If there is a word that seems like it might be too legal or technical, it probably is. Break it down into a simpler explanation.

This will not necessarily make the instruction shorter. In fact, in many cases it will make the instruction a little longer. One of the chief problems in drafting jury instructions is that they are legal terms of art that can't be explained to a jury only by using ten or maybe fifteen words of plain English. Lawyers may understand what a "life in being" is for purposes of the Rule Against Perpetuities, but a jury is going to have to have that explained to them. Lawyers understand what an easement is, but it takes a little bit more verbiage to tell a jury what that is.

Take the time to help the jury understand the instruction so they can help you win your case.

Can I Translate the Pattern Instructions?

You may run into trouble if you started with a pattern instruction and tried to translate it into English. Judges are often afraid to depart from the pattern instructions. Trial judges hate being reversed more than just about anything in the world, and they generally feel that they cannot be reversed (or at least are not likely to be reversed) if they just read an instruction straight out of the applicable pattern instructions. It is safer that way.

But if the pattern instruction is not written in plain English, the jury won't get it. Most trial judges seem to genuinely appreciate the effort to put the instructions into plain English for the jury, and some actually will translate the pattern instructions into plain English if you can convince them that you are doing it for the good of the judicial process, rather than some strategic advantage (although sometimes the two go hand in hand).

The Charging Conference and Objections to Instructions

Before the judge reads the instructions to the jury, you and your opponent will have a chance to debate the instructions. This is called the "charging conference." Some judges hold the charging conference in chambers, others hold it in the courtroom. Most judges will not have a record made of the entire debate; they will only record each side's objections to the instructions after the debate is over and the judge has decided which instructions to give.

In order to be prepared for the charging conference, you obviously have to have read and understand both your own proposed instructions and your opponent's proposed instructions. If you understand the law that governs the case, you should have some sense of whether your opponent's proposed instructions are fair statements of the law or not.

Judges don't like uptight lawyers at the charging conference. Be relaxed and confident when you argue for your proposed instructions.

Obviously, you will want to object to any of your opponent's instructions that do not accurately and fairly set out the law. You must be prepared to explain to the judge exactly what it is that is inaccurate or unfair about your opponent's instructions.

Three of the more common objections to instructions are as follows:

1. Incorrect statement of the law

This one is fairly straightforward. If your opponent's proposed instruction is simply incorrect on the law, you need to point that out to the judge and be prepared with citations to cases that do accurately cite the law. For example, if your opponent is relying on New York case law but Ohio law is different, you will need to explain that to the judge.

2. Unfair statement of the law

Some proposed instructions are technically accurate, but they are biased or skewed in some way. It is hard to explain all the ways in which this can happen, but you know it when you see it. An example might be an instruction taken from a case that explicitly confined the rule set out in the case to the facts in that case. Obviously, trying to have that instruction read in a case where the facts are different would be inappropriate. You should be prepared to make that objection.

3. Unfair focus on one party's theory of the case

Some proposed instructions are accurate, but they unduly highlight particular theories of the case. You can fight some of your opponent's instructions that you don't like by arguing to the judge that a general instruction is better than a specific one, because the judge should not put too much emphasis on anyone's particular theory of the case.

Have a copy of the case for the judge so she can understand your objection.

Object or Not?

Typically, by the time you arrive at the charging conference, all the evidence will be admitted and the parties will be preparing for closing argument. You will probably have a sense by the time of the charging conference how you are doing in your case, and you may even be able to tell whether you are winning or losing the trial.

A common strategic question is what to do about the jury instructions when you know that you are probably winning the case. Do you try to object to as many of your opponent's instructions as you can? Or do you limit your objections only to the proposed instructions that are clearly improper for some reason? This issue becomes important because if you are truly winning the trial, your opponent may be taking an appeal, and you want to give your opponent as little to talk about on appeal as possible.

If most of your opponent's instructions are read to the jury, then your opponent cannot complain that the verdict was caused by instructional error, and that is one potential appeal point that your opponent loses. To avoid any appeal problems, wouldn't you rather win with your opponent's instructions than with yours?

Insulating your winning verdict from appeal is a noble goal, but you also want to make sure you win your case at trial, and not on appeal. You do not want to kick the stuffing out of your opponent on the evidence, only to lose in the end because your opponent received extremely favorable (and maybe even inappropriate) jury instructions, thereby causing the jury to decide the case against you.

Unfortunately, this is a judgment call that depends on how the entire trial went. The closer the case, the more likely it is that you will want to object to as many of your opponent's instructions as you reasonably can. But if you are four touchdowns ahead, you probably will not want to sweat your opponent's instructions unless they are patently incorrect or you simply cannot live with them.

When in doubt, object to as many of your opponent's instructions as you reasonably can. Dealing with your opponent's arguments about instructional error on appeal from a jury verdict in your favor is far preferable to watching the jury decide the case against you and having to decide what points *you* will make on appeal.

Make Your Record

At the end of the charging conference, the judge will decide what instructions she will read to the jury, and she'll give you a chance to object to those instructions on the record. Make sure to put a formal objection on the record for every one of your instructions that the judge rejected, and every one of your opponent's instructions the judge accepted and to which you objected.

You need not go into great detail. It is acceptable to describe briefly the instruction at issue and state that you object to the giving or not giving of the instruction, with perhaps a one-sentence explanation of why you object. For example:

Make sure you really are "four touchdowns ahead" before deferring to bad instructions.

> Your Honor, I object to the Court giving the plaintiff's requested instruction No. 17 because I believe that it does not accurately state the law for reasons that I mentioned during the charging conference. I believe that our proposed instruction No. 21 is a more accurate statement of the law, and should be read to the jury instead of the plaintiff's instruction.

The reason why you are placing your objection on the record is that you need to do so in order to preserve it for appeal. If you fail to object to the giving or withholding of an instruction at trial, you have waived that objection and cannot complain about it on appeal. Thus, you want to make sure that you are on record with all your objections to the jury instructions so that you can raise it as an issue on appeal in the unhappy event that you lose the trial.

Let the Jurors Have a Copy of the Instructions

In the old days, the jurors did not receive a hard copy of the instructions to take back to the jury room. Imagine that! How in the world can we expect jurors to *memorize* the legal points that the judge reads to them during the charge? The jurors had to be really attentive when the judge was reading the instructions to them, or else they had to rely on their own ideas of what the law was.

Appeals are no fun when you forget to place objections in the record.

Today, most courts allow the jury to take at least one copy of the instructions into the deliberating room. You should always make sure to ask if this will be the case, however. It is very important that the jurors have the chance to not only hear the instructions, but to read them (and re-read them if necessary) as they deliberate. If the judge says that that is not her practice, ask that it be done in your case. The argument for it is simple. It will lead to a jury that is more well-versed in the legal rules, and therefore will lead to a higher quality outcome than if the jurors can't see the instructions after retiring and have to go from memory.

PTM

Chapter 12

Closing Arguments That Work

Closing argument gives you your best chance at connecting with the jury and winning your case once and for all. In this chapter, you'll learn:

▲ what you can and cannot argue

▲ how to make your best arguments

▲ what strategic calls you need to make

What's the Point of Closing Argument?

The main purpose of your closing argument is to summarize the evidence for the jury and persuade the jurors that you should win the case. It's your chance to tell the story of your case and make the jurors want to find in your favor. All the loose ends at trial, all the lurking factual inferences, and all of the subtle points that you hoped the jury was realizing during the trial now can be tied together and explained. It is the last word you will have before the jury retires to decide the case.

How Should You Act?

The jury will trust you only if you present your persuasive self. They will detect any attempt at a personality overhaul.

Remember to be your persuasive self (chapter 2). Are you naturally loud, boisterous, and dramatic? Or are you kind of quiet, reserved, and distinctly understated? Whatever your personality, your closing argument should reflect it. And it should reflect the same personality and demeanor that you displayed during the trial. It is jarring for the jury to see an attorney who has been quiet and soft-spoken during the trial suddenly leap to his feet and start screaming at them during the closing argument, and vice versa. You should use whatever manner of presentation meshes best with your personality.

What Can You Argue?

You can make almost any argument, as long as it is based on the evidence at trial. In general (and subject to the exceptions discussed later in this chapter), closing argument is generally a gloves-are-off, no-holds-barred affair.

1. Facts and evidence

The first thing that you can argue, of course, is the facts and the evidence. This will be the primary content of your closing argument. The jury is there to resolve factual disputes, so you want to focus on the facts that favor your side. Better yet, since the jury has already heard the evidence, you don't have to keep saying "the evidence will show," like you did during opening statement. You may *want* to say things like "the evidence showed" or "you heard at trial" or "we proved." But you don't have to do so. It's your choice.

The most persuasive facts will be the ones that favored your side and that the other side did not dispute.

Good Example

Ladies and gentlemen, you heard Ms. Jones testify that she did a scientific analysis of the soil under the Love Canal site, and that it was contaminated with benzene. Acme Chemical Company does not dispute that. You also heard expert testimony from Dr. Dreben, and she testified that benzene is one of the most cancer-causing chemicals known to mankind. Acme doesn't dispute that either.

Not all the facts will be undisputed, of course, and thus much of your argument will consist of disputed facts. You needn't give the other side equal time by saying, "He said this, but we say this" for every disputed fact. But you may want to explain why the jury should believe your witnesses and discount the testimony from the other side's witnesses.

Good Example

We found two witnesses to the car accident, Jane Austen and Charles Dickens, both of whom say that T.S. Eliot had the red light when he entered the intersection, and that he was going well over thirty miles an hour when he hit E.M. Forster's car. Both Ms. Austen and Mr. Dickens were standing at the intersection when the crash happened, and each of them had a clear view of the accident from about thirty-five feet away. Now Mr. Eliot called witnesses who say that he had the green light when the accident happened, but both of those witnesses were approximately a hundred yards from the accident when it happened, and they did not have as good a view of the accident as Ms. Austen and Mr. Dickens had.

---

2. Inferences

Another important part of closing argument is drawing inferences from the facts. This is important because inferences are more subtle, and some or all of the jurors may not have drawn the inference you wanted them to draw from the evidence.

The general rule is: Don't make the jury figure it out, explain it to them.

Good Example

You heard Ms. Towson testify that after my client called her and asked if he could examine the cows that Ms. Towson's company seized, Ms. Towson immediately ordered the cows to be transported to a stockyard in South Dakota and sold. Now why do you think she did that? It's very simple: because she knew that if my client examined the cows, he would determine that they belonged to him. Ms. Towson ordered the cows sold and slaughtered so that she could destroy the evidence that the cows belonged to my client.

Good Example

Ladies and Gentlemen, you heard that my client, George Vosburg, was subjected to stern discipline for every minor infraction that he committed. When he was five minutes late for work one day, he was suspended for a day without pay. When he had to leave early to pick up his sick child at day care, he was suspended two days. When he complained about the suspension, he was suspended an additional day for insubordination. And the list goes on. Nobody else at Acme Chemical Company was subjected to this kind of treatment for minor infractions. It's clear what was going on. Acme wanted to get rid of George Vosburg, and it was looking for excuses to justify his firing.

Circumstantial evidence also needs explaining in many cases.

> ### Good Example
>
> You heard testimony that the first three shipments of spark plugs worked just fine, but the fourth shipment had an extraordinarily high rate of failure. The fourth shipment of spark plugs was supposed to be the same as the prior three. There were no changes in the design of the spark plugs, no changes in the way the spark plugs were used, and no changes in the way my client installed the spark plugs. The only change from the first three shipments to the fourth was that Sparkie Company started using cheaper aluminum contacts rather than brass contacts in the spark plugs. It stands to reason that that change, and not anything that my client did, caused the spark plugs in the fourth shipment to fail.

3. Discuss specific testimony

You can also highlight the witnesses who may have been less than truthful, which is especially useful if their untruthfulness was subtle during the trial.

Good Example

You heard Colonel Jessup testify that he was arranging to transfer Private Santiago off the base for his own protection. But Colonel Jessup also testified that he had previously ordered his men not to harm Private Santiago, and that his orders were always followed. Ladies and Gentlemen, if Colonel Jessup's orders are always followed, and if he ordered his men not to harm Private Santiago, then there was no need to transfer Private Santiago off the base for his protection. In reality, Colonel Jessup is not being truthful when he says that he was about to transfer Private Santiago in order to protect him. There was no transfer in the works. This was a story that Colonel Jessup made up after Private Santiago's death in order to cover the fact that he ordered his men to discipline Private Santiago, and that discipline cost Private Santiago his life.

As discussed in chapter 6, you should refrain from gloating or otherwise commenting on your impeachment of a witness *during the examination*. But during closing argument, you have an opportunity to rub it in a bit.

Good Example

And do you remember Mr. Blatner's testimony in this courtroom? He was under oath, sworn to tell the truth before you, yet his testimony was 180 degrees different from what he told me at his deposition eight months ago. He told me in his deposition that he wasn't sure what color the light was. Now he says he's sure it was green. He told me in his deposition that he was in a hurry, traveling about foty miles an hour. Now he says he was out for a leisurely drive, going about twenty-five miles an hour. To be perfectly blunt, Mr. Blatner's story keeps changing, and a changing story is not an honest one. My client, by contrast, has always told the same story: the light was red for Mr. Blatner, and he ran the light and plowed into her car at around forty miles per hour. The consistent story is the believable story, and it's my client's story.

4. The law

The law is another good thing to discuss during closing argument. This requires some care, though. You have to be careful to accurately state the law. The judge has already decided on the instructions prior to closing, and thus you know exactly how the judge is going to instruct the jury. It's even better if the judge instructs the jury *before* closings, so you can integrate what the judge actually said to the jurors in your closing.

Don't deviate from the judge's instructions, or you could draw an objection and appear as if you're trying to mislead the jury on the law. Jurors don't like that. But it's perfectly appropriate to tell the jury exactly what the judge is going to instruct them, and then tie that into the facts.

> **Good Example**
>
> Judge Doohickey is going to instruct you on the law. And one of the things he's going to tell you is that whenever someone sells goods in Minnesota, there is something called an "implied warranty of merchantability," which means a promise that the goods are going to be fit for their usual purposes. Now you've heard evidence that Acme Company broke that warranty by selling plastic tubes that cracked and broke when my client used them. Obviously, a cracked and broken tube is not fit for its usual purpose.

You also want to discuss the law in a manner the jury can understand. A technical legal discussion will do no good. For example, telling the jury "The law under Rule 10b-5, promulgated by the SEC under the Securities Exchange Act of 1934, prohibits the making of any false and deceptive statements in connection with the purchase or sale of a security," is too technical and stuffy. Why not say simply, "The law says that people can't make false statements when they sell stock," or words to that effect?

5. Use the special verdict form

One good way to work the law into your closing argument is to use the special verdict form, if the judge is going to give one to the jury. Discussing the special verdict form during your closing argument does four main things. First, it gets the jury familiar with the format of the special verdict form and what it asks them to do. Second, it gives you a chance to tell the jurors how to answer the questions in the form, and *why* they should answer the questions they way you want them to. Third, it gives you a chance to integrate the law and the facts in your closing and relate both of them to the "questionnaire" that they'll be asked to fill out. Finally, keying off the special verdict form is a decent way to organize your closing argument if no other method of organization jumps out at you.

What Can't You Argue?

Closing argument is generally a no-holds-barred affair. But there are some things that are off limits.

1. Misstating the evidence

Closing argument is definitely a time to tell your story, but it's not a time to make one up. If you can't tie each factual statement in your closing to something that a witness said, an exhibit that the jury saw, or a fair inference from one of those things, then you probably shouldn't include it in your closing. With most judges, the lawyers receive plenty of latitude in their closings, which makes it a bit risky to object to a closing argument on the ground it misstates the evidence unless your opponent says someting that's blatantly untrue or unsupported by any evidence.

Most objections to a closing argument on the ground of misstatement of the evidence are met with the judge overruling the objection and telling the jurors that they will just have to rely on their recollection of the evidence. You should be sure that what your opponent is saying is actually *unsupported* by anything that happened at trial. You can't object on the ground of misstatement just because you disagree with your opponent's statement, or you have a witness who contradicted what your opponent just said. The facts are almost *always* in dispute at trial; otherwise, someone would have won summary judgment. Even the slightest support is enough to base factual argument on in closing.

Setting aside any objections, the jury will reject arguments that are based on imaginary facts. Don't make such arguments.

If someone objects during your closing on the ground of misstatement and the judge sustains the objection, tell the jury that you don't mean to misstate the evidence, that they should rely on their recollection of the evidence, and that you are simply telling them what you believe the evidence showed. And be sure not to misstate the evidence again.

2. Misstating the law

You receive less latitude on arguing the law as opposed to arguing the facts because the judge knows what the law is (or at least appears to the jury to know what the law is, which is what really matters) and can cut you off in a hurry if you're starting to play fast and loose with the judge's interpretation of the law. If the judge sustains an objection that you are misstating the law, the jury will think you are breaking the rules and they will hold it against you.

Treat instructions like impeaching documents (chapter 6). Use the exact words from the instructions when talking to the jury.

One of the best ways to ensure that you are stating the law accurately is to have an enlargement of one or two of the judge's key instructions to show to the jury—if you have the time to prepare it. That way, you're absolutely certain to give the jury the correct law. If you draw an objection that is sustained, apologize to the judge for misstating the law (perhaps you just inadvertently misunderstood it), and remind the jury that they should listen to the judge for the final word on the law.

3. Arguing the "Golden Rule"

Another area that is off-limits in closings is "golden rule" arguments—*i.e.,* "How would you feel if this happened to you?" or "What if you were in the plaintiff's shoes?" There are crafty ways to make the same sort of argument without it being a true "golden rule" argument.

Instead of	*You could try*
How would you feel if you had been treated this way?	Most reasonable people would have been offended to be treated like that.
Put yourself in the plaintiff's shoes.	You can imagine how the plaintiff must have felt.
I'm sure that's not the way you would have wanted to be treated if you were the defendant.	The defendant was right to feel like he was being picked on. Any normal person would have.

The key is to avoid *directly* urging the jury to decide the case based on how he or she would want to be treated. Note the word "directly" in the last sentence, though. Part of the whole point of closing is to make the jury empathize with your client. If your closing persuades the jury to decide the case in part because they would never want to be treated as shabbily as your client was treated, then you have done a great closing.

4. Unfairly inflaming the passion of the jury

Inflaming the passion of the jury is pretty much what closing argument is about in many cases, and it is legitimate to connect with the jury on an emotional level. But you can't use "unfair means" to get there.

What are "unfair means"? It is hard to describe. Appeals to racial, sexual, and religious prejudices are certainly off-limits. Some other examples of prohibited arguments:

If it feels slimy, then you probably shouldn't make the point in your closing.

▲ suggesting the plaintiff should get a lot of money because he's poor;

▲ arguing that the defendant should have to pay a lot of money because she's rich (unless you're in a trial involving punitive damages, in which case the defendant's wealth may be a legitimate subject);

▲ asking for a large award because insurance will pay for the claim;

▲ relying on salacious details of your opponent's personal life (unless it's relevant to the case and came into evidence at the trial).

Perhaps the best way to sum it up is that you cannot base your closing on "hot-button" factors that are completely irrelevant to the legal and factual issues in the case. But it's admittedly a fine line. Appealing to the jurors' sensibilities and feelings is part of the deal (chapter 3). How far is "too far" will vary from judge to judge.

How Should You Argue?

The biggest and toughest question is *how* you should argue the case to the jury. This encompasses everything from your demeanor to your speaking style to the substantive content and organization of your closing argument.

As with virtually everything in the PTM approach, *remember that you're speaking to a jury*. Better yet, remember that you're speaking to a jury that has just sat through a trial—perhaps a lengthy one— for the princely sum of about $40 or so per day. They've got a lot of undone work waiting for them back at the office. They're probably tired of hearing evidence, and even more tired of hearing lawyers talk (chapter 2).

The case may have been complicated, but your job as a lawyer is to make it uncomplicated and keep your closing as concise and simple as possible.

The general admonition to respect the jury leads to the following guidelines for closing arguments.

1. Keep it short

Your should be as short as possible. Make sure you hit all the important points, but don't talk about everything that happened during the trial. When someone asks you what a movie was about, you don't (or at least shouldn't) take as long as the movie was to explain it. People don't want the blow-by-blow of a movie, they just want a synopsis. Hit the high points, perhaps go into a little detail on one or two important scenes, and that's about it. The same applies to closing arguments.

This will be challenging in your first few trials. Do your best to keep it as short as possible.

Some judges impose time limits on closing arguments. Federal judges routinely limit you to one hour of closing, whether the trial took two days or two weeks. Even when the judge sets a limit, don't feel like you have to use it all. And if there's no time limit (as is often the case in state court), that does not mean that you get to talk all day.

Different people have different rules on the outer time limit of a closing argument. A good maximum is two hours. Try not to ever exceed two hours in closing argument. There's a reason most movies are about two hours long, and why critics always make a point of calling even the best movies "a bit long" if they go over two hours. Two hours seems to be about the most time that people can watch or listen to something before it starts to feel like it's taking too long. To paraphrase Sam Goldwyn (and to end the movie analogies for now): If you can't do your closing argument in two hours or less, you don't understand your case, and the jury won't either.

2. Keep it simple

How would you tell the story to a stranger you met at a party? You'd hit the high points. You'd leave out irrelevant detail and complicated legal points. That is exactly what you should do in your closing argument. Your entire closing argument should be built around your themes (Chapter 3).

The jurors are tired and want to go home. Don't waste their time.

Perhaps your theme will be the very first line of your closing argument.

> ### Good Example
>
> You remember that I told you in my opening statement that this case is about a company that actually admitted that a house it built had a major construction defect, but then the company refused to fix the defect. And the evidence you've heard and seen over the last four days has proven that to be true.

The rest of your closing should focus on the evidence that supports your theme. And you might want to restate the theme a couple of times during your closing just to refocus on it.

Good Example

[At the start of the closing argument:] On Monday I told you that this was a case about a company that broke a very simple rule: don't take things that don't belong to you. And for the last three days, you've heard how Acme Company took something that didn't belong to it.

* * *

[After a discussion about two pieces of evidence showing that Acme took something that didn't belong to it] Then you heard Mr. Gooseley testify that his boss told him to take all of the cows up on that land in Brainerd, and ask questions later. Mr. Gooseley said that he did that, despite the fact that he suspected some of the cows belonged to somebody else. Again, Acme taking something that didn't belong to it.

* * *

[After further discussion about the facts] So I come back to the place I started. It's a very simple rule. Don't take things that don't belong to you. Acme broke that rule, and it broke the rule on purpose. The way to fix the situation is equally simple. Acme has to pay for what it took.

3. Use plain, conversational English

Closely related to the idea of keeping the closing argument simple is the idea of using plain, conversational English in your argument. Avoid technical, dense prose.

Bad Example

You've heard all the evidence, and it's clear that the central issue is whether Acme Company breached its implied warranty of merchantability in the sale of wood brackets to Woodland Company. And the evidence shows that Acme breached its warranty because the warpage of the wood that Acme sold exceeded both the contractual specifications and the standard tolerances set forth by the Wood Window and Door Association when the warpage is measured at the midpoint of the chord formed by laying the brackets on a flat surface. You heard expert testimony that this condition was caused by a moisture gradient that existed between the laminated portions of the bracket—a delta M of approximately 15.6 percent, I think Dr. Jones testified—and that this moisture gradient was the fault of Acme Company in not maintaining a proper relative humidity in its plant in months when the relative humidity exceeds 40 percent.

Good Example

The judge has just instructed you that the main issue in this case is whether the wood brackets that Acme Company sold to Woodland Company were fit for use as wood brackets in the industry. And you heard a whole lot of evidence showing that the answer to that question is "no." Witness after witness testified that the problem was that the brackets warped. Now Acme and Woodland had a contract allowing the brackets to warp somewhat, but you heard evidence that the brackets actually warped far more than that contract allowed. And they warped far more than the industry standard. You heard expert testimony that the problem was that Acme didn't control the humidity in its plant, and that led to the pieces of wood that were laminated—or glued—together having much different moisture contents. Dr. Jones testified that when you glue two pieces of wood with different moisture contents together, you get warping. And that's exactly what happened in this case.

The second example is much more understandable to a lay jury (and to most other people). There is no need to dazzle or impress the jury with your detailed knowledge of the facts of the case if the jury is not going to follow what you're saying.

4. Make it interesting

This is easy to understand. Trials are seldom as interesting as they are on television or in the movies, but jurors certainly would like them to be. And while we can't usually achieve the gut-wrenching excitement of TV, we can at least make our cases as interesting as possible to the jurors.

As long as the jurors think you are trying to make the case interesting, they'll stick with you for awhile.

Some cases are more interesting than others. The challenging ones are cases involving civil disputes between two large corporations. To spice things up, remember that corporations are run by people, and that they are generally trying to accomplish something when they act. All you need to do is tell the story in as noble a way as possible, and do the opposite for your opponent.

Take a patent case, for example. They can get very dry and technical. If you focus too much on the science, the story won't be interesting. But there's usually a story hidden somewhere underneath the science.

Good Example

MediVent decided fifteen years ago that it wanted to go into the medical device business because it believed it could make the best products in the world, and that those products would help people who have heart disease. MediVent hired the best scientists it could find—people with Ph.Ds and other advanced degrees—to develop cutting edge products. Those people don't come cheap. It cost MediVent a lot of money to do that. But they kept on going, because they wanted to be the leaders in this field. Some of those top scientists came up with some great inventions—great enough that the United States Patent and Trademark Office gave MediVent three patents. MediVent had finally turned the corner. It was poised to become the world leader in this type of technology. MediVent was excited about introducing its products—the products that it spent so long working on—at the Vienna Medical Product Show in August of 1998. But that excitement turned to shock and disappointment when MediVent got to the show and saw that its competitor, VediMent, was showing virtually the same products that Medi-Vent was about to introduce. The Kong Dual-Lumen Catheterization Stent was MediVent's idea. It got the patent. VediMent took that idea and stole MediVent's business away.

5. Use demonstrative exhibits

A good visual aid is worth its weight in gold in closing argument. For more on the use of such exhibits, see chapter 8.

6. Use analogies and anecdotes

A good analogy or anecdote is often an effective way to get a complex point across. Take, for example, a case where the plaintiffs allege that a corporation diluted the plaintiffs' interest in the company by selling stock to other people without the plaintiffs' consent. Here's an analogy that illustrates the case:

Good Example

The plaintiffs are complaining that the company sold stock to more people, which led to the plaintiffs getting a smaller share of the company. And I could understand the plaintiffs' concern if they were really getting a smaller piece of the pie. But they are not. If you make a pie larger, you can cut it into more pieces and still give everyone the same amount as if the pie was smaller and cut into fewer pieces. That is exactly what happened here. When the new investors came in, they invested money in the company. That made the pie bigger, so you can cut it up into more pieces, and everyone still gets about the same amount of pie.

Make sure the analogy is a good logical fit. And make sure it's appropriate for a jury trial. "This guy walks into a bar . . ." is usually not the best start for an appropriate analogy.

7. Organize your thoughts

Part of keeping the story interesting and understandable is choosing the organization of the story. There are a million different ways to do it. We won't discuss all of them. Here are a few:

- ▲ *Chronological.* People tend to remember things best when they are presented in order of their occurrence. A chronological presentation is very understandable, but might not be the most interesting method of presentation.

- ▲ *Flashback.* Sometimes the most interesting way to tell a story is to talk about the end, then jump to the beginning. This works best when the last part of the story sheds a new light on the earlier part of the story.

- ▲ *Topical.* Perhaps you feel that the clearest presentation calls for organizing the evidence into broad topics. This approach lends itself very well to using the special verdict form as a guide to your closing argument, since the special verdict form will likely divide the issues into legal topics.

5 Ways To Tell if You're Being Too Dramatic

1. The jurors are rolling their eyes at you.

2. The judge laughs out loud during the climactic moment in your closing.

3. Opposing counsel asks the judge for leave to vomit.

4. The judge's clerk begins loudly humming "The Way We Were" as you speak.

5. You're Sally Field.

▲ *Order of Proof at Trial.* If you liked how the evidence was presented at trial, you may want your closing argument to track the order of the trial so that you can have the jury relive the whole experience. This is also effective in refreshing the jurors' recollection of the evidence, since they may well remember the order in which they met the witnesses and will remember the testimony once they are reminded of the order of presentation.

▲ *Liability, Then Damages.* This organizational technique can be used in combination with other organization techniques discussed in this chapter (for example, you may want to discuss liability through a flashback presentation before moving to damages).

Practice your closing with a non-lawyer, if possible. If they don't get it, neither will the jury.

There are many, many ways to organize a story. The ones above are the most common. Every case is different, and each calls for its own method of organizing the story. Think about which organizational method resonates with you. Try a few out on friends or loved ones and see what they think. The central issue is always the same: what will get the jury to understand the case best?

8. Tell them what you want

At some point in the closing, usually the very end, you must clearly and concisely tell the jury what you want them to do. If there is a special verdict form, tell the jury exactly how it should answer the special verdict questions.

Good Example

The first question on the special verdict form is: "Did Sergeant Bilko act reasonably when he arrested Mortimer Snerd on August 13, 1998?" As I explained to you earlier, the evidence in this case requires you to answer that question "No." The second question on the verdict form asks, "How much money will fairly compensate Mr. Snerd for the injury (if any) that he suffered on August 13, 1998?" The evidence requires you to answer that question "$200,000."

If there is no special verdict form, you must simply tell the jury how you want them to decide on liability (in favor of the plaintiff or in favor of the defendant), and (if you're the plaintiff or liability is conceded) how much the jury should award in damages.

9. Consider left brain and right brain

A truly great closing argument should please both halves of the juror's brain. It should not be too dry and clinical, but should not be too emotional and histrionic either. The true art of a closing argument is striking the right balance of evidence and emotions. A dramatic, Perry Mason-type closing that reduces the jury to tears is rarely possible, but it is usually possible to inject some emotion into your client's case.

Suppose you are defending a huge corporation against an employment discrimination claim where the corporation says that the employee is trying to turn minor annoyances in the workplace into a trumped-up charge of discrimination in order to make some money. The employee's lawyer, of course, will easily be able to work emotion into the closing argument. But you can too:

Good Example

You've heard Mr. Bradwell testify that he believes that all of the things that happened to him were because Acme Company was discriminating against him. But what he's really complaining about are the minor annoyances that all of us encounter in the workplace from time to time. They're unfortunate, but they're not discrimination. Acme Company is made up of people. Hundreds of workers like Mr. Bradwell wake up each morning, punch the clock, and work hard all day to make money to support their families. They understand that there are going to be some annoyances and inconveniences at work. They work through them. They don't sue over them. They make their money through hard work, and they count on their co-workers to do the same. Mr. Bradwell is asking to make his money through a lawsuit—a lawsuit over the types of incidents that his co-workers work through without asking for a dime. That's not fair to the hundreds of other people at Acme Company.

The more dramatic the underlying facts in the case, of course, the more dramatic your closing can be.

Good Example

On the morning of June 15, 2000, Anna Blatz woke up in a room filled with light from the rising sun and fresh air from a spring breeze. She had breakfast and prepared for work. It was an ordinary morning in all ways but one. It was her last morning alive. Before the sun set that night, Anna Blatz would be dead. When she stood at the bathroom mirror that morning and brushed her hair, she did not know that she had less than twelve hours to live.

Be careful with drama, though. There is such a thing as being over-dramatic, and that will backfire on you by making the jury think that you are trying to hard to evoke their sympathy.

In general, the more naturally dramatic the facts of the case, the less you should think about and work on making the closing dramatic. The great actor Sir John Gielgud said that the audience cried more as a tragic character cried less. The same goes for your closing in a naturally dramatic case. Let the case speak for itself. That's drama enough.

What's Your Strategy?

As we discussed above, you can argue just about anything in closing. But *should* you argue certain things? There are no clear answers; again, each case is different. But here are some typical strategic calls that every trial lawyer has to make in closing argument from time to time.

1. Mentioning the weaknesses in your case

Every case has weak spots. In general, the stronger the weak spots in your case, the more likely you will be to mention them in closing and try to explain them. If you don't have a plausible explanation for the big weak points, the jury will either assume you have no answer, or think that you are not being candid with them. Either conclusion will hurt you.

The flip side is that admitting your weak points will win you credibility with the jury, and make it more likely that they will believe what you are telling them about the *good* points of your case.

Good Example

You've heard a lot in this trial about how my client violated the environmental laws. And I'm here to tell you that all of that evidence is absolutely true. Acme did violate the environmental laws. Acme admitted to the violations, and paid over $15 million in fines for its violations. Acme isn't proud of that. It made a lot of mistakes, and has paid for those mistakes. It has been working to make sure that those mistakes never happen again. But all the talk about our violations of the environmental laws should not distract you from what this case is really about. It's an employment discrimination case. And the question isn't whether Acme violated the environmental laws, it's whether Acme violated the employment laws. And the answer to that question is "no" for the reasons that I'll review with you now.

Good Example

Wood Guy Company has made a big deal out of the fact that ABC Company did not thoroughly inspect the wood that Wood Guy shipped to ABC. And that's quite true. But it made no difference, because no amount of inspection would have uncovered the defects in the wood that Wood Guy shipped to ABC. So don't be misled by the whole inspection argument. It's a red herring, and nothing more.

Whether to address weaknesses (and if so, which ones to address) is usually easier when you are the plaintiff, since you generally give your closing last and so have had a chance to hear your opponent's closing before you deliver yours. If your opponent didn't touch on certain weaknesses, you'll probably be safest not touching on them either. There's no sense in making a big deal out of a bad point that your opponent didn't bother to mention. The strategic call is much tougher when you're the defendant and you have to give your closing first.

2. "Going negative"

What about your opponent's weak spots? How much do you dwell on them in your closing? The answer, as always, varies. But generally, you should spend some of your closing argument pointing out the weaknesses in the other side's case. You should, however, do this only after discussing the strengths of your case. If you spend too long rebutting your opponent's case, the jury may believe that your opponent has you on the ropes. And you also won't have much time to argue the affirmative side of your case.

Jurors don't like purely negative arguments. Give them something positive.

The extent to which you address your opponent's specific arguments constitutes a pure judgment call. The usual rule of thumb is not to haul off on your opponent too badly unless: (a) you're confident that the jury hates your opponent as much as you do; or (b) you're so far behind that you've got nothing to lose. The main reason not to hammer on your opponent is that it may offend the jury. They may see it as rude or just a "lawyer acting like a lawyer." Either way, it's usually not an effective tactic.

That being said, you should definitely not hesitate to attack weaknesses in your opponent's arguments. If your opponent has taken an implausible or weakly supported position at the trial, by all means point that out in closing and go after it. But do it politely and logically.

Good Example

Mr. Childress testified that he was handcuffed with his hands behind his head, and that he was wearing nothing on his head and only a light jacket at the time. But as the videotape of the arrest clearly shows, Mr. Childress was handcuffed with his hands behind his *back*, and he was wearing a winter coat with a hood at the time of his arrest. You can assume that Mr. Childress simply can't recall the event; I'm not asking you to find that he was lying. But the point is the same either way. His testimony is inconsistent with all the other evidence you heard, so you can't give it any weight.

Bad Example

Mr. Childress testified that he was handcuffed with his hands behind his head, wearing nothing on his head and only a light jacket. What bunk! You saw the videotape as well as I did. He had a winter coat with a hood, and his hands were behind his back. Did he really expect us to believe his story? Does he really expect us to believe anything he says? He lied about that, and he's lying about everything else, I tell you. You can't believe a word this guy says.

Again, these are general rules, and part of being a good trial lawyer is knowing when to break the general rules. But especially when you are just starting out with trial work, you should err on the side of politeness and rationality, since it is much less likely to alienate the jury.

3. Your opponent's failure to deliver

If your opponent made promises in his closing argument that she was not able to deliver on—perhaps because some evidence was excluded or perhaps because she couldn't get a key witness to testify the way she expected—your opponent has given you a good opportunity to tell the jury to remember the promise that your opponent made, and to point out that your opponent was unable to deliver.

Good Example

In her opening statement, Ms. Haversham told you that you would hear from the chief engineer in charge of the pacemaker project that Acme Pacemakers' engineers developed the pacemaker on their own. But you never heard from that chief engineer, did you? That's extremely important. The person that they identified as their key witness on one of the most important issues in the case never showed up to testify. What does that tell you about their case? It tells you that they know they have no case, because if the chief engineer had been able to contradict our evidence, he surely would have come here to testify. The fact that he didn't testify tells you that he and Ms. Haversham knew that his testimony would have been bad for Acme.

Good Example

Ms. Haversham promised you in her closing that she would prove that my client knew that its products were defective. She was not able to deliver on that promise. Ms. Haversham produced no evidence that anyone at Acme knew that its products were defective. Every witness from Acme testified that they had no idea that there was any defect in the product, and Ms. Haversham could not come up with a single witness or exhibit to the contrary.

---

4. The burden of proof

If you are the defendant, you should mention the burden of proof in your closing argument. It seems obvious to you that your opponent has the burden of proof, but it is not necessarily obvious to the jury. Remind them. Make sure they understand that if the defendant either wins *or fights to a draw*, the verdict has to go to the defendant.

5. Objections to your opponent's closing

Objections during closing are generally frowned upon, for two main reasons. First, it tends to make it look as though you are trying to interfere with the other side telling its story. Second, it is difficult to persuade a judge to sustain an objection during closing argument, so you are likely to be overruled and look bad in front of the jury.

Nonetheless, there are times when an objection is warranted. The most common are when opposing counsel is blatantly misstating the law or the facts. Be careful: make these objections cautiously, and only when you are confident that you have a good chance of prevailing on the objection.

Closing Thoughts

A great closing argument can be simply magical. In a complicated case where the jury did not fully understand the evidence as it came in, an effective closing argument can actually spell the difference between winning and losing. It is the last word in the case, and the last thing the jury will hear before it retires to deliberate. Give a great deal of thought—and a lot of practice—to your closing argument, and you'll go out with a bang.

Chapter 13

The End is Near

Your trial is about to end. Now what do you do? In this chapter, you'll learn:

▲ what to do once the jury starts deliberating

▲ how to handle questions from the jury

▲ how to react to the jury verdict (win or lose)

The case has gone to the jury. But you can't catch up on your sleep just yet. There are a few more details to attend to.

What's Going to Happen?

Will you be notified when the jury reaches its verdict? And if so, how long will you have to get to the courtroom? The most common answers are, "Yes, if you leave a number where you can be reached," and "About twenty minutes at most." Most judges want the jurors to be able to go home quickly once they have reached a verdict. They'll give you twenty minutes to show up in person, but they don't want to have the jurors cool their heels for two hours waiting for the lawyers who have already taken enough of the jury's time. Make sure and let the Court's clerk know if you want to be contacted when the jury reaches its verdict and where you can be reached.

You should also ask the judge how the verdict will be taken. Will it be in open court, or will the judge just have the jury give its verdict to the bailiff for delivery to the judge without further ceremony? Usually, the judge takes the verdict in open court.

Where Should I Wait?

Regardless of what you do, it's a good idea to keep the client away from the jurors.

Should you keep vigil outside the courtroom? And if so, do you keep vigil where the jury can see you? If you're more than twenty minutes away from the courthouse, you may have to keep vigil if you want to be present when the jury returns its verdict. If not, the question is whether you want to keep vigil to impress the jury. Thoughts differ.

Many think that it's a little creepy to be sitting outside the courtroom like a vulture whenever the jurors go to and return from lunch. Others believe that it shows the jury that you really care. Nobody knows for sure. You should follow your instincts and do what feels right for you. If you keep vigil, make sure you don't cross the line into invading the physical or psychological space of the jurors.

Questions from the Jury

How do you handle questions from the jury? The typical practice is that the judge will call counsel from both sides if the jury has a question, read the question to counsel, and ask for input on the proper response. After discussing the issue with available counsel, the judge will draft a response and either give the written response to the jury or read the respond to the jury in open court. The jury is typically not allowed to ask any follow up questions in open court but must rely on additional written questions. Rather than write down such follow up questions, the jury ususally moves on and tries to reach a verdict, even if the response was not particularly helpful.

Be careful. You can win or lose a case by mishandling a jury question.

The questions usually involve a request for clarification on an evidentiary point. Seven times out of ten the answer to the jury is something like, "You must rely on your recollection of the evidence at trial," which obviously doesn't help the jury (they wouldn't have asked the question if they recalled the evidence at trial), but is the safe answer, because it is error to give the jury an answer that suggests which way it should decide the case, or that unduly highlights one piece of evidence. If counsel agree on what the response should be, then obviously the judge can read that response to the jury with more freedom. If the response is legally dictated (*e.g.,* "Do we have to find for the plaintiff on all three elements of his case, or is two out of three okay?"), then the judge may tell the jury what to do even if someone (the poor plaintiff, in this example) would rather just say words to the effect, "Do what your heart is telling you to do."

Jury Question That
Makes Plaintiff Smile

*Can we give the
plaintiff more money
than she wants?*

Jury Question That
Makes Defendant
Smile

*Does the plaintiff really
have to meet his burden
of proof?*

When called upon for input on a response to the jury, you need to figure out what the jury is hung up on (sometimes it's obvious, sometimes not) and to propose an answer that guides the jury in the direction most favorable for you. You seldom get to do this, though, because the more you guide them, the more likely your opponent will object and the more likely the judge will simply tell the jury to rest on their best recollection.

Reacting to the Verdict

What should you do after the jury returns their verdict?

If you lose, do you poll the jurors (*i.e.*, have the judge ask each juror if the verdict is his or her true verdict)? The answer is generally "yes," because you have nothing to lose. Once in a blue moon a juror will actually say (á la Perry Mason), "No! The others made me do it! They tortured me! I wanted to vote the other way!" Mostly, though, the jurors all just say "Yes." Have the jurors polled, though, just in case lightning strikes, or you have a juror who honestly doesn't have the guts to own up to his or her decision when your client is sitting there live and in person.

If you win, don't gloat to opposing counsel. Shake hands and leave the courtroom. Fast.

If you win, just shut up. Don't thank the jurors or give them a big smile. They don't want to look like they did you a big favor (even if they did and even if they thought so in the jury room). They want to return the verdict and leave the courtroom. Let them do so.

In the days following the trial, can you call the jurors to ask them what they thought of your stunning performance? The best practice is to ask the judge first. Most judges don't like this practice, even though it can be *extremely* helpful—especially for new trial lawyers. Talking to the decision-makers about what motivated them to do what they did is a *gold mine* of great information for your development as a lawyer (or possibly a *silver mine*, since jurors sometimes tell counsel what they think counsel wants to hear). But judges still hate it, because they want to protect the jurors.

Some judges say, "Don't do it or I'll have you sanctioned," which is probably not appropriate, but is also probably not worth challenging (*i.e.*, don't call the judge's bluff on this). Many judges say, "I'd prefer that you not, but I can't stop you." This is what we call "grumbling acceptance," which means it's okay to contact the jurors, just don't go making a big deal out of it. Other judges will say they think it's a fine idea.

One important point holds true in all cases, though: always be polite and nonthreatening to the jurors. If you are abusive or suggest that the jurors *must* talk to you, then the judge will come down on you like a ton of bricks. The jurors do not have to talk to you if they don't want to, and you should make that clear at the beginning of your conversation with them. Remember: you impinged on the jurors' time for however long it took to try the case because they were legally required to give you their time, but now you're impinging on time they're not legally required to give you. So be *nice*. Explain to them that their input would greatly aid your development as a lawyer, scholar, and human being. And thank them for their time.

Listen to what they say. Don't argue with them or otherwise appear defensive.

Chapter 14

Are You Mocking My Jury Trial?

Like anything else in life, practice makes a jury trial perfect (or at least better). In this chapter, you'll Learn:

▲ different ways to practice or "mock" your trial

▲ how to use consultants to get more bang for your mock trial buck

▲ what type of potential problems may result from your mock experience

To Mock or Not to Mock?

Your trial is just around the corner. You and your client would really love some feedback on your themes and witnesses.

C.K. Rowland, Ph.D., of Litigation Insights graciously provided substantial contributions to this chapter.

What are your options?

Apart from bouncing ideas of friends and colleagues, you may want to consider some type of mock trial exercise. The decision to go this route depends on a variety of factors, the most obvious of which is cost. Is your case worth it? Are the damages or monetary importance high enough to justify a full blown mock trial?

Even if your client can afford the cost of a mock trial, does it make sense to go through all the time and trouble of conducting such an exercise? Most importantly, are you and the client ready, willing and able to make a full commitment to carrying out a mock trial exercise? Going forward with the exercise may require a lot of preparation time with important business executives—does your client want to take these witnesses away from their current projects? Going forward may also require you, the trial lawyer, to prepare an opening statement, witness examinations, and a closing argument *right now*. You may have to cancel a vacation or otherwise rearrange your life due to a mock, as opposed to real, trial. Do you want to do this? Or do you plan merely to go through the motions and deliver a "rough draft" or "work in progress" at the mock exercise?

And even if you get past all of the above obstacles, do you really need to mock your trial? Is there an issue or a set of issues that require specific feedback from a mock jury? In short, do you know *why* you want to conduct the mock trial exercise?

It is almost always a mistake to simply "tee it up and see what a jury says" without identifying specific questions to which you want answers at the end of your exercise. Rather, you want to learn how jurors resolve specific evidentiary and legal issues, and what you can to do anticipate and influence jurors on those issues.

Should We Do It Alone or With Some Help?

With rare exceptions, this is an easy one. Unless exposure is too small to justify even modest outsourced research, it is almost always better to hire a professional jury consulting firm and to work collaboratively with them on the design, implementation and analysis of research aimed at your core goals and questions. Although jury consultants have never tried a case and are often naïve regarding the most basic rules of evidence and procedure, they bring a quantity and quality of experience that is not shared by even the most experienced trial lawyer. While you have been trying those cases, the trial consultant has been facilitating focus groups and watching literally thousands of mock jurors debate questions similar to the questions that define your need for jury research.

Using consultants is almost always a good idea.

Mock Jury Feedback You Could Do Without:

Mock Juror No. 1:   I hated that one lawyer, you know, [describes you in detail]. I just hated that lawyer.

Mock Juror No. 2:   So I wasnt the only one? Gosh, that lawyer was terrible.

Mock Juror No. 3:   You know, I think they always have one pretend lawyer in the group to see if we can pick them out. I'm sure that lawyer was the pretend one.

Mock Juror No. 1:   You're probably right. All I can say about that lawyer is "ick." I mean, "ick, ick, ick, ick."

How Do I Pick a Consultant?

Having decided to use a jury consultant, how do you decide which one to use? This is a difficult question, made more difficult by the fact that there are no jury consulting analogues to law schools, bar exams, and continuing legal education. Technically, anyone can hang out a shingle and call himself or herself a jury consultant. For example, the reluctance of many HMOs to support extended mental health treatment triggered the transformation of many counseling psychologists into novice jury consultants.

As you think about consultants, consider the following factors:

In-person interview. Consulting is a collaborative effort. You need to make judgments about compatibility and how your consultant will think on his/her feet when unexpected challenges or opportunities present themselves. You also need to get a feel for how your consultant will interact with your client.

Take time to pick the right consultant. It matters.

Experience. Experience putting on a lot of mocks is neither rare nor particularly important. The mechanics are not that difficult. You need to feel comfortable that your consultant has the quantity and quality of experience necessary to add significant value to your joint endeavor. Has the consultant worked in the state or region where your case is to be tried? To what extent has he/she worked on cases that address exposures, research questions and legal issues similar to those you face? Finally, and most important, with whom has he/she worked and is he/she willing for you to call them? Any experienced, effective consultant should be able to offer on-point references.

Education and Expertise. In the early days of trial consulting, a number of consultants entered the field with bachelor degrees, sometimes in a field that had little to do with American juries. Some of these folks learned on the job and became the kinds of consultants who can give you a good set of references. But today this is very much the exception. When hiring a consultant today, it helps to find someone with a graduate degree, preferably a Ph.D., in psychology or communications. Moreover, it would be great if their training and areas of specialization focused on certain "fancy-pants" subjects, such as the psychology of human judgment,

217

rhetoric and persuasion, or other areas that will help them connect their academic training to the real-world challenges you face.

Institutional Capacity and Commitment. You want a commitment from your consultant to be personally involved in your case, especially the design of the research and the analysis of the results. But you also want a consulting firm with the institutional capacity to conduct large-scale research and offer whatever ancillary services are suggested by the results of that research—e.g., a forensic animation reconstructing a controversial medical procedure. It is important to establish both sides of this equation before committing to a firm and a consultant. You need to feel comfortable that the firm has the capacity you need and that the firm's consulting will be led by the consultant you hire.

Now What?

Mock exercises come in all shapes and sizes.

Once you select a consultant, sit down and decide, "What research model fits my unique research needs?" Discussions with focus groups? Presentations to mock jury panels who then decide selected issues? Witness examinations with feedback from mock jury panels? Full-blown mock trials with openings, witness examintions, and closing arguments? This list goes on and on.

If you have selected the right consultant, he/she will be able to identify research questions that have not occurred to you. Some of these questions will offer important insights. Others will have been rendered moot or irrelevant by judicial decisions. Some of the questions will be slightly off point, but will open other, productive avenues of inquiry. The point is that you will always come up with a better research model if you put in the time required to blend your consultant's expertise and experience with your own rather than simply imposing or accepting a cookbook research design.

How Do You Use the Results?

The manner in which your consultant designs the jury research (being sure the right questions are being addressed the right way), analyzes the results, and then helps you learn from those results, is what distinguishes the best trial consultants from their more pedestrian counterparts. You should insist that your consultant's work product include a set of research-based thematic and strategic recommendations that go beyond "Here's what we learned," to "Here's what we think you can do to improve your case." Ideally, this work product should include a written report that is passed along to your client and a face-to-face brainstorming session designed to incorporate the jury-research results into your trial themes, presentation strategies, witness preparation, and courtroom graphics.

A Note of Caution

If designed, implemented and analyzed correctly, jury research can improve greatly the probability of a favorable trial outcome. Certainly a litigant who has the benefit of jury research has an advantage over the litigant who has not previewed juror response to key issues. But one should never forget that a mock trial is just that—a mock trial. By definition it cannot account for unanticipated interventions, such as a judge's decision to include or exclude a damaging piece of evidence. Nor can jury research account for the impact of certain untested variables, such as an exceptional animation or other exhibits prepared by the other side. But you can minimize the potential disconnects between your jury research and your jury trial if you follow two rules of thumb. First, avoid "false positives" by making the other side's mock case as strong as possible. If you are unsure about the admissibility of a document that will help the other side, include it in their mock case. You don't want to cheat by winning the mock battle only to lose the real war at trial.

Don't cheat your way to a mock trial win.

Second, focus less on the verdict and damages outcomes of jury research than on the reasoning and emotional responses that produce these outcomes. If your consultant helps you understand the emotional and cognitive reasons behind a verdict, he/she should be able to help you adjust to the inevitable changes in the litigation landscape that occur between your jury simulation and your jury trial.

A good mock trial can mean the difference between winning or losing. Or it might simply mean you had a good mock trial. You won't know how much the mock trial helped your case until you receive a verdict from a real jury in a real courtroom.

Appendix A

Federal Rules of Evidence

RULES OF EVIDENCE FOR UNITED STATES COURTS AND MAGISTRATES

Rule 101. **Scope.** These rules govern proceedings in the courts of the United States and before the United States bankruptcy judges and the United States magistrate judges, to the extent and with the exceptions stated in rule 1101.

Rule 102. **Purpose and Construction.** These rules shall be construed to secure fairness in administration, elimination of unjustifiable expense and delay, and promotion of growth and development of the law of evidence to the end that the truth may be ascertained and proceedings justly determined.

Rule 103. **Rulings on Evidence.**

(a) **Effect of erroneous ruling.** Error may not be predicated upon a ruling which admits or excludes evidence unless a substantial right of the party is affected, and

(1) **Objection.** In case the ruling is one admitting evidence, a timely objection or motion to strike appears of record, stating the specific ground of objection, if the specific ground was not apparent from the context; or

(2) **Offer of proof.** In case the ruling is one excluding evidence, the substance of the evidence was made known to the court by offer or was apparent from the context within which questions were asked.

(b) **Record of offer and ruling.** The court may add any other or further statement which shows the character of the evidence, the form in which it was offered, the objection made, and the ruling thereon. It may direct the making of an offer in question and answer form.

(c) **Hearing of jury.** In jury cases, proceedings shall be conducted, to the extent practicable, so as to prevent inadmissible evidence from being suggested to the jury by any means, such as making statements or offers of proof or asking questions in the hearing of the jury.

(d) **Plain error.** Nothing in this rule precludes taking notice of plain errors affecting substantial rights although they were not brought to the attention of the court.

Rule 104. **Preliminary Questions.**

(a) **Questions of admissibility generally.** Preliminary questions concerning the qualification of a person to be a witness, the existence of a privilege, or the admissibility of evidence shall be determined by the court, subject to the provisions of subdivision (b). In making its determination it is not bound by the rules of evidence except those with respect to privileges.

(b)   **Relevancy conditioned in fact.** When the relevancy of evidence depends upon the fulfillment of a condition of fact, the court shall admit it upon, or subject to, the introduction of evidence sufficient to support a finding of the fulfillment of the condition.

(c)   **Hearing of jury.** Hearings on the admissibility of confessions shall in all cases be conducted out of the hearing of the jury. Hearings on other preliminary matters shall be so conducted when the interests of justice require, or when an accused is a witness and so requests.

(d)   **Testimony by accused.** The accused does not, by testifying upon a preliminary matter, become subject to cross-examination as to other issues in the case.

(e)   **Weight and credibility.** This rule does not limit the right of a party to introduce before the jury evidence relevant to weight or credibility.

Rule 105.   **Limited Admissibility.** When evidence which is admissible as to one party or for one purpose but not admissible as to another party or for another purpose is admitted, the court, upon request, shall restrict the evidence to its proper scope and instruct the jury accordingly.

Rule 106.   **Remainder of or Related Writings or Recorded Statements.** When a writing or recorded statement or part thereof is introduced by a party, an adverse party may require the introduction at that time of any other part or any other writing or recorded statement which ought in fairness to be considered contemporaneously with it.

Rule 201.   **Judicial Notice of Adjudicative Facts.**

(a)   **Scope of rule.** This rule governs only judicial notice of adjudicative facts.

(b)   **Kinds of facts.** A judicially noticed fact must be one not subject to reasonable dispute in that it is either (1) generally known within the territorial jurisdiction of the trial court or (2) capable of accurate and ready determination by resort to sources whose accuracy cannot reasonably be questioned.

(c)   **When discretionary.** A court may take judicial notice, whether requested or not.

(d)   **When mandatory.** A court shall take judicial notice if requested by a party and supplied with the necessary information.

(e)   **Opportunity to be heard.** A party is entitled upon timely request to an opportunity to be heard as to the propriety of taking judicial notice and the tenor of the matter noticed. In the absence of prior notification, the request may be made after judicial notice has been taken.

(f) **Time of taking notice.** Judicial notice may be taken at any stage of the proceeding.

(g) **Instructing jury.** In a civil action or proceeding, the court shall instruct the jury to accept as conclusive any fact judicially noticed. In a criminal case, the court shall instruct the jury that it may, but is not required to, accept as conclusive any fact judicially noticed.

Rule 301. **Presumptions in General in Civil Actions and Proceedings.** In all civil actions and proceedings not otherwise provided for by Act of Congress or by these rules, a presumption imposes on the party against whom it is directed the burden of going forward with evidence to rebut or meet the presumption, but does not shift to such party the burden of proof in the sense of the risk of nonpersuasion, which remains throughout the trial upon the party on whom it was originally cast.

Rule 302. **Applicability of State Law in Civil Actions and Proceedings.** In civil actions and proceedings, the effect of a presumption respecting a fact which is an element of a claim or defense as to which State law supplies the rule of decision is determined in accordance with State law.

Rule 401. **Definition of "Relevant Evidence."** "Relevant evidence" means evidence having any tendency to make the existence of any fact that is of consequence to the determination of the action more probable or less probable than it would be without the evidence.

Rule 402. **Relevant Evidence Generally Admissible; Irrelevant Evidence Inadmissible.** All relevant evidence is admissible, except as otherwise provided by the Constitution of the United States, by Act of Congress, by these rules, or by other rules prescribed by the Supreme Court pursuant to statutory authority. Evidence which is not relevant is not admissible.

Rule 403. **Exclusion of Relevant Evidence on Grounds of Prejudice, Confusion, or Waste of Time.** Although relevant, evidence may be excluded if its probative value is substantially outweighed by the danger of unfair prejudice, confusion of the issues, or misleading the jury, or by considerations of undue delay, waste of time, or needless presentation of cumulative evidence.

Rule 404. **Character Evidence Not Admissible To Prove Conduct; Exceptions; Other Crimes.**

(a) **Character evidence generally.** Evidence of a person's character or a trait of character is not admissible for the purpose of proving action in conformity therewith on a particular occasion, except:

(1)   **Character of accused.** Evidence of a pertinent trait of character offered by an accused, or by the prosecution to rebut the same;

(2)   **Character of victim.** Evidence of a pertinent trait of character of the victim of the crime offered by an accused, or by the prosecution to rebut the same, or evidence of a character trait of peacefulness of the victim offered by the prosecution in a homicide case to rebut evidence that the victim was the first aggressor;

(3)   **Character of witness.** Evidence of the character of a witness, as provided in   rules 607, 608, and 609.

(b)   **Other crimes, wrongs, or acts.** Evidence of other crimes, wrongs, or acts is not admissible to prove the character of a person in order to show action in conformity therewith. It may, however, be admissible for other purposes, such as proof of motive, opportunity, intent, preparation, plan, knowledge, identity, or absence of mistake or accident, provided that upon request by the accused, the prosecution in a criminal case shall provide reasonable notice in advance of trial, or during trial if the court excuses pretrial notice on good cause shown, of the general nature of any such evidence it intends to introduce at trial.

Rule 405.   Methods of Proving Character.

(a)   **Reputation or opinion.** In all cases in which evidence of character or a trait of character of a person is admissible, proof may be made by testimony as to reputation or by testimony in the form of an opinion. On cross-examination, inquiry is allowable into relevant specific instances of conduct.

(b)   **Specific instances of conduct.** In cases in which character or a trait of character of a person is an essential element of a charge, claim, or defense, proof may also be made of specific instances of that person's conduct.

Rule 406.   Habit; Routine Practice. Evidence of the habit of a person or

of the routine practice of an organization, whether corroborated or not and regardless of the presence of eyewitnesses, is relevant to prove that the conduct of the person or organization on a particular occasion was in conformity with the habit or routine practice.

Rule 407.   Subsequent Remedial Measures. When, after an injury or harm

allegedly caused by an event, measures are taken that, if taken previously, would have made the injury or harm less likely to occur, evidence of the subsequent measures is not admissible to prove negligence, culpable conduct, a defect in a product, a defect in a product's design, or a need for a warning or instruction. This rule does not require the exclusion of evidence of subsequent measures when offered for another purpose, such as proving ownership, control, or feasibility of precautionary measures, if controverted, or impeachment.

Rule 408. **Compromise and Offers to Compromise.** Evidence of (1) furnishing or offering or promising to furnish, or (2) accepting or offering or promising to accept, a valuable consideration in compromising or attempting to compromise a claim which was disputed as to either validity or amount, is not admissible to prove liability for or invalidity of the claim or its amount. Evidence of conduct or statements made in compromise negotiations is likewise not admissible. This rule does not require the exclusion of any evidence otherwise discoverable merely because it is presented in the course of compromise negotiations. This rule also does not require exclusion when the evidence is offered for another purpose, such as proving bias or prejudice of a witness, negativing a contention of undue delay, or proving an effort to obstruct a criminal investigation or prosecution.

Rule 409. **Payment of Medical and Similar Expenses.** Evidence of furnishing or offering or promising to pay medical, hospital, or similar expenses occasioned by an injury is not admissible to prove liability for the injury.

Rule 410. **Inadmissibility of Pleas, Plea Discussions, and Related Statements.** Except as otherwise provided in this rule, evidence of the following is not, in any civil or criminal proceeding, admissible against the defendant who made the plea or was a participant in the plea discussions:

(1)   a plea of guilty which was later withdrawn;

(2)   a plea of nolo contendere;

(3)   any statement made in the course of any proceedings under Rule 11 of the Federal Rules of Criminal Procedure or comparable state procedure regarding either of the foregoing pleas; or

(4)   any statement made in the course of plea discussions with an attorney for the prosecuting authority which do not result in a plea of guilty or which result in a plea of guilty later withdrawn.

However, such a statement is admissible (i) in any proceeding wherein another statement made in the course of the same plea or plea discussions has been introduced and the statement ought in fairness be considered contemporaneously with it, or (ii) in a criminal proceeding for perjury or false statement if the statement was made by the defendant under oath, on the record and in the presence of counsel.

Rule 411. **Liability Insurance.** Evidence that a person was or was not insured against liability is not admissible upon the issue whether the person acted negligently or otherwise wrongfully. This rule does not require the exclusion of evidence of insurance against liability when offered for another purpose, such as proof of agency, ownership, or control, or bias or prejudice of a witness.

Rule 412.   Sex Offense Cases; Relevance of Alleged Victim's Past Sexual Behavior or Alleged Sexual Predisposition.

(a)   Evidence generally inadmissible. The following evidence is not admissible in any civil or criminal proceeding involving alleged sexual misconduct except as provided in subdivisions (b) and (c):

(1)   Evidence offered to prove that any alleged victim engaged in other sexual behavior.

(2)   Evidence offered to prove any alleged victim's sexual predisposition.

(b)   Exceptions.

(1)   In a criminal case, the following evidence is admissible, if otherwise admissible under these rules:

(A)   evidence of specific instances of sexual behavior by the alleged victim offered to prove that a person other than the accused was the source of semen, injury, or other physical evidence;

(B)   evidence of specific instances of sexual behavior by the alleged victim with respect to the person accused of the sexual misconduct offered by the accused to prove consent or by the prosecution; and

(C)   evidence the exclusion of which would violate the constitutional rights of the defendant.

(2)   In a civil case, evidence offered to prove the sexual behavior or sexual predisposition of any alleged victim is admissible if it is otherwise admissible under these rules and its probative value substantially outweighs the danger of harm to any victim and of unfair prejudice to any party. Evidence of an alleged victim's reputation is admissible only if it has been placed in controversy by the alleged victim.

(c)   Procedure to determine admissibility.

(1)   A party intending to offer evidence under subdivision (b) must –

(A)   file a written motion at least 14 days before trial specifically describing the evidence and stating the purpose for which it is offered unless the court, for good cause requires a different time for filing or permits filing during trial; and

(B)   serve the motion on all parties and notify the alleged victim or, when appropriate, the alleged victim's guardian or representative.

(2)   Before admitting evidence under this rule the court must conduct a hearing in camera and afford the victim and parties a right to attend and be heard. The motion, related papers, and the record of the hearing must be sealed and remain under seal unless the court orders otherwise.

Rule 413.   Evidence of Similar Crimes in Sexual Assault Cases.

(a)   In a criminal case in which the defendant is accused of an offense of sexual assault, evidence of the defendant's commission of another offense or offenses of sexual assault is admissible, and may be considered for its bearing on any matter to which it is relevant.

(b)   In a case in which the Government intends to offer evidence under this rule, the attorney for the Government shall disclose the evidence to the defendant, including statements of witnesses or a summary of the substance of any testimony that is expected to be offered, at least fifteen days before the scheduled date of trial or at such later time as the court may allow for good cause.

(c)   This rule shall not be construed to limit the admission or consideration of evidence under any other rule.

(d)   For purposes of this rule and Rule 415, "offense of sexual assault" means a crime under Federal law or the law of a State (as defined in section 513 of title 18, United States Code) that involved—

(1)   any conduct proscribed by chapter 109A of title 18, United States Code;

(2)   contact, without consent, between any part of the defendant's body or an object and the genitals or anus of another person;

(3)   contact, without consent, between the genitals or anus of the defendant and any part of another person's body;

(4)   deriving sexual pleasure or gratification from the infliction of death, bodily injury, or physical pain on another person; or

(5)   an attempt or conspiracy to engage in conduct described in paragraphs (1)-(4).

Rule 414.   Evidence of Similar Crimes in Child Molestation Cases.

(a)   In a criminal case in which the defendant is accused of an offense of child molestation, evidence of the defendant's commission of another offense or offenses of child molestation is admissible, and may be considered for its bearing on any matter to which it is relevant.

(b)   In a case in which the Government intends to offer evidence under this rule, the attorney for the Government shall disclose the evidence to the defendant, including statements of witnesses or a summary of the substance of any testimony that is expected to be offered, at least fifteen days before the scheduled date of trial or at such later time as the court may allow for good cause.

(c)   This rule shall not be construed to limit the admission or consideration of evidence under any other rule.

(d)   For purposes of this rule and Rule 415, "child" means a person below the age of fourteen, and "offense of child molestation" means a crime under Federal law or the law of a State (as defined in section 513 of title 18, United States Code) that involved–

(1)   any conduct proscribed by chapter 109A of title 18, United States Code, that was committed in relation to a child;

(2)   any conduct proscribed by chapter 110 of title 18, United States Code;

(3)   contact between any part of the defendant's body or an object and the genitals or anus of a child;

(4)   contact between the genitals or anus of the defendant and any part of the body of a child;

(5)   deriving sexual pleasure or gratification from the infliction of death, bodily injury, or physical pain on a child; or

(6)   an attempt or conspiracy to engage in conduct prescribed in paragraphs (1)-(5).

Rule 415.   Evidence of Similar Acts in Civil Cases Concerning Sexual Assault or Child Molestation.

(a)   In a civil case in which a claim for damages or other relief is predicated on a party's alleged commission of conduct constituting an offense of sexual assault or child molestation, evidence of that party's commission of another offense or offenses of sexual assault or child molestation is admissible and may be considered as provided in Rule 413 and Rule 414 of these rules.

(b)   A party who intends to offer evidence under this Rule shall disclose the evidence to the party against whom it will be offered, including statements of witnesses or a summary of the substance of any testimony that is expected to be offered, at least fifteen days before the scheduled date of trial or at such later time as the court may allow for good cause.

(c)   This rule shall not be construed to limit the admission or consideration of evidence under any other rule.

Rule 501.   General Rule. Except as otherwise required by the Constitution of the United States or provided by Act of Congress or in rules prescribed by the Supreme Court pursuant to statutory authority, the privilege of a witness, person, government, State, or political subdivision thereof shall be governed by the principles of the common law as they may be interpreted by the courts of the United States in the light of reason and experience. However, in civil actions and proceedings, with respect to an element of a claim or defense as to which State law supplies the rule of decision, the privilege of a witness, person, government, State, or political subdivision thereof shall be determined in accordance with State law. (Pub.L. 93-595, § 1, Jan. 2, 1975, 88 Stat. 1933.)

Rule 601.   General Rule of Competency. Every person is competent to be a witness except as otherwise provided in these rules. However, in civil actions and proceedings, with respect to an element of a claim or defense as to which State law supplies the rule of decision, the competency of a witness shall be determined in accordance with State law.

Rule 602.   Lack of Personal Knowledge. A witness may not testify to a matter unless evidence is introduced sufficient to support a finding that the witness has personal knowledge of the matter. Evidence to prove personal knowledge may, but need not, consist of the witness' own testimony. This rule is subject to the provisions of rule 703, relating to opinion testimony by expert witnesses.

Rule 603.   Oath or Affirmation. Before testifying, every witness shall be required to declare that the witness will testify truthfully, by oath or affirmation administered in a form calculated to awaken the witness' conscience and impress the witness' mind with the duty to do so.

Rule 604.   Interpreters. An interpreter is subject to the provisions of these rules relating to qualification as an expert and the administration of an oath or affirmation to make a true translation.

Rule 605.   Competency of Judge as Witness. The judge presiding at the trial may not testify in that trial as a witness. No objection need be made in order to preserve the point.

Rule 606.   Competency of Juror as Witness.

(a)   At the trial. A member of the jury may not testify as a witness before that jury in the trial of the case in which the juror is sitting. If the juror is called so to testify, the opposing party shall be afforded an opportunity to object out of the presence of the jury.

(b)   Inquiry into validity of verdict or indictment. Upon an inquiry into the validity of a verdict or indictment, a juror may not testify as to any matter or statement occurring during the course of the jury's deliberations or to the effect of anything upon that or any other juror's mind or emotions as influencing the juror to assent to or dissent from the verdict or indictment or concerning the juror's mental processes in connection therewith, except that a juror may testify on the question whether extraneous prejudicial information was improperly brought to the jury's attention or whether any outside influence was improperly brought to bear upon any juror. Nor may a juror's affidavit or evidence of any statement by the juror concerning a matter about which the juror would be precluded from testifying be received for these purposes.

Rule 607.   Who May Impeach. The credibility of a witness may be attacked by any party, including the party calling the witness.

Rule 608.   Evidence of Character and Conduct of Witness.

(a)   Opinion and reputation evidence of character. The credibility of a witness may be attacked or supported by evidence in the form of opinion or reputation, but subject to these limitations: (1) the evidence may refer only to character for truthfulness or untruthfulness, and (2) evidence of truthful character is admissible only after the character of the witness for truthfulness has been attacked by opinion or reputation evidence or otherwise.

(b)   Specific instances of conduct. Specific instances of the conduct of a witness, for the purpose of attacking or supporting the witness' credibility, other than conviction of crime as provided in rule 609, may not be proved by extrinsic evidence. They may, however, in the discretion of the court, if probative of truthfulness or untruthfulness, be inquired into on cross-examination of the witness (1) concerning the witness' character for truthfulness or untruthfulness, or (2) concerning the character for truthfulness or untruthfulness of another witness as to which character the witness being cross-examined has testified.

The giving of testimony, whether by an accused or by any other witness, does not operate as a waiver of the accused's or the witness' privilege against self-incrimination when examined with respect to matters which relate only to credibility.

Rule 609.   Impeachment by Evidence of Conviction of Crime.

(a)   General rule. For the purpose of attacking the credibility of a witness,

(1)   evidence that a witness other than an accused has been convicted of a crime shall be admitted, subject to Rule 403, if the crime was punishable by death or imprisonment in excess of one year under the law under which the witness was convicted, and evidence that an accused has been convicted of such a crime shall be admitted if the court determines that the probative value of admitting this evidence outweighs its prejudicial effect to the accused; and

(2)   evidence that any witness has been convicted of a crime shall be admitted if it involved dishonesty or false statement, regardless of the punishment.

(b)   Time limit. Evidence of a conviction under this rule is not admissible if a period of more than ten years has elapsed since the date of the conviction or of the release of the witness from the confinement imposed for that conviction, whichever is the later date, unless the court determines, in the interests of justice, that the probative value of the conviction supported by specific facts and circumstances substantially outweighs its prejudicial effect. However, evidence of a conviction more than 10 years old as calculated herein, is not admissible unless the proponent gives to the adverse party sufficient advance written notice of intent to use such evidence to provide the adverse party with a fair opportunity to contest the use of such evidence.

(c)   Effect of pardon, annulment, or certificate of rehabilitation. Evidence of a conviction is not admissible under this rule if (1) the conviction has been the subject of a pardon, annulment, certificate of rehabilitation, or other equivalent procedure based on a finding of the rehabilitation of the person convicted, and that person has not been convicted of a subsequent crime which was punishable by death or imprisonment in excess of one year, or (2) the conviction has been the subject of a pardon, annulment, or other equivalent procedure based on a finding of innocence.

(d)   Juvenile adjudications. Evidence of juvenile adjudications is generally not admissible under this rule. The court may, however, in a criminal case allow evidence of a juvenile adjudication of a witness other than the accused if conviction of the offense would be admissible to attack the credibility of an adult and the court is satisfied that admission in evidence is necessary for a fair determination of the issue of guilt or innocence.

(e)   **Pendency of appeal.** The pendency of an appeal therefrom does not render evidence of a conviction inadmissible. Evidence of the pendency of an appeal is admissible.

Rule 610.   Religious Beliefs or Opinions. Evidence of the beliefs or opinions of a witness on matters of religion is not admissible for the purpose of showing that by reason of their nature the witness' credibility is impaired or enhanced.

Rule 611.   Mode and Order of Interrogation and Presentation.

(a)   **Control by court.** The court shall exercise reasonable control over the mode and order of interrogating witnesses and presenting evidence so as to (1) make the interrogation and presentation effective for the ascertainment of the truth, (2) avoid needless consumption of time, and (3) protect witnesses from harassment or undue embarrassment.

(b)   **Scope of cross-examination.** Cross-examination should be limited to the subject matter of the direct examination and matters affecting the credibility of the witness. The court may, in the exercise of discretion, permit inquiry into additional matters as if on direct examination.

(c)   **Leading questions.** Leading questions should not be used on the direct examination of a witness except as may be necessary to develop the witness' testimony. Ordinarily leading questions should be permitted on cross-examination. When a party calls a hostile witness, an adverse party, or a witness identified with an adverse party, interrogation may be by leading questions.

Rule 612.   Writing Used to Refresh Memory. Except as otherwise provided in criminal proceedings by section 3500 of title 18, United States Code, if a witness uses a writing to refresh memory for the purpose of testifying, either—

(1)   while testifying, or

(2)   before testifying, if the court in its discretion determines it is necessary in the interests of justice,

an adverse party is entitled to have the writing produced at the hearing, to inspect it, to cross-examine the witness thereon, and to introduce in evidence those portions which relate to the testimony of the witness. If it is claimed that the writing contains matters not related to the subject matter of the testimony the court shall examine the writing in camera, excise any portions not so related, and order delivery of the remainder to the party entitled thereto. Any portion withheld over objections shall be preserved and made available to the appellate court in the event of an appeal. If a writing is not produced or delivered pursuant to order under this rule, the court shall make any order justice requires, except that in criminal cases when the prosecution elects not to comply, the order shall be one striking the testimony or, if the court in its discretion determines that the interests of justice so require, declaring a mistrial.

Rule 613.   Prior Statements of Witnesses.

(a)   Examining witness concerning prior statement. In examining a witness concerning a prior statement made by the witness, whether written or not, the statement need not be shown nor its contents disclosed to the witness at that time, but on request the same shall be shown or disclosed to opposing counsel.

(b)   Extrinsic evidence of prior inconsistent statement of witness. Extrinsic evidence of a prior inconsistent statement by a witness is not admissible unless the witness is afforded an opportunity to explain or deny the same and the opposite party is afforded an opportunity to interrogate the witness thereon, or the interests of justice otherwise require. This provision does not apply to admissions of a party-opponent as defined in rule 801(d)(2).

Rule 614.   Calling and Interrogation of Witnesses by Court.

(a)   Calling by court. The court may, on its own motion or at the suggestion of a party, call witnesses, and all parties are entitled to cross-examine witnesses thus called.

(b)   Interrogation by court. The court may interrogate witnesses, whether called by itself or by a party.

(c)   Objections. Objections to the calling of witnesses by the court or to interrogation by it may be made at the time or at the next available opportunity when the jury is not present.

Rule 615.   Exclusion of Witnesses. At the request of a party the court shall order witnesses excluded so that they cannot hear the testimony of other witnesses, and it may make the order of its own motion. This rule does not authorize exclusion of (1) a party who is a natural person, or (2) an officer or employee of a party which is not a natural person designated as its representative by its attorney, or (3) a person whose presence is shown by a party to be essential to the presentation of the party's cause, or (4) a person authorized by statute to be present.

Rule 701.   Opinion Testimony by Lay Witnesses. If the witness is not testifying as an expert, the witness' testimony in the form of opinions or inferences is limited to those opinions or inferences which are (a) rationally based on the perception of the witness and (b) helpful to a clear understanding of the witness' testimony or the determination of a fact in issue.

Rule 702.   Testimony by Experts. If scientific, technical, or other specialized knowledge will assist the trier of fact to understand the evidence or to determine a fact in issue, a witness qualified as an expert by knowledge, skill, experience, training, or education, may testify thereto in the form of an opinion or otherwise.

Rule 703.   Bases of Opinion Testimony by Experts. The facts or data in the particular case upon which an expert bases an opinion or inference may be those perceived by or made known to the expert at or before the hearing. If of a type reasonably relied upon by experts in the particular field in forming opinions or inferences upon the subject, the facts or data need not be admissible in evidence.

Rule 704.   Opinion on Ultimate Issue.

(a)   Except as provided in subdivision (b), testimony in the form of an opinion or inference otherwise admissible is not objectionable because it embraces an ultimate issue to be decided by the trier of fact.

(b)   No expert witness testifying with respect to the mental state or condition of a defendant in a criminal case may state an opinion or inference as to whether the defendant did or did not have the mental state or condition constituting an element of the crime charged or of a defense thereto. Such ultimate issues are matters for the trier of fact alone.

Rule 705.   Disclosure of Facts or Data Underlying Expert Opinion. The expert may testify in terms of opinion or inference and give reasons therefor without first testifying to the underlying facts or data, unless the court requires otherwise. The expert may in any event be required to disclose the underlying facts or data on cross-examination.

Rule 706.   Court Appointed Experts.

(a)   Appointment. The court may on its own motion or on the motion of any party enter an order to show cause why expert witnesses should not be appointed, and may request the parties to submit nominations. The court may appoint any expert witnesses agreed upon by the parties, and may appoint expert witnesses of its own selection. An expert witness shall not be appointed by the court unless the witness consents to act. A witness so appointed shall be informed of the witness' duties by the court in writing, a copy of which shall be filed with the clerk, or at a conference in which the parties shall have opportunity to participate. A witness so appointed shall advise the parties of the witness' findings, if any; the witness' deposition may be taken by any party; and the witness may be called to testify by the court or any party. The witness shall be subject to cross-examination by each party, including a party calling the witness.

(b) **Compensation.** Expert witnesses so appointed are entitled to reasonable compensation in whatever sum the court may allow. The compensation thus fixed is payable from funds which may be provided by law in criminal cases and civil actions and proceedings involving just compensation under the fifth amendment. In other civil actions and proceedings the compensation shall be paid by the parties in such proportion and at such time as the court directs, and thereafter charged in like manner as other costs.

(c) **Disclosure of appointment.** In the exercise of its discretion, the court may authorize disclosure to the jury of the fact that the court appointed the expert witness.

(d) **Parties' experts of own selection.** Nothing in this rule limits the parties in calling expert witnesses of their own selection.

Rule 801. **Definitions.** The following definitions apply under this article:

(a) **Statement.** A "statement" is (1) an oral or written assertion or (2) nonverbal conduct of a person, if it is intended by the person as an assertion.

(b) **Declarant.** A "declarant" is a person who makes a statement.

(c) **Hearsay.** "Hearsay" is a statement, other than one made by the declarant while testifying at the trial or hearing, offered in evidence to prove the truth of the matter asserted.

(d) **Statements which are not hearsay.** A statement is not hearsay if—

(1) **Prior statement by witness.** The declarant testifies at the trial or hearing and is subject to cross-examination concerning the statement, and the statement is (A) inconsistent with the declarant's testimony, and was given under oath subject to the penalty of perjury at a trial, hearing, or other proceeding, or in a deposition, or (B) consistent with the declarant's testimony and is offered to rebut an express or implied charge against the declarant of recent fabrication or improper influence or motive, or (C) one of identification of a person made after perceiving the person; or

(2) **Admission by party-opponent.** The statement is offered against a party and is (A) the party's own statement, in either an individual or a representative capacity or (B) a statement of which the party has manifested an adoption or belief in its truth, or (C) a statement by a person authorized by the party to make a statement concerning the subject, or (D) a statement by the party's agent or servant concerning a matter within the scope of the agency or employment, made during the existence of the relationship, or (E) a statement by a coconspirator of a party during the course and in furtherance of the conspiracy. The contents of the statement shall be considered but are not alone sufficient to establish the declarant's authority under subdivision (C), the agency or employment relationship and scope thereof under subdivision (D), or the existence of the conspiracy and the participation therein of the declarant and the party against whom the statement is offered under subdivision (E).

Rule 802.   Hearsay Rule. Hearsay is not admissible except as provided by these rules or by other rules prescribed by the Supreme Court pursuant to statutory authority or by Act of Congress.

Rule 803.   Hearsay Exceptions; Availability of Declarant Immaterial. The following are not excluded by the hearsay rule, even though the declarant is available as a witness:

(1)   **Present sense impression.** A statement describing or explaining an event or condition made while the declarant was perceiving the event or condition, or immediately thereafter.

(2)   **Excited utterance.** A statement relating to a startling event or condition made while the declarant was under the stress of excitement caused by the event or condition.

(3)   **Then existing mental, emotional, or physical condition.** A statement of the declarant's then existing state of mind, emotion, sensation, or physical condition (such as intent, plan, motive, design, mental feeling, pain, and bodily health), but not including a statement of memory or belief to prove the fact remembered or believed unless it relates to the execution, revocation, identification, or terms of declarant's will.

(4)   **Statements for purposes of medical diagnosis or treatment.** Statements made for purposes of medical diagnosis or treatment and describing medical history, or past or present symptoms, pain, or sensations, or the inception or general character of the cause or external source thereof insofar as reasonably pertinent to diagnosis or treatment.

(5)   **Recorded recollection.** A memorandum or record concerning a matter about which a witness once had knowledge but now has insufficient recollection to enable the witness to testify fully and accurately, shown to have been made or adopted by the witness when the matter was fresh in the witness' memory and to reflect that knowledge correctly. If admitted, the memorandum or record may be read into evidence but may not itself be received as an exhibit unless offered by an adverse party.

(6)   **Records of regularly conducted activity.** A memorandum, report, record, or data compilation, in any form, of acts, events, conditions, opinions,

or diagnoses, made at or near the time by, or from information transmitted by, a person with knowledge, if kept in the course of a regularly conducted business activity, and if it was the regular practice of that business activity to make the memorandum, report, record, or data compilation, all as shown by the testimony of the custodian or other qualified witness, unless the source of information or the method or circumstances of preparation indicate lack of trustworthiness. The term "business" as used in this paragraph includes business, institution, association, profession, occupation, and calling of every kind, whether or not conducted for profit.

(7) **Absence of entry in records kept in accordance with the provisions of paragraph (6)**. Evidence that a matter is not included in the memoranda reports, records, or data compilations, in any form, kept in accordance with the provisions of paragraph (6), to prove the nonoccurrence or nonexistence of the matter, if the matter was of a kind of which a memorandum, report, record, or data compilation was regularly made and preserved, unless the sources of information or other circumstances indicate lack of trustworthiness.

(8) **Public records and reports**. Records, reports, statements, or data compilations, in any form, of public offices or agencies, setting forth (A) the activities of the office or agency, or (B) matters observed pursuant to duty imposed by law as to which matters there was a duty to report, excluding, however, in criminal cases matters observed by police officers and other law enforcement personnel, or (C) in civil actions and proceedings and against the Government in criminal cases, factual findings resulting from an investigation made pursuant to authority granted by law, unless the sources of information or other circumstances indicate lack of trustworthiness.

(9) **Records of vital statistics**. Records or data compilations, in any form, of births, fetal deaths, deaths, or marriages, if the report thereof was made to a public office pursuant to requirements of law.

(10) **Absence of public record or entry**. To prove the absence of a record, report, statement, or data compilation, in any form, or the nonoccurrence or nonexistence of a matter of which a record, report, statement, or data compilation, in any form, was regularly made and preserved by a public office or agency, evidence in the form of a certification in accordance with rule 902, or testimony, that diligent search failed to disclose the record, report, statement, or data compilation, or entry.

(11) **Records of religious organizations**. Statements of births, marriages, divorces, deaths, legitimacy, ancestry, relationship by blood or marriage, or other similar facts of personal or family history, contained in a regularly kept record of a religious organization.

(12)   **Marriage, baptismal, and similar certificates**. Statements of fact contained in a certificate that the maker performed a marriage or other ceremony or administered a sacrament, made by a clergyman, public official, or other person authorized by the rules or practices of a religious organization or by law to perform the act certified, and purporting to have been issued at the time of the act or within a reasonable time thereafter.

(13)   **Family records**. Statements of fact concerning personal or family history contained in family Bibles, genealogies, charts, engravings on rings, inscriptions on family portraits, engravings on urns, crypts, or tombstones, or the like.

(14)   **Records of documents affecting an interest in property**. The record of a document purporting to establish or affect an interest in property, as proof of the content of the original recorded document and its execution and delivery by each person by whom it purports to have been executed, if the record is a record of a public office and an applicable statute authorizes the recording of documents of that kind in that office.

(15)   **Statements in documents affecting an interest in property**. A statement contained in a document purporting to establish or affect an interest in property if the matter stated was relevant to the purpose of the document, unless dealings with the property since the document was made have been inconsistent with the truth of the statement or the purport of the document.

(16)   **Statements in ancient documents**. Statements in a document in existence twenty years or more the authenticity of which is established.

(17)   **Market reports, commercial publications**. Market quotations, tabulations, lists, directories, or other published compilations, generally used and relied upon by the public or by persons in particular occupations.

(18)   **Learned treatises**. To the extent called to the attention of an expert witness upon cross-examination or relied upon by the expert witness in direct examination, statements contained in published treatises, periodicals, or pamphlets on a subject of history, medicine, or other science or art, established as a reliable authority by the testimony or admission of the witness or by other expert testimony or by judicial notice. If admitted, the statements may be read into evidence but may not be received as exhibits.

(19)   **Reputation concerning personal or family history**. Reputation among members of a person's family by blood, adoption, or marriage, or among a person's associates, or in the community, concerning a person's birth, adoption, marriage, divorce, death, legitimacy, relationship by blood, adoption, or marriage,

ancestry, or other similar fact of personal or family history.

(20) **Reputation concerning boundaries or general history**. Reputation in a community, arising before the controversy, as to boundaries of or customs affecting lands in the community, and reputation as to events of general history important to the community or State or nation in which located.

(21) **Reputation as to character**. Reputation of a person's character among associates or in the community.

(22) **Judgment of previous conviction**. Evidence of a final judgment, entered after a trial or upon a plea of guilty (but not upon a plea of nolo contendere), adjudging a person guilty of a crime punishable by death or imprisonment in excess of one year, to prove any fact essential to sustain the judgment, but not including, when offered by the Government in a criminal prosecution for purposes other than impeachment, judgments against persons other than the accused. The pendency of an appeal may be shown but does not affect admissibility.

(23) **Judgment as to personal, family or general history, or boundaries**. Judgments as proof of matters of personal, family or general history, or boundaries, essential to the judgment, if the same would be provable by evidence of reputation.

(24)   [Transferred to Rule 807]

Rule 804.   Hearsay Exceptions; Declarant Unavailable.

(a)   **Definition of unavailability.** "Unavailability as a witness" includes situations in which the declarant—

(1)   is exempted by ruling of the court on the ground of privilege from testifying concerning the subject matter of the declarant's statement; or

(2)   persists in refusing to testify concerning the subject matter of the declarant's statement despite an order of the court to do so; or

(3)   testifies to a lack of memory of the subject matter of the declarant's statement; or

(4)   is unable to be present or to testify at the hearing because of death or then existing physical or mental illness or infirmity; or

(5)   is absent from the hearing and the proponent of a statement has

been unable to procure the declarant's attendance (or in the case of a hearsay exception under subdivision (b)(2), (3), or (4), the declarant's attendance or testimony) by process or other reasonable means.

A declarant is not unavailable as a witness if exemption, refusal, claim of lack of memory, inability, or absence is due to the procurement or wrongdoing of the proponent of a statement for the purpose of preventing the witness from attending or testifying.

(b)   **Hearsay exceptions.** The following are not excluded by the hearsay rule if the declarant is unavailable as a witness:

(1)   **Former testimony.** Testimony given as a witness at another hearing of the same or a different proceeding, or in a deposition taken in compliance with law in the course of the same or another proceeding, if the party against whom the testimony is now offered, or, in a civil action or proceeding, a predecessor in interest, had an opportunity and similar motive to develop the testimony by direct, cross, or redirect examination.

(2)   **Statement under belief of impending death.** In a prosecution for homicide or in a civil action or proceeding, a statement made by a declarant while believing that the declarant's death was imminent, concerning the cause or circumstances of what the declarant believed to be impending death.

(3)   **Statement against interest.** A statement which was at the time of its making so far contrary to the declarant's pecuniary or proprietary interest, or so far tended to subject the declarant to civil or criminal liability, or to render invalid a claim by the declarant against another, that a reasonable person in the declarant's position would not have made the statement unless believing it to be true. A statement tending to expose the declarant to criminal liability and offered to exculpate the accused is not admissible unless corroborating circumstances clearly indicate the trustworthiness of the statement.

(4)   **Statement of personal or family history.** (A) A statement concerning the declarant's own birth, adoption, marriage, divorce, legitimacy, relationship by blood, adoption, or marriage, ancestry, or other similar fact of personal or family history, even though declarant had no means of acquiring personal knowledge of the matter stated; or (B) a statement concerning the foregoing matters, and death also, of another person, if the declarant was related to the other by blood, adoption, or marriage or was so intimately associated with the other's family as to be likely to have accurate information concerning the matter declared.

(5)   [Transferred to Rule 507]

(6)   Forfeiture by wrongdoing. A statement offered against a party that has engaged or acquiesced in wrongdoing that was intended to, and did, procure the unavailability of the declarant as a witness.

Rule 805.   Hearsay Within Hearsay. Hearsay included within hearsay is not excluded under the hearsay rule if each part of the combined statements conforms with an exception to the hearsay rule provided in these rules.

Rule 806.   Attacking and Supporting Credibility of Declarant. When a hearsay statement, or a statement defined in Rule 801(d)(2)(C), (D), or (E), has been admitted in evidence, the credibility of the declarant may be attacked, and if attacked may be supported, by any evidence which would be admissible for those purposes if declarant had testified as a witness. Evidence of a statement or conduct by the declarant at any time, inconsistent with the declarant's hearsay statement, is not subject to any requirement that the declarant may have been afforded an opportunity to deny or explain. If the party against whom a hearsay statement has been admitted calls the declarant as a witness, the party is entitled to examine the declarant on the statement as if under cross-examination.

Rule 807.   Residual Exception. A statement not specifically covered by Rule 803 or 804 but having equivalent circumstantial guarantees of trustworthiness, is not excluded by the hearsay rule, if the court determines that (A) the statement is offered as evidence of a material fact; (B) the statement is more probative on the point for which it is offered than any other evidence which the proponent can procure through reasonable efforts; and (C) the general purposes of these rules and the interests of justice will best be served by admission of the statement into evidence. However, a statement may not be admitted under this exception unless the proponent of it makes known to the adverse party sufficiently in advance of the trial or hearing to provide the adverse party with a fair opportunity to prepare to meet it, the proponent's intention to offer the statement and the particulars of it, including the name and address of the declarant.

Rule 901.   Requirement of Authentication or Identification.

(a)   General provision. The requirement of authentication or identification as a condition precedent to admissibility is satisfied by evidence sufficient to support a finding that the matter in question is what its proponent claims.

(b)   Illustrations. By way of illustration only, and not by way of limitation, the following are examples of authentication or identification conforming with the requirements of this rule:

(1)   Testimony of witness with knowledge. Testimony that a matter is what it is claimed to be.

(2)   Nonexpert opinion on handwriting. Nonexpert opinion as to the genuineness of handwriting, based upon familiarity not acquired for purposes of the litigation.

(3)   Comparison by trier or expert witness. Comparison by the trier of fact or by expert witnesses with specimens which have been authenticated.

(4)   Distinctive characteristics and the like. Appearance, contents, substance, internal patterns, or other distinctive characteristics, taken in conjunction with circumstances.

(5)   Voice identification. Identification of a voice, whether heard firsthand or through mechanical or electronic transmission or recording, by opinion based upon hearing the voice at any time under circumstances connecting it with the alleged speaker.

(6)   Telephone conversations. Telephone conversations, by evidence that a call was made to the number assigned at the time by the telephone company to a particular person or business, if (A) in the case of a person, circumstances, including self-identification, show the person answering to be the one called, or (B) in the case of a business, the call was made to a place of business and the conversation related to business reasonably transacted over the telephone.

(7)   Public records or reports. Evidence that a writing authorized by law to be recorded or filed and in fact recorded or filed in a public office, or a purported public record, report, statement, or data compilation, in any form, is from the public office where items of this nature are kept.

(8)   Ancient documents or data compilation. Evidence that a document or data compilation, in any form, (A) is in such condition as to create no suspicion concerning its authenticity, (B) was in a place where it, if authentic, would likely be, and (C) has been in existence 20 years or more at the time it is offered.

(9)   Process or system. Evidence describing a process or system used to produce a result and showing that the process or system produces an accurate result.

(10)   Methods provided by statute or rule. Any method of authentication or identification provided by Act of Congress or by other rules prescribed by the Supreme Court pursuant to statutory authority.

Rule 902.   **Self-authentication.** Extrinsic evidence of authenticity as a condition precedent to admissibility is not required with respect to the following:

(1)   **Domestic public documents under seal.** A document bearing a seal purporting to be that of the United States, or of any State, district, Commonwealth, territory, or insular possession thereof, or the Panama Canal Zone, or the Trust Territory of the Pacific Islands, or of a political subdivision, department, officer, or agency thereof, and a signature purporting to be an attestation or execution.

(2)   **Domestic public documents not under seal.** A document purporting to bear the signature in the official capacity of an officer or employee of any entity included in paragraph (1) hereof, having no seal, if a public officer having a seal and having official duties in the district or political subdivision of the officer or employee certifies under seal that the signer has the official capacity and that the signature is genuine.

(3)   **Foreign public documents.** A document purporting to be executed or attested in an official capacity by a person authorized by the laws of a foreign country to make the execution or attestation, and accompanied by a final certification as to the genuineness of the signature and official position (A) of the executing or attesting person, or (B) of any foreign official whose certificate of genuineness of signature and official position relates to the execution or attestation or is in a chain of certificates of genuineness of signature and official position relating to the execution or attestation. A final certification may be made by a secretary of an embassy or legation, consul general, consul, vice consul, or consular agent of the United States, or a diplomatic or consular official of the foreign country assigned or accredited to the United States. If reasonable opportunity has been given to all parties to investigate the authenticity and accuracy of official documents, the court may, for good cause shown, order that they be treated as presumptively authentic without final certification or permit them to be evidenced by an attested summary with or without final certification.

(4)   **Certified copies of public records.** A copy of an official record or report or entry therein, or of a document authorized by law to be recorded or filed and actually recorded or filed in a public office, including data compilations in any form, certified as correct by the custodian or other person authorized to make the certification, by certificate complying with paragraph (1), (2), or (3) of this rule or complying with any Act of Congress or rule prescribed by the Supreme Court pursuant to statutory authority.

(5)   **Official publications.** Books, pamphlets, or other publications purporting to be issued by public authority.

(6)   **Newspapers and periodicals.** Printed materials purporting to be newspapers or periodicals.

(7)   **Trade inscriptions and the like.** Inscriptions, signs, tags, or labels purporting to have been affixed in the course of business and indicating ownership, control, or origin.

(8)   **Acknowledged documents.** Documents accompanied by a certificate of acknowledgment executed in the manner provided by law by a notary public or other officer authorized by law to take acknowledgments.

(9)   **Commercial paper and related documents.** Commercial paper, signatures thereon, and documents relating thereto to the extent provided by general commercial law.

(10)   **Presumptions under Acts of Congress.** Any signature, document, or other matter declared by Act of Congress to be presumptively or prima facie genuine or authentic.

Rule 903.   **Subscribing Witness' Testimony Unnecessary.** The testimony of a subscribing witness is not necessary to authenticate a writing unless required by the laws of the jurisdiction whose laws govern the validity of the writing.

Rule 1001.   **Definitions.** For purposes of this article the following definitions are applicable:

(1)   **Writings and recordings.** "Writings" and "recordings" consist of letters, words, or numbers, or their equivalent, set down by handwriting, typewriting, printing, photostating, photographing, magnetic impulse, mechanical or electronic recording, or other form of data compilation.

(2)   **Photographs.** "Photographs" include still photographs, X-ray films, video tapes, and motion pictures.

(3)   **Original.** An "original" of a writing or recording is the writing or recording itself or any counterpart intended to have the same effect by a person executing or issuing it. An "original" of a photograph includes the negative or any print therefrom. If data are stored in a computer or similar device, any printout or other output readable by sight, shown to reflect the data accurately, is an "original".

(4)   **Duplicate.** A "duplicate" is a counterpart produced by the same impression as the original, or from the same matrix, or by means of photography, including enlargements and miniatures, or by mechanical or electronic

re-recording, or by chemical reproduction, or by other equivalent techniques which accurately reproduces the original.

Rule 1002. **Requirement of Original.** To prove the content of a writing, recording, or photograph, the original writing, recording, or photograph is required, except as otherwise provided in these rules or by Act of Congress.

Rule 1003. **Admissibility of Duplicates.** A duplicate is admissible to the same extent as an original unless (1) a genuine question is raised as to the authenticity of the original or (2) in the circumstances it would be unfair to admit the duplicate in lieu of the original.

Rule 1004. **Admissibility of Other Evidence of Contents.** The original is not required, and other evidence of the contents of a writing, recording, or photograph is admissible if—

    (1) **Originals lost or destroyed.** All originals are lost or have been destroyed, unless the proponent lost or destroyed them in bad faith; or

    (2) **Original not obtainable.** No original can be obtained by any available judicial process or procedure; or

    (3) **Original in possession of opponent.** At a time when an original was under the control of the party against whom offered, that party was put on notice, by the pleadings or otherwise, that the contents would be a subject of proof at the hearing, and that party does not produce the original at the hearing; or

    (4) **Collateral matters.** The writing, recording, or photograph is not closely related to a controlling issue.

Rule 1005. **Public Records.** The contents of an official record, or of a document authorized to be recorded or filed and actually recorded or filed, including data compilations in any form, if otherwise admissible, may be proved by copy, certified as correct in accordance with rule 902 or testified to be correct by a witness who has compared it with the original. If a copy which complies with the foregoing cannot be obtained by the exercise of reasonable diligence, then other evidence of the contents may be given.

Rule 1006. **Summaries.** The contents of voluminous writings, recordings, or photographs which cannot conveniently be examined in court may be presented in the form of a chart, summary, or calculation. The originals, or duplicates, shall be made available for examination or copying, or both, by other parties at reasonable time and place. The court may order that they be produced in court.

Rule 1007.   Testimony or Written Admission of Party. Contents of writings, recordings, or photographs may be proved by the testimony or deposition of the party against whom offered or by that party's written admission, without accounting for the nonproduction of the original.

Rule 1008.   Functions of Court and Jury. When the admissibility of other evidence of contents of writings, recordings, or photographs under these rules depends upon the fulfillment of a condition of fact, the question whether the condition has been fulfilled is ordinarily for the court to determine in accordance with the provisions of rule 104. However, when an issue is raised (a) whether the asserted writing ever existed, or (b) whether another writing, recording, or photograph produced at the trial is the original, or (c) whether other evidence of contents correctly reflects the contents, the issue is for the trier of fact to determine as in the case of other issues of fact.

Rule 1101.   Applicability of Rules.

(a)   Courts and judges. These rules apply to the United States district courts, the District Court of Guam, the District Court of the Virgin Islands, the District Court for the Northern Mariana Islands, the United States courts of appeals, the United States Claims Court, and to the United States bankruptcy judges and United States magistrate judges, in the actions, cases, and proceedings and to the extent hereinafter set forth. The terms "judge" and "court" in these rules include United States bankruptcy judges and United States magistrate judges.

(b)   Proceedings generally. These rules apply generally to civil actions and proceedings, including admiralty and maritime cases, to criminal cases and proceedings, to contempt proceedings except those in which the court may act summarily, and to proceedings and cases under title 11, United States Code [11 USCS §§ 1 et seq.].

(c)   Rule of privilege. The rule with respect to privileges applies at all stages of all actions, cases, and proceedings.

(d)   Rules inapplicable. The rules (other than with respect to privileges) do not apply in the following situations:

(1)   Preliminary questions of fact. The determination of questions of fact preliminary to admissibility of evidence when the issue is to be determined by the court under rule 104.

(2)   Grand jury. Proceedings before grand juries.

(3)   Miscellaneous proceedings. Proceedings for extradition or rendition; preliminary examinations in criminal cases; sentencing, or granting or revoking probation; issuance of warrants for arrest, criminal summonses, and search warrants; and proceedings with respect to release on bail or otherwise.

(e) **Rules applicable in part.** In the following proceedings these rules apply to the extent that matters of evidence are not provided for in the statutes which govern procedure therein or in other rules prescribed by the Supreme Court pursuant to statutory authority: the trial of misdemeanors and other petty offenses before United States magistrate judge; review of agency actions when the facts are subject to trail de novo under section 107(2)(F) of title 5, United States Code; review of orders of the Secretary of Agriculture under section 2 of the Act entitled "An Act to authorize association of producers of agricultural products" approved February 18, 1922 (7 U.S.C. 292), and under section 6 and 7(c) of the Perishable Agricultural Commodities Act, 1930 (7 U.S.C. 499f, 499g(c))); naturalization and revocation of naturalization under sections 310—318 of the Immigration and Nationality Act (8 U.S.C. 1421—1429); prize proceedings in admiralty under sections 7651—7681 of title 10, United States Code; review of orders of the Secretary of the Interior under section 2 of the Act entitled "An Act authorizing associations of producers of aquatic products" approved June 25, 1934 (15 U.S.C. 533); review of orders of petroleum control boards under section 5 of the Act entitled "An act to regulate interstate and foreign commerce in petroleum and its products by prohibiting the shipment in such commerce of petroleum and its products produced in violation of State law, and for other purposes", approved February 22, 1935 (15 U.S.C. 715d); actions for fines, penalties, or forfeitures under part V of title IV of the Tariff Act of 1930 (19 U.S.C. 1581—1624), or under the Anti-Smuggling Act (19 U.S.C. 1701—1711); criminal libel for condemnation, exclusion of imports, or other proceedings under the Federal Food, Drug, and Cosmetic Act (21 U.S.C. 301—392); disputes between seamen under sections 4079, 4080, and 4081 of the Revised Statutes (22 U.S.C. 256—258); habeas corpus under sections 2241—2254 of title 28, United States Code; motions to vacate, set aside or correct sentence under section 2255 of title 28, United States Code; actions for penalties for refusal to transport destitute seamen under section 4578 of the Revised Statutes (46 U.S.C. 679); actions against the United States under the Act entitled "An Act authorizing suits against the United States in admiralty for damage caused by and salvage service rendered to public vessels belonging to the United States, and for other purposes", approved March 3, 1925 (46 U.S.C. 781—790), as implemented by section 7730 of title 10, United States Code.

Rule 1102. **Amendments.** Amendments to the Federal Rules of Evidence may be made as provided in section 2072 of title 28 of the United States Code.

Rule 1103. **Title.** These rules may be known and cited as the Federal Rules of Evidence.

PTM

Appendix B

Sample Civil Trial Rules

SAMPLE CIVIL TRIAL RULES

Note: These rules are based on the Minnesota Civil Trialbook.

Section 1.   Scope; Policy

This trialbook is a declaration of practical policies and procedures to be followed in civil trials. It has been written to standardize practices and procedures throughout the state with the hope, and expectation, that trial time and expense will be reduced and that justice to the litigants and public acceptance of trial procedures will be increased.

It is recommended that the policies and procedures be generally and uniformly used. However, it is recognized that situations will arise where their use would violate the purpose for which they were drafted. In such circumstances, the policies and procedures should be disregarded so that justice, not form, may prevail.

Section 5.   Pretrial Conferences

(a)   Settlement Procedures. Settlement conferences are encouraged and recommended for case disposition. However, because of the diversity of approaches to be used, specific procedures are not set forth.

Lawyers will be notified by the court of the procedures to be followed in any action where settlement conferences are to be held.

(b)   Procedures to be Followed. In those courts where a formal pretrial conference is held prior to assignment for trial, a trial date shall be set and the conference shall cover those matters set forth in paragraphs (d) and (e) of this section.

(c)   Settlement Discussions with Court. The court may request counsel to explore settlement between themselves further and may engage in settlement discussions.

(d)   Pretrial Chambers Conferences. At an informal chambers conference before trial the trial court shall:

    (1)   determine whether settlement possibilities have been exhausted;

    (2)   determine whether all pleadings have been filed;

    (3)   ascertain the relevance to each party of each cause of action; and

    (4)   with a view to ascertaining and reducing the issues to be tried, shall inquire:

(i)   whether the issues in the case may be narrowed or modified by stipulations or motions;

(ii)   whether dismissal of any of the causes of actions or parties will be requested;

(iii)   whether stipulations may be reached as to those facts about which there is no substantial controversy;

(iv)   whether stipulations may be reached for waiver of foundation and other objections regarding exhibits, tests, or experiments;

(v)   whether there are any requests for producing evidence out of order;

(vi)   whether motions *in limine* to exclude or admit specified evidence or bar reference thereto will be requested; and

(vii)   whether there are any unusual or critical legal or evidentiary issues anticipated;

(5)   direct the parties to disclose the number and names of witnesses they anticipate calling, and to make good faith estimates as to the length of testimony and arguments;

(6)   inquire whether the number of experts or other witnesses may be reduced;

(7)   ascertain whether there may be time problems in presentation of the case, e.g., because of other commitments of counsel, witnesses, or the court and advise counsel of the hours and days for trial; and

(8)   ascertain whether counsel have graphic devices they want to use during opening statements; and

(9)   ascertain whether a jury, if previously demanded, will be waived. If a jury is requested, the judge shall make inquiries with a view to determining:

(i)   the areas of proposed voir dire interrogation to be directed to prospective jurors, and whether there is any contention that the case is one of "unusual circumstances";

(ii)   the substance of a brief statement to be made by the trial court to the prospective jurors outlining the case, the contentions of the parties, and the anticipated issues to be tried;

(iii)   the number of alternate jurors (it is suggested that the identity of the alternates not be disclosed to the jury); and

(iv)   in multiple party cases, whether there are issues as to the number of "sides" and allocation of peremptory challenges.

(e)   **Formal Conference.** After conclusion of the informal chambers conference and any review of the court file and preliminary research the court finds advisable, a formal record shall be made of:

(1)   arguments and rulings upon motions, bifurcation, and order of proof;

(2)   statement of stipulations, including whether graphic devices can be used during opening statement; and

(3)   in a jury trial, specification of:

(i)   the brief statement the trial court proposes to make to prospective jurors outlining the case, contentions of the parties, and anticipated issues to be tried;

(ii)   the areas of proposed voir dire interrogation to be directed to the prospective jurors;

(iii)   whether any of the defendants have adverse interests to warrant individual peremptory challenges and number of them;

(iv)   the number of alternate jurors, if any, and the method by which the alternates shall be determined;

(v)   the need for any preliminary jury instructions.

Section 6.   Voir Dire of Jurors

(a)   **Swearing Jurors to Answer.** The entire panel shall be sworn by the clerk to truthfully answer the voir dire questions put to them. The clerk shall then draw the names of the necessary persons who shall take their appropriate seats in the jury box.

(b)   **Statement of the Case to and Examination of Prospective Jurors.** The court shall make a brief statement to the prospective jurors introducing the counsel and parties and outlining the case, contentions of the parties, and anticipated issues to be tried and may then permit the parties or their lawyers to conduct voir dire or may itself do so.

In the latter event, the court shall permit the parties or their lawyers to supplement the voir dire by such further nonrepetitive inquiry as it deems proper.

(c)   **Challenges for Cause.** A challenge for cause may be made at any time during voir dire by any party or at the close of voir dire by all parties.

(d)   **Peremptory Challenges.** Each adverse party shall be entitled to two peremptory challenges, which shall be made alternately beginning with the defendant. The parties to the action shall be deemed two, plaintiffs being one party, defendants the other. If the court finds that two or more defendants have adverse interests, the court shall allow each adverse defendant additional peremptory challenges. When there are multiple adverse parties, the court shall determine the order of exercising peremptory challenges.

(e)   **Voir dire of Replacements.** When a prospective juror is excused, the replacement shall be asked by the court:

(1)   whether he or she heard and understood the brief statement of the case previously made by the judge;

(2)   whether he or she heard and understood the questions;

(3)   whether, other than to personal matters such as prior jury service, area of residence, employment, and family, the replacement's answers would be different from the previous answers in any substantial respect.

If the replacement answers in the affirmative to (3) above, the court shall inquire further as to those differing answers and counsel may make such supplemental examination as the court deems proper.

(f)   **Alternates.** In any trial the court may allow alternate jurors to be seated. The alternate or alternates shall be the last juror or jurors seated. Any alternates shall be excused before the jury retires to deliberate and shall not participate in deliberations unless all parties agree on the record or in writing to have alternates participate in deliberations.

Section 7.   Preliminary Instructions

After the jury is sworn, but before opening statements, the judge shall instruct the jurors generally as follows:

(1)   to refrain from communicating in writing or by other means about the case, to use the jury room rather than remaining in the courtroom or hallway,

and to avoid approaching, or conversations with counsel, litigants, or witnesses, and that they must not discuss the case, or any aspect of it among themselves or with other persons;

(2)   that if a juror has a question or communication for the court (e.g., as regards time scheduling), it should be taken up with, or transmitted through, the appropriate court personnel who is in charge of the jurors as to their physical facilities and supplies;

(3)   that the jurors will be supplied with note pads and pencils, on request, and that they may only take notes on the subject of the case for their personal use, though they may bring such notes with them into the jury room once they commence deliberations in the case. The jury should receive a cautionary instruction that they are to rely primarily on their collective recollection of what they saw and heard in the courtroom and that extensive note taking may distract them from properly fulfilling this function;

(4)   as to law which the judge determines to be appropriate; and

(5)   that, as with other statements of counsel, the opening statement is not evidence but only an outline of what counsel expect to prove.

Upon submission of the case to the jury, the judge shall instruct the jury that they shall converse among themselves about the case only in the jury room and only after the entire jury has assembled.

Section 8.   Opening Statement and Final Arguments

(a)   Scope of Opening. Counsel on each side, in opening the case to the jury, shall only state the facts proposed to be proven. During opening statement counsel may use a blackboard or paper for illustration only. There shall be no display to the jury of, nor reference to, any chart, graph, map, picture, model or any other graphic device unless, outside the presence of the jurors:

(1)   it has been admitted into evidence; or

(2)   such display or reference has been stipulated to; or

(3)   leave of court for such reference or display has been obtained.

(b)   Final Arguments. Final arguments to the jury shall not misstate the evidence. During final argument counsel may use a blackboard or paper for illustration only. A graphic device, such as a chart, summary or model, which is to be used for illustration only in argument shall be prepared and shown to opposing counsel before commencement of the argument. Upon request by opposing counsel, it shall remain available for reference and be marked for identification.

(c)   **Objections.** Objections to remarks by counsel either in the opening statement to the jury or in the closing argument shall be made while such statement or argument is in progress or at the close of the statement or argument. Any objection shall be argued outside the juror's hearing. If the court is uncertain whether there has been a misstatement of the evidence in final argument, the jurors shall be instructed to rely on their own recollections.

Section 9.   Availability of Witnesses

(a)   **Exchange of Information as to Future Scheduling.** In order to facilitate efficient scheduling of future witnesses and court time, all parties shall communicate with one another and exchange good faith estimates as to the length of witness examinations together with any other information pertinent to trial scheduling.

(b)   **"On-Call" Witnesses.** It is the responsibility of an "on-call" witness proponent to have the witness present in court when needed.

(c)   **Completion of Witness' Testimony.** Except with the court's approval, a witness's testimony shall be pursued to its conclusion and not interrupted by the taking of other evidence.

Upon the conclusion of a witness's testimony the court should inquire of all counsel whether the witness may be excused from further attendance and if affirmative responses are given, the court may then excuse the witness.

(d)   **Excluding Witnesses.** Exclusion of witnesses shall be in accordance with Minn.R.Evid. 615.

(e)   **Issuance of Warrants.** A warrant for arrest or body attachment for failure of a witness to attend shall not be released for service unless it is shown by the applicant party, in a hearing outside the presence of jurors, that (1) service of the process compelling attendance was made at a time providing the witness with reasonable notice and opportunity to respond, and (2) no reasonable excuse exists for the failure to attend or, if the reason for the failure to attend is unknown to the applicant party, due diligence was used in attempting to communicate with such witness to ascertain the reason for the failure to attend.

Section 10.   Examination of Witnesses

(a)   **Objections.** Lawyers shall state objections succinctly, stating only the specific legal grounds for the objection without argument. Argument, if allowed by the court, and any offer of proof shall be made outside of the hearing of the jury and on the record.

(b)   Caution to Witnesses. Before taking the stand and outside of the hearing of the jury, a witness called by counsel shall be cautioned by such counsel to be responsive to the questions and to wait in answering until a question is completed and a ruling made on any objection. Lawyers should advise their clients and witnesses of the formalities of court appearances.

Counsel may request the court to caution a witness while on the stand as to the manner of answering questions.

(c)   Questions Not to be Interrupted. A question shall not be interrupted by objection unless then patently objectionable.

(d)   Effect of Asking Another Question. An examiner shall not repeat the witness' answer to the prior question before asking another question.

An examiner shall wait until the witness has completed answering before asking another question. If a question is asked before the preceding question of the same examiner is answered or any objection is ruled upon, it shall be deemed a withdrawal of the earlier question.

(e)   Number of Examinations. On the trial of actions only one counsel on each side shall examine or cross-examine a witness, and one counsel only on each side shall sum up the case to the jury, unless the judge otherwise orders.

(f)   Counsel's Use of Graphic Devices. Counsel may use a graphic device to diagram, calculate, or outline chronology from witnesses' testimony.

(g)   Familiarity with Witnesses, Jurors and Opposing Counsel. Lawyers and judges shall not exhibit undue familiarity with adult witnesses, parties, jurors or opposing counsel, or each other and the use of first names shall be avoided. In arguments to the jury, no juror shall be singled out and addressed individually. When addressing the jury, the lawyers shall first address the court, who shall recognize the lawyer.

(h)   Matters to be Out of Jury's Hearing. The following matters shall be held outside the hearing of jurors. Counsel wishing to argue such matters shall request leave from the court. The first time this request is granted in a trial, the judge shall advise the jurors that matters of law are for the court rather than the jury and that discussions as to law outside the jurors' hearing are necessary and proper for counsel to request.

(1)   Arguments: Evidentiary arguments and offers of proof as provided for in section 10(a) of this Trialbook;

(2)   Offers to Stipulate: Counsel shall not confer about stipulations within possible jury hearing, nor without leave of the court when such conference would impede trial progress;

(3)   Requests for Objects: Other than requests to a witness during testimony, requests by a party to opposing counsel for objects or information purportedly in the possession of the opposing counsel or party shall be made outside the hearing of jurors;

(4)   Motions: Motions for judgments on the pleadings, to exclude evidence, directed verdict, and mistrial shall be made and argued outside the hearing of the jurors. If the ruling affects the issues to be tried by the jury, the court, after consulting with counsel, shall advise the jurors. Immediately upon granting a motion to strike any evidence or arguments to the jury, the court shall instruct the jury to disregard the matter stricken; and

(5)   Sensitive Areas of Inquiry: Areas of inquiry reasonably anticipated to be inflammatory, highly prejudicial, or inadmissible, shall be brought to the attention of opposing counsel and the court outside the hearing of jurors before inquiry. A question of a witness shall be framed to avoid the suggestion of any inadmissible matter.

(i)   **Questioning by Judge.** The judge shall not examine a witness until the parties have completed their questions of such witness and then only for the purpose of clarifying the evidence. When the judge finishes questioning, all parties shall have the opportunity to examine the matters touched upon by the judge. If a lawyer wants to object to a question posed by the court, he or she shall make an objection on the record outside the presence of the jury. The lawyer shall make a "motion to strike" and ask for a curative instruction.

(j)   **Advice of Court as to Self-Incrimination.** Whenever there is a likelihood of self-incrimination by a witness, the court shall advise the witness outside the hearing of the jurors of the privilege against self-incrimination.

(k)   **Policy Against Indication as to Testimony.** Persons in the courtroom shall not indicate by facial expression, shaking of the head, gesturing, shouts or other conduct disagreement or approval of testimony or other evidence being given, and counsel shall so instruct parties they represent, witnesses they call, and persons accompanying them.

(l)   **Policy on Approaching the Bench.** Except with approval of the court, persons in the courtroom shall not traverse the area between the bench and counsel table, and counsel shall so instruct parties they represent, witnesses they call, and persons accompanying them.

(m)   **Use of Depositions and Interrogatories.** A party, before reading into evidence from depositions or interrogatories, shall cite page and line numbers to be read, and pause briefly for review by opposing counsel and the court and for any objections. The court may require designation of portions of depositions to be used at trial in a pretrial order.

Section 11.   Interpreters

The party calling a witness for whom an interpreter is required shall advise the court in advance of the need for an interpreter. Parties shall not use a relative or friend as an interpreter in a contested proceeding, except as approved by the court.

Section 12.   Exhibits

(a)   **Pretrial Exchange of Lists of Exhibits.** Each party shall prepare a list of exhibits to be offered in evidence, and exchange copies of such lists with other counsel prior to the pretrial conference. Such lists shall briefly describe each exhibit anticipated to be offered in evidence. Prior to the commencement of trial, copies of all documents on the list of exhibits shall be made available by the proponent for examination and copying by any other party.

(b)   **Counsel to Organize Numerous Exhibits.** If it can reasonably be anticipated that numerous exhibits will be offered in a trial, all counsel shall meet with designated court personnel shortly prior to or during a recess of the trial for the purpose of organizing and marking the exhibits.

All exhibits shall be marked for identification before any reference by counsel or by a witness.

(c)   **Marking of Exhibits First Disclosed During Trial.** When an exhibit is first disclosed, the proponent shall have it marked for identification before referring to it.

(d)   **Collections of similar and Related or Integrated Documents.** Each collection of similar and related or integrated documents shall be marked with a single designation. If reference is made to a specific document or page in such collection, it shall be marked with a letter the arabic exhibit number assigned to the collection, e.g., "1-a," "21-b," "2-g," etc.

(e)   **Oral Identification of Exhibits at First Reference.** Upon first reference to an exhibit the proponent shall briefly refer to its general nature, without describing the contents.

(f)   **When Exhibits to be Given to Jurors.** Exhibits admitted into evidence, subject to cursory examination, such as photographs and some other demonstrative evidence, may be handed to jurors only after leave is obtained from the court.

Other exhibits admitted into evidence, not subject to cursory examination, such as writings, shall not be handed to jurors until they retire to the jury room upon the cause being submitted to them. If a party contends that an exhibit not subject to cursory examination is critical and should be handed to jurors in the jury box during the course of the trial, counsel shall request leave from the court. Such party shall be prepared to furnish sufficient copies of the exhibit, if reasonably practicable, for all jurors in the event such leave is granted; and upon concluding their examination, the jurors should return the copies to the bailiff. In lieu of copies, and if reasonably practicable, enlargements or projections of such exhibits may be utilized. The court may permit counsel to read short exhibits or portions of exhibits to the jury.

(g)   **Exhibits Admitted in Part.** If an exhibit admitted into evidence contains some inadmissible matter, e.g., a reference to insurance, excluded hearsay, opinion or other evidence lacking foundation, the court, outside the hearing of the jury, shall specify the excluded matter and withhold delivery of such exhibit to the jurors unless and until the inadmissible matter is physically deleted.

Such redaction may be accomplished by photocopying or other copying which deletes the inadmissible portions, and in such event, the proponent of such exhibit shall prepare and furnish a copy.

If redaction by such copying is not accomplished, the parties shall seek to reach a stipulation as to other means; and failing so to do, the admissible matter may be read into evidence with leave of the court.

(h)   **Evidence Admitted for a Limited Purpose.** When evidence is received for a limited purpose or against less than all other parties, the court shall so instruct the jury at the time of admission and, if requested by counsel, during final instructions.

Section 13.   Custody of Exhibits

(a)   **Return of Exhibits to Court Personnel.** Immediately after conclusion of the examination of a witness regarding an exhibit shown to a witness, counsel shall return it to the court personnel.

(b)   **Exhibits after Trial.** Upon the completion of trial, the administrator shall index and retain all exhibits until the case is finally disposed of and all times for appeal have expired and they are either retrieved by the party offering them or destroyed pursuant to Minn. Gen. R. Prac. 128. In the event an appeal is taken, the court administrator shall deliver the exhibits to the Clerk of Appellate Courts in accordance with the procedures of the appellate courts.

(c)   **Bulky Exhibits.** Any time after trial and upon the agreement of all parties, the court administrator may arrange the return of bulky exhibits to the party offering them at trial.

Section 14.   Sealing and Handling of Confidential Exhibits

When briefs, depositions, and other documents or an exhibit such as a trade secret, formula or model are to be treated as confidential, if size permits, such an exhibit shall be placed in a sealed envelope clearly labeled as follows:

> "This envelope contains Exhibits _____ which are confidential and sealed by order of the court. This envelope shall not be opened, nor the contents hereof revealed, except by order of the court."

Such an envelope and other confidential exhibits shall be kept in a locked container such as a file cabinet or some other secure location under the supervision of the administration until released by order of the court.

If testimony is taken which would reveal the substance of confidential exhibits, the courtroom shall be cleared of all persons other than parties, their lawyers, and court personnel. Those present, including jurors, shall be directed by the court to refrain from disclosing the substance of the confidential exhibits.

The pertinent portions of the reporter's notes or transcript shall be kept in a locked container after being placed in a sealed envelope clearly labeled as follows:

> "This envelope contains confidential references sealed by order of the court. This envelope shall not be opened, nor the contents hereof revealed, except by order of the court."

Briefs and other papers submitted in or after trial ordinarily should not describe the substance of confidential exhibits but should refer to them only by number or letter designation pursuant to the uniform method of marking exhibits.

Section 15.   Instructions

(a)   **When Jury Instructions to be Submitted.** Jury instructions shall be submitted in accordance with R. Civ. P. 51. Written requests for instructions shall list authorities.

(b) **Conference Regarding Instructions and Verdicts.** Before final argument and after submission to the court of all proposed jury instructions and verdict forms, a conference shall be held outside the presence of jurors.

A reporter is not required at the beginning of the conference while the court reviews with counsel any proposed instructions or verdict forms and discusses;

>   (1)   whether any proposed instructions or verdict forms are inappropriate and will be voluntarily withdrawn;

>   (2)   whether there is any omission of instructions or verdict forms which are appropriate and shall be offered and given without objection; and

>   (3)   whether there is any other modification of instructions or verdict forms to which the parties will stipulate.

Thereafter, the conference shall be reported and the court shall:

>   (1)   specify those instructions and verdict forms the court proposes to give, refuse, or modify, wither at the request of a party or on its own initiative;

>   (2)   hear formal argument, and rule upon any objections to, and offers of, the proposed instruction and verdict forms.

(c) **Specifying Disposition of Instructions.** Upon determining the instructions to be given, refused, or modified, the court shall indicate the disposition and sign or initial them.

(d) **Stipulations Regarding Further Procedure.** At a conference prior to the submission of the case to the jury, the court may request that the parties consider stipulating:

>   (1)   that in the absence of any counsel the court may, upon request of the jury, read to the jury any and all instructions previously given;

>   (2)   that in the absence of the court after the original submission of the case to the jury, any judge of the court may act in the court's place up to and including the time of dismissal of the jury;

>   (3)   that a stay of entry of judgment for an agreed upon number of days shall be granted after a verdict;

>   (4)   that a sealed verdict may be returned; and

(5)   that the presence of the clerk and reporter, the right to poll the jury, and the right to have the verdict immediately recorded and filed in open court are waived.

(e)   **Changing Jury Instructions.** If, after the chambers conference and at any time before giving the instructions and verdict form to the jurors, the court determines to make any substantive change the court shall so advise all parties outside the hearing of jurors. If the court determines to make a substantive change after final argument, the court shall permit additional final argument. The court shall also make a statement on the record regarding any changes.

(f)   **Use of Jury Instructions in Jury Room.** Jury instructions may be sent to the jury room for use by the jurors if the court so directs. The number, title, citation of authority, and history shall be removed from each instruction. Stricken portions shall be totally obliterated and any additions shall be completely legible.

Section 16.   Questions by Jurors

If the jury has a question regarding the case during deliberations, the court shall instruct the foreperson to reduce it to writing and submit it through appropriate court personnel. Upon receipt of such a written question, the court shall review the propriety of an answer with counsel, unless counsel have waived the right to participate or cannot be found after reasonable and diligent search documented by the court. Such review may be in person or by telephone, and shall be on the record outside the hearing of the jury. The written question and answer shall be made a part of the record. The answer shall be given in open court, absent a stipulation to the contrary.

Section 17.   Special Verdicts

(a)   **Special Verdict Forms.** A party requesting a special verdict form should prepare the proposed form and submit it to the court and serve it upon the other counsel prior to the chambers conference referred to in section 15 of this Trialbook.

(b)   **Filing.** Proposed special verdict forms shall be filed and made part of the record in the case.

(c)   **Copies of Verdict.** The court may provide copies of the verdict form to the jury or to each juror for use during arguments or instruction.

Section 18.   Polling and Discharge

(a)   **Polling the Jury.** Upon the return of any verdict and at the request of a party the jury shall be polled. Polling shall be conducted by the trial court or by the clerk at the trial court's direction by asking each juror: "Is the verdict read your verdict?"

(b) **Discharge of the Jury.** In discharging the jury, the court shall:

(1) Thank the jury for its service;

(2) Not comment on the propriety of any verdict or failure to reach same;

(3) Advise the jurors that they may, but need not, speak with anyone about the case; and

(4) Specify where and when any jurors are to return for further service.

PTM

Appendix C

Sample Exhibit List

Case Type: Contract

STATE OF STATE

DISTRICT COURT

COUNTY OF COUNTY

TENTH JUDICIAL DISTRICT

The Window Company,

Case No. C5-01-3098

Plaintiff,

v.

THE WINDOW COMPANY'S
EXHIBIT LIST

Wood Supplier, Inc.,

Defendant.

Pursuant to the Court's order dated March 20, 2001, plaintiff The Window Company ("Window Company") submits the following list of exhibits that it may introduce at trial. Window Company reserves the right not to introduce any exhibits listed and to offer additional or alternative exhibits at trial for rebuttal, impeachment, foundation, or other purposes. Window Company also reserves the right to offer any exhibit identified on defendant's exhibit list, which is hereby incorporated by reference. Window Company further reserves the right to supplement this list at any time before trial if the need arises.

Dated: April 10, 2001

LAW FIRM, LLP

Mary Roe (#208772)
John Doe (#215247)
90 South Seventh Street
Anywhere, USA 98765
Telephone: (555) 555-1212

Attorneys for The Window Company

The Window Company v. Wood Supplier, Inc.

Plaintiff's Trial Exhibits

Presiding Judge	Plaintiff's Attorneys	Defendant's Attorneys
The Honorable Douglas Bruce	Mary Roe John Doe LAW FIRM, LLP 90 South Seventh Street Anywhere, USA 98765 (555) 555-1212	John A. McDonald THE OTHER FIRM, LLP 42 Universal Tower 715 10th Avenue South Anywhere, USA 98761
Trial Date(s)	Court Reporter	Courtroom Deputy

PLTF. EXHIBIT NO.	DATE	DESCRIPTION	OFFERED	ADMITTED
1	--	Wood Supplier's drawing of original design of Series 302 side sash, Part No. 4-34-28 (cross-section)		
2	--	Wood Supplier's drawing of original design of Series 203 side sash, Part No. 4-34-28 (cross-section)		

PLTF. EXHIBIT NO.	DATE	DESCRIPTION	OFFERED	ADMITTED
3	2/4/99	"Pilot Purchase Order" from The Window Company to Wood Supplier, Inc.		
4	8/5/99	Letter from Wood Supplier to Chris Frank (Konkel Depo. Ex. 25)		
5	9/15/99	Fax from Dave Wethering to Jeff Kross with attached Purchase Order #10185 and drawings		
6	4/9/00	Wood Supplier's Print No. S-4994		
7	9/28/00	Fax from Dave Wethering to Jeff Kross		
8	9/27/00	Fax from Lawrence Sherman to Dave Wethering with attached drawings (Sherman Depo. Ex. 20)		
9	1/31/01	Fax from Lawrence Sherman to Dave Wethering		
10	2/7/01	Fax from Dave Wethering to Lawrence Sherman (Sherman Depo. Ex. 22)		
11	7/7/01	Letter from Peter Douglas to Jeff Kross		
12	8/4/01	Letter from Peter Douglas to Jeff Kross re defective wood		

Appendix D

Sample Witness List

Case Type: Contract

STATE OF STATE   DISTRICT COURT

COUNTY OF COUNTY   TENTH JUDICIAL DISTRICT

The Window Company,   Case No. C5-01-3098

                Plaintiff,

v.   THE WINDOW COMPANY'S
                              WITNESS LIST

Wood Supplier, Inc.,

                Defendant.

       Pursuant to the Court's order dated March 20, 2001, plaintiff The Window Company ("Window Company") submits the attached list of witnesses it may introduce at trial. Window Company reserves the right not to call any witness listed and to offer testimony of additional or alternative witnesses at trial for rebuttal, impeachment, foundation, or other purposes. Window Company also reserves the right to call any witness identified on defendant's witness list, which is hereby incorporated by reference. Window Company further reserves the right to supplement this list at any time before trial if the need arises.

Dated: April 10, 2001   **LAW FIRM, LLP**

                               Mary Roe (#208772)
                               John Doe (#215247)
                               90 South Seventh Street
                               Anywhere, USA 98765
                               Telephone: (555) 555-1212

                               Attorneys for The Window Company

Plaintiff's Witness List

1.   Chelsea Frank

2.   Hayley Wethering

3.   Isabelle Kross

4.   Teresa Sheerman

5.   Noelle Douglas

6.   Marie Johnson

7.   Jack Henry Erickson

8.   Kevin Rhodes

9.   Hildy Bowbeer

10. Chuck Osland

11. Denise Earl

12. Daniel Griffin

13. Michael Andrews

14. Karen Wilson

15. Kenny Barrow

16. All witnesses listed by defendant

17. Rebuttal witnesses

PTM

Appendix E

Sample Proposed Jury Instructions

Case Type: Contract

STATE OF STATE   DISTRICT COURT

COUNTY OF COUNTY   TENTH JUDICIAL DISTRICT

The Window Company,   Case No. C5-01-3098

                  Plaintiff,

v.   THE WINDOW COMPANY'S
                                                    PROPOSED JURY INSTRUCTIONS

Wood Supplier, Inc.,

                  Defendant.

Pursuant to Rule 51 of the State Rules of Civil Procedure, and the Court's order dated March 20, 2001, plaintiff The Window Company ("Window Company") hereby submits its proposed jury instructions. Window Company respectfully reserves the right to amend, delete, or add to these proposed jury instructions depending upon the evidence adduced at trial.

In addition, Window Company requests that the Court give the following general instructions directly from *State Jury Instruction Guides (Civil)* (3d ed.) ("JIG III").

WINDOW COMPANY INSTR. NO.	JIG III NO.	DESCRIPTION
1	1	Preliminary Statement – Before Trial
2	2	Preliminary Statement – Duties of Judge and Jury
3	3	Instructions to be Considered as a Whole

Dated: April 10, 2001

LAW FIRM, LLP

Mary Roe (#208772)
John Doe (#215247)
90 South Seventh Street
Anywhere, USA 98765
Telephone: (555) 555-1212

Attorneys for The Window Company

THE WINDOW COMPANY'S PROPOSED INSTRUCTION NO. 18

Pretrial Statement – Nature of the Lawsuit

The plaintiff in this case is The Window Company. Window Company is located in City, State. It manufactures windows.

The defendant in this case is Wood Supplier, Inc. Wood Supplier is located in City, State. It manufactures wood.

Window Company purchased wood from Wood Supplier and used the wood to make windows for Window Company's customers. Window Company alleges that windows containing wood made by Wood Supplier warped, or "bowed," after the windows were installed into the homes and businesses of Window Company's customers. Window Company had to replace the windows that warped. Window Company filed this lawsuit to recover the damages and expenses it incurred in replacing the warped windows and taking other steps to respond to the problem and to recover profits that Window Company lost as a result of the problems it experienced with warping windows.

Wood Supplier denies that it is liable to Window Company. Wood Supplier has also counter-sued Window Company to recover payment for three shipments of wood that it claims Window Company should have paid for. Window Company denies that it was required to pay for the three shipments of wood.

THE WINDOW COMPANY'S PROPOSED INSTRUCTION NO. 19

<u>Express Warranty</u>

Window Company alleges that Wood Supplier made certain express warranties about the wood that Wood Supplier sold to Window Company. Any affirmation of fact or promise made by the seller to the buyer which relates to the goods being sold becomes part of the basis of the bargain between the parties and creates an express warranty that the goods being sold will conform to the affirmation or promise. In addition, any sample or model which is made part of the basis of the bargain creates an express warranty that all of the goods will conform to the sample or model.

JIG III 640 (modified); State Stat. § 336.2-313.

THE WINDOW COMPANY'S PROPOSED INSTRUCTION NO. 20

Implied Warranty of Merchantability

Window Company also alleges that Wood Supplier breached a warranty called the implied warranty of merchantability. An "implied" warranty is one that arises by operation of law from a sale of goods. It does not depend on the affirmative intention or agreement of the parties to the transaction—that is, the seller need not specifically give such a warranty to the buyer. It is automatically part of the sale transaction.

When a sale of goods is made, the seller warrants or guarantees that the goods purchased will pass without objection in the trade under the contract description and are fit for the ordinary purposes for which such goods are used. If the goods would not pass without objection in the trade under the contract description, or are not fit for the ordinary purposes for which such goods are used, then the seller has breached the implied warranty of merchantability.

In order to find that the seller has breached the implied warranty of merchantability, you need not find a specific defect in the goods purchased. A breach of an implied warranty of merchantability may occur even if the seller was not aware of any defect at the time of the sale.

A buyer may recover for a breach of the implied warranty of merchantability without proving that the seller was negligent or at fault.

JIG III 641 (modified); State Stat. § 2-314; *Liebman v. Erdman*, 946 N.E.2d 349 (State 1994).

Appendix F

Sample Special Verdict Form

UNITED STATES DISTRICT COURT
DISTRICT OF STATE
01-CV-761 (JMR/FLN)

Felicity J. Boyd   )
)
)   VERDICT
v.   )
)
Kramer Refining Co.   )

We, the jury, answer the questions submitted to us as follows:

     1.   Did the defendant Kramer Refining Co., retaliate against the plaintiff, Felicity J. Boyd, in violation of the State Whistleblower Statute?

          _____ Yes _____ No

Note: If your answer to question 1 was "yes," proceed to question 2. Otherwise, sign and date the verdict form, as you have completed your deliberations.

     2.   What amount of damages, if any, do you find Ms. Boyd suffered?

     (a)   Lost wages and benefits to date: $_____

     (b)   Loss of future wages and benefits: $_____

     (c)   Emotional distress: $_____

Dated: January 19, 2001

             _____
             Foreperson

Appendix G

Sample Motion in Limine Brief

Case Type: Civil Rights

STATE OF STATE

COUNTY OF COUNTY

Jimmy Poradek,

Plaintiff,

v.

Officer Tom Kahnke,

Defendant.

DISTRICT COURT

FIRST JUDICIAL DISTRICT

File No. 00-2566

DEFENDANT'S MEMORANDUM
IN SUPPORT OF MOTION IN
LIMINE TO EXCLUDE
EVIDENCE OF PRIOR ACTS

The plaintiff has attempted to offer evidence of prior conduct by Officer Kahnke in different cases dealing with different people. This evidence is inadmissible and must be excluded.

Rule 404(b) of the State Rules of Evidence provides that "[e]vidence of another crime, wrong, or act is not admissible to prove the character of a person in order to show conformity therewith." The Eighth Circuit has joined other courts across the nation in holding that Rule 404(b) requires exclusion of evidence of an officer's past conduct in Section 1983 cases. *Hopson v. Fredericksen*, 961 F.2d 1374, 1379 (8th Cir. 1992); *Morgan v. City of Marmaduke*, 958 F.2d 207, 211 & n.2 (8th Cir. 1992); *Carter v. District of Columbia*, 795 F.2d 116, 129-31 (D.C. Cir. 1986) (reversing verdict in favor of plaintiffs because of admission of evidence of officer's prior conduct); *Berkovich v. Hicks*, 922 F.2d 1019, 1022-23 (2d Cir. 1991).

The most common rationale offered by plaintiffs seeking to introduce such evidence against police officers is that it is relevant to show the officer's motive or intent in acting, which is an exception to the exclusionary provision of Rule 404(b). But this argument is no longer valid in light of *Graham v. Connor*, 490 U.S. 386 (1989), which held that the Fourth Amendment standard that applies to excessive force cases is purely objective and that an officer's actions must be judged "without regard to their underlying intent or motivation." *Graham*, 490 U.S. at 397. *See also Ohio v. Robinette*, 117 S. Ct. 417, 421 (1996) (officer's subjective motivations are irrelevant to Fourth Amendment inquiry); *Whren v. United States*, 116 S. Ct. 1769, 1774, 1775 (1996) (same); *Scott v. United States*, 436 U.S. 128, 137-39 (1978) (same). The Eighth Circuit has explicitly held that any argument that evidence of an officer's prior acts is relevant to show motive or intent "is foreclosed by the Supreme Court's recent decision in [*Graham*]." *Robinson v. City of St. Charles*, 972 F.2d 974, 976 (8th Cir. 1992).

None of the other exceptions to Rule 404(b)—opportunity, preparation, plan, knowledge, identity, or absence of mistake or accident—applies in this case. Thus, the evidence must be excluded pursuant to Minn. R. Evid. 404(b).

Dated: August 22, 1996   LAW FIRM, LLP

_____

Carl Litsey (#208772)
Lea Pulju (#215247)
90 South Seventh Street
Anywhere, USA 98765
Telephone: (555) 555-1212

PTM

Appendix H

Sample Opening Statement

SAMPLE OPENING STATEMENT

THE COURT: Now we have the opportunity to hear from the Defendants and hear their opening statement.

Counsel?

MR. WEBBER: Good morning, ladies and gentlemen. My name is Chuck Webber. I am one of the attorneys representing Ampersand, and I know that you have already met the others that I am sitting with here. Jerry Snider you met during jury selection and Jenny Erickson Murphy from Ampersand, he will be sitting with us through the trial.

I'll tell you something that will probably surprise you. This is an easy case. You may not be thinking that right now, but I want to spend a few minutes talking with you about the case, take you through it, and I think that you will begin to see what the evidence is about. And what the evidence will show in this case is that the two Plaintiffs here, the Lenon Family Trust and Best Trust, took a gamble. They took a gamble on a stock warrant and they lost. Another way to say it is they made a deal with Ampersand and it didn't turn out the way they wanted, and they came to Ampersand and tried to get Ampersand to change the deal to make it more profitable, and Ampersand said no, the deal we entered into is the deal we entered into. And the Plaintiffs decided to sue instead, to try to get back the profit that they wish they would have made. That is all the case is about and I think the evidence will show that by the end of the day.

Let me step back for a minute. You heard a lot about Ampersand, heard the name a lot and it occurs to me nobody really told you too much about it. We haven't been properly introduced, so to speak. Let me give you a proper introduction.

Ampersand is a Minnesota corporation whose headquarters are in Brooklyn Center. Used to be Plymouth, but they just moved recently. Started in '86, started by three people who came over from another big medical company called Medtrix. Medtrix is sort of a bigwig in medical products. They are a division headquartered in Fridley, and employ about twelve thousand people. Ampersand employs about 250 people. Ampersand is not a bigwig, but a small player.

The folks that started up Ampersand started it up with the idea that they could maybe start a company that would be able to do more innovative things with medical technology than some of the big players in the market, and that is why they started the company. Ampersand in its early days tried out different products, tried to develop a lot of things, but by early '90 what they started to focus on is defibrillators. You heard that in the jury selection. A lot of people didn't know what we were talking about. You probably know what it is, but you don't know it. If you watch *ER* or some other hospital show and there is a scene where somebody's heart stops or there is some problem, the doctors take out two metal paddles, yell "clear", put it on the chest of the person involved. That is a defibrillator. A defibrillator is something that literally jolts the heart back into action if there is a problem, if the heart stops or starts beating irregularly. There are some people who have a number of chronic heart problems or a number of heart attacks where they need to have a defibrillator, and obviously that is not always possible. So in the 1980s people came up with the idea of an implantable defibrillator, kind of like a pacemaker surgically implanted inside, so people who need it can get jolts to their heart in case something happens.

In the 1980s, you are going to hear defibrillators were kind of big things. They were big clunky things and had to be implanted right here at waistline, and you will hear people that had these defibrillators implanted had to buy pants that were four sizes too big to fit over this great big lump.

The surgery to put these things in was really intrusive open heart surgery, literally open chest, run wires from the defibrillator down at the waist line all the way to the heart. Really intrusive.

In 1990 Ampersand decided it was going to try to get the defibrillators smaller and smarter and make use of technology to do that. Ampersand, as I said, tried a bunch of different products but in the '90s decided the defibrillator was going to be a core product, and tried to focus on that.

After years of research and after years of development and testing Ampersand manufactured a defibrillator that is much smaller and much smarter, and I am holding in my hands right now what these defibrillators look like today. That is all that they are. This defibrillator is one of the newest ones, and you will hear in the trial that this particular one, one just like this, was implanted for the first time in the United States last week in Cleveland. This defibrillator is actually implanted up kind of towards somebody's shoulder, not down in the waistline, and it can be so far that it leaves just a tiny bump. You wouldn't even know it when somebody is wearing a shirt over it. And the leads or wires that go to the heart are much shorter. This can now be implanted by a surgeon in about 45 minutes.

Your Honor, may I pass this to the jury so they can take a look at it?

THE COURT: No objection, Counsel?

MR. MCCARTNEY: No objection.

THE COURT: You may do so.

MR. WEBBER: You should note on the back it says not for human use. It is for human use, but this one isn't. This one hasn't been implanted in anyone. Look at it. That is what they make. Their claim to fame is making a defibrillator. So I wanted to start out by giving you an introduction of Ampersand, tell you what it does so you will understand the kind of things we are talking about here.

Well, now that we have been properly introduced to Ampersand, let me take a minute or two and talk with you about the case. Like I said, it turns out that this is really an easy case and I sense that you may not get that idea right now, and I want to explain why that is. I start the story at the top and it's not because I want to give you the story first but because I have some information that I think is going to come out at this trial that I think will help you understand the whole story going on here. As Mr. McCartney said, the story kind of starts in 1990 and starts with a company called Dayfield. Dayfield International. Mr. McCartney said Dayfield is a company owned by Mr. George Starr and Mr. Harrison who are with you today. They own Dayfield and really kind of were the corporation. They set up Dayfield to provide financial advisory services to companies. I'll explain that in a second.

As Mr. McCartney said, in 1990 Dayfield and Ampersand entered into a contract. Dayfield was going to provide financial advisory services to Ampersand. Let me tell you why. Like I said, Ampersand started out in 1986. By 1990 it was only four years old. That is pretty young, kind of a baby company. It's what we call a start-up company. You will hear testimony that one thing start-up companies need more than anything else in the world is they need money. They need money to research and develop and test their products and to try to sell them to people. They need a lot of money. They generally don't have a lot of assets. Start-up companies generally have a good idea, hopefully a good idea, but not a lot of money to try to make it a go. Start-up companies need money. And Ampersand was a start-up company and needed money. Dayfield, run by Mr. Starr and Mr. Harrison, was set up to provide financing services. Mr. Starr and Mr. Best, you will hear, and as Mr. McCartney told you, are very, very experienced in the financial world. These are sophisticated, savvy guys, and they have a lot of contacts in the investment world. They know people who have money to invest in start-up companies like Ampersand, and they set up Dayfield in order to try to contact their investors with the people they know and put them together with companies like Ampersand that needed money. That is exactly what the parties did in 1990.

Dayfield and Ampersand signed a contract in 1990. It's not the contract that is at issue here but it's just a little background. Signed a contract in 1990 when Dayfield said we will provide five million dollars in financing for Ampersand. Mr. Starr and Mr. Harrison were going to go out and kind of tap their contacts in the investment world and try to come up with five million dollars of financing for Ampersand. And the contract said if Dayfield raised five million dollars Dayfield would get two things. First it would get $60,000 in cash and the second thing is that it would get a warrant. What Dayfield is going to try to do is get people to invest money in Ampersand. Now Ampersand is a start-up company, couldn't really go to a bank, you will hear, to get financing. Banks don't like to lend to start-up companies. They don't have a lot of assets. So if you are a start-up company and need money, you need people to invest money. When people invest money you give them shares of stock.

Let me stop for a minute and talk about what stock is. You probably all know, but I want to make sure everybody starts on the same page under these terms. Stock is a piece of ownership of the company. If I own one share of IBM, for example, I own a piece of IBM. It's a little bitty piece of IBM, but I own a piece of IBM, and if IBM has a terrific year, they make lots of dough, I get a little piece of that. Maybe my stock goes up in value or I actually get a share of the profits. But by the same token, if they have a lousy year my ownership isn't worth all that much. Stock is a gamble. I think that is something we all know. If you buy stock it can go up, it can go down. It's risky. It's a gamble.

Now what Dayfield was trying to do is get people to invest money in Ampersand in exchange for stock. The people would put their money into Ampersand, they'd get Ampersand stock in return. As I said, Dayfield got compensation for doing that, $60,000 cash and a warrant.

Let me stop again, and let's talk about what a warrant is, because I don't know that that has been particularly defined, and since we're talking about a warrant in this case you will need to know what that is. A warrant is not stock. What a warrant is, it's a right to buy stock in the future. Now let me give you an example again with IBM. Say that I have a warrant to buy a hundred shares of IBM stock for a hundred dollars a share for three years. That means that any time I want to during that three year period I can go take my warrant and say "I would like to buy my hundred shares of stock now for a hundred dollars a share." I can do that any time I want to during that three year period no matter what IBM is selling for on the market.

So say IBM goes up to one hundred fifty and my next door neighbor who wants to buy IBM stock has to pay a hundred and fifty a share for his, and I got it for a hundred bucks because I have a contract that says I can get it for a hundred bucks. That is what a warrant is. It's very simple. If I hold a warrant, what I am hoping is that the stock goes up, because if the stock goes up I get a better deal. If the stock goes up to two hundred and I have a warrant for a hundred, I get to buy it for a hundred dollars a share less than everybody else does. But what if the stock goes down? If the stock goes down my warrant becomes worthless. If I have a warrant to buy a hundred dollars of stock at a hundred dollars, then the stock price goes down to eighty, I'd have to be nuts to buy it under my warrants, because I can just go down to Piper, Jaffray or Dain, Bosworth and buy it for eighty bucks. Why would I want to pay a hundred when I can get it for eighty?

A warrant is sort of like a coupon in that regard. If you have a coupon to buy Cheerios for two dollars and you go to the store and they are a dollar and a half, what do you need a coupon for if you can get it for buck and a half? A warrant is not stock. When you have a warrant you don't own a piece of the company, but you can buy the stock. It's unlike stock in that regard but it's kind of like stock in that it's a gamble. Like I said, if the stock goes up you win. If the stock goes down your warrants can become worthless.

Let's get back to the story. Dayfield is supposed to raise $5 million in cash for Ampersand. You are going to hear evidence that Dayfield didn't do that. Dayfield didn't raise the $5 million that it was supposed to raise. It only raised $1.6 million, and that is something that is not disputed. It only raised about a third of what it was supposed to raise. But you know what? They got paid anyway. Ampersand gave Dayfield the $60,000 and gave Dayfield that warrant for Ampersand stock, despite the fact that Dayfield hadn't raised all the money they were supposed to raise. On December 1 of 1990 Ampersand gave Dayfield its warrants, and the warrant that Dayfield got was to buy 250,000 shares of Ampersand stock at $3.87½ cents per share for three years. Like I said, what that means is if any time during that three-year period that that warrant was good, Dayfield could go to Ampersand and say we want to buy our 250,000 shares and here's a check for, you know, whatever 250,000 multiplied by $3.87½ cents is. Okay, pretty close to a million dollars. Any time during that three-year period, and it was up to Dayfield whether it wanted to exercise that warrant. Obviously when Dayfield gets the warrants it's hoping Ampersand stock goes up because if Ampersand stock goes up to $6 they get to buy it at $3.87, but by the same token if the stock goes down to $2 it's worthless, because they can buy stock on the market. That is an important point we'll come back to. If the warrant is worthless they can buy the stock on the market. I am going to come back to that.

So Dayfield has its warrants. Dayfield had to pay for this warrant. That was part of the deal. They had to buy the warrants from Ampersand. You know what Dayfield paid was a total of a thousand dollars. That is it. Ampersand only saw a thousand dollars from that warrant. That is all that Dayfield paid.

Now as Mr. McCartney said, almost immediately after Dayfield got the warrant it split it up, sold pieces of it to a bunch of different people and entities. Kind of whacked up the 250,000 shares and pieced them out to other people. One of the pieces went to the Lenon Family Trusts. That is one of the plaintiffs in this case. The Lenon Family Trusts got a piece of the warrant for 100,000 shares. The rest of the deal was the same, same price, $3.87½ cents, same time period. Another piece of the warrant went to the William Best 1993 Irrevocable Trust, which we are probably just going to call the Best Trust because it takes too long to say the other one. The Best Trust got a piece of this warrant for 85,000 shares.

These are the two plaintiffs we have here today. That is what this case is about. It's about 100,000 shares of warrants and 85,000 shares worth of warrants. The Lenon Family Trust paid for their warrant. You want to know what they paid? It was $10,000. But the money, you will hear, went to Dayfield, because Dayfield owned the only warrant, the whole 250,000 shares, and Dayfield is the one that sold pieces of it off to these other trusts. The Lenon Family Trust paid $10,000 to Dayfield, not to Ampersand. Remember all that

Ampersand ever saw for this warrant, all that Dayfield ever paid for it was $1,000. So you can see what has happened right away. Almost immediately Dayfield has already made $9,000 profit right out of the gate by selling a piece of the warrant to the Lenon Family Trust for $10,000. Dayfield already made nine. The Best Trust with its warrant for 85,000 shares paid zero.

I think the evidence is going to show the Best Trust didn't pay money for its warrant at all. Just got it for free. So the Lenon Trusts and Best Trusts now both have their warrant. Later on this three-year period was extended out by six months. Parties agreed to do that. Ampersand asked the Plaintiffs if they would agree not to exercise their warrant for a certain period of time in exchange for getting an extra six months on the warrant and the Plaintiffs agreed to that. So these warrants, folks, expired on June 1, 1994. It's the last day that those warrants could be exercised.

Well, 1991 comes and goes and the warrants aren't exercised. 1992 comes and goes. The warrants aren't exercised. 1993 comes and goes. The warrants aren't exercised.

Mr. McCartney showed you this chart, this is a chart of Ampersand stock price. Mr. McCartney has drawn a yellow line on this to show what the price of the warrants was. $3.87½. Here's the start of the warrant period and here's the end of the warrant period. And you can see that a good portion of that time Ampersand stock was above $3.87½, which means that at a lot of these times these Plaintiffs could have gone in and exercised their warrants and bought Ampersand stock at a discount because the price was above $3.87½, but they didn't do it. They didn't do it. They just waited. And nothing happened until a couple months, eight or nine months before the warrants were going to expire in August of 1993. We're kind of getting to the end of the warrant period and they still haven't exercised the warrants, and for the first time Mr. Starr and Mr. Harrison write a letter to Ampersand, as Mr. McCartney said, and they said to Ampersand, we'd like you to change the deal. We don't like the $3.87½-price anymore. What we'd like you to do, Ampersand, is we'd like you to lower that price to $2.50 a share. We'd like a bigger discount, if we can, on the stock. And do you know what else they said? We'd also like you to give us an extra eighteen months on the warrants, extend them out to the end of 1996. Give us more time to exercise these.

The evidence is going to show that Mr. Starr and Mr. Harrison just came to Ampersand and said we'd really like it if you'd reduce the price to two-and-a-half dollars. No reason. Just wanted to, I suspect. And I think the evidence will show what the reason was, and it's pretty obvious that Ampersand stock was below $3.87½ in August of '93 and the warrants weren't any good, and I think the evidence is going to show that the plaintiffs were starting to get nervous and thought maybe the stock wasn't going to go back above $3.87½, and they came to Ampersand and said, can we change the deal? A couple weeks later they followed up with another letter and they renewed their request and they said, "We'd really like you to reduce the price of the stock—or the warrant, so that we can exercise it." Ampersand said no to this. And I want to tell you why Ampersand said no. There is a couple reasons why.

One reason is that Ampersand really hadn't been given any good reason for the reduction. All of these events that Mr. McCartney told you about that they think should have made us give them a break on the warrant, none of those had been mentioned at that time. Nobody ever came to Ampersand on behalf of the plaintiffs and said you know, that stock manipulation scheme really should—you know, we're upset about that. That should really lead you to reduce the price. Nobody said the fact that Ampersand sold some of its medical products to another company should have led to a reduction in the price. None of the events that Mr. McCartney mentioned ever came up. They just didn't mention them. The plaintiffs simply came and asked Ampersand for a better deal. Ampersand said no, as I said, because there really wasn't any reason presented to do it.

There is a second reason. You are going to hear that Ampersand has never ever changed the price of a warrant. It's just not done. And it's not done for reasons I mentioned at the very beginning—a deal is a deal, and nobody wants to be hard-nosed about it but a warrant is a gamble. That is the deal. That is the price you pay. If the stock goes up you win. If the stock goes down the warrant becomes worthless, and you can't go back later and say, no, look, I really want this warrant to be changed so that I can make some money with it. That is the risk you take. Ampersand had never adjusted warrants for anybody else who had warrants, and I am going to suggest it would be unfair to Ampersand to do it for one person and not another.

* * *

And finally you are going to hear the plaintiffs complain that during the three-year period Ampersand issued stock to more people, let more shareholders in the club, and that they believed that that reduced their piece of the pie. Mr. McCartney called it dilution. D-I-L-U-T-I-O-N, not D-E-L-U-D-E-D like you are crazy. Dilution.

I want to take a minute to tell you what dilution is, and you will hear testimony about this. Let me start with an easy one. If you get a half-glass of Scotch and top it off with water you have diluted the scotch. That is easy. The percentage of Scotch is less then with the water than it was before. Easy example of dilution. Let me give you another example of dilution. Say I went to a family reunion in the summer. It was a hot day and we got one of those big tubs of ice cream and we were all getting ready to have the ice cream, and then the side of the family that nobody really wanted to show up showed up. And one reason why we don't like this side of the family to show up is because they never bring anything. They never bring anything to these family reunions. And we are all sitting there, a hot day, ice cream ready to go, and we're thinking, great, we'll get less ice cream than we want. And much to our surprise and delight they brought with them their own big tub of ice cream and we all end up enjoying the day. Turned out fine. Okay, we were afraid of being diluted. We were afraid our respective share of the ice cream was going to get smaller because we brought new people to the party, but it turned out to be okay because the people brought their own ice cream to the party.

Those are two examples of dilution. The plaintiffs are complaining that Ampersand sold more stock to people during the warrant period and that led to their slice of the Ampersand pie getting smaller. Sort of think of Ampersand as a pie divided up into pieces. Each shareholder has a piece. If you let more shareholders in you are dividing the pie into more pieces. Well, that is true. We did let more shareholders in. Couple things about it. First you will hear testimony, that is what start-up companies do for crying out loud. You have to raise money by buying stock. If somebody invests in you, you have to give them stock in return. Mr. Starr and Mr. Harrison knew that. As a matter of fact that is what they were doing in 1990. That is why they originally came on to the scene, to help Ampersand raise money by selling stock. But there is a more important point. When Ampersand takes on more stockholders it's dividing the pie into more pieces, true enough, but the pie is getting big because the shareholders are bringing in money. So if this is Ampersand before we take on new shareholders, that might be Ampersand afterwards—more pieces of pie but a bigger pie. Another way to put it for my family reunion is the new people should bring their own ice cream to the party. They bring money to Ampersand and add that to Ampersand's value and make the pie bigger, so you are dividing it into more pieces but everybody gets about the same amount of pie.

You are going to hear an expert witness testify that the things that Ampersand did during the three-year warrant period did not dilute the plaintiffs' interests at all. You are also going to hear that none of the other events that Mr. McCartney described to you, events that the plaintiffs came up with after the fact, just before they filed the lawsuit, none of those events hurt them at all. And you are going to hear testimony that none of the events that Mr. McCartney mentioned should have led Ampersand to adjust the price of that warrant to give the plaintiffs a better deal.

Let me finish up now where I started off. The case is about a deal that didn't work out the way the Plaintiffs wanted it to. It's about the plaintiffs taking a gamble that didn't work out. And it's unfortunate that deals sometimes don't go the way people plan and that gambles don't work out the way people want them to, but that is the nature of the deal. That is the nature of the gamble. That is what investing in stock is like. And you can't come back later and change the terms just because you wish it had gone better. At the end of the case the plaintiffs are going to come to you and I think they are going to ask you to give them over a million dollars. They are going to ask you to give them over a million dollars on the grounds that if Ampersand had reduced the price of the warrant to make it profitable for them they would have bought Ampersand stock and they would have held the Ampersand stock and they would have sold it at the height of the market, and everybody would love to do that, obviously. I mean when you buy stock that is what you want to have happen. But these guys never bought stock. They didn't exercise the warrant, and they never went out on the market and bought the stock themselves. What they are asking you to do is give them all of the reward but none of the risk, and that is not something that happens in life and it's not something that happens with the stock market either. They are going to ask you for almost a million dollars on their lost investment in the warrant of $10,000 for the Lenon Trust and zero for the Best Trust.

When you have heard all the evidence, you have seen the exhibits and the witnesses testify, we're going to come back and ask you to come back with a ruling, come back with a verdict that says, look, a deal is a deal and you can't adjust it later just because you don't like how it turned out, and you can't get unlimited reward without taking risk, and these plaintiffs didn't take any risk and they are not entitled to recover a fortune from Ampersand.

Thank you very much.

THE COURT: Thank you, Mr. Webber.

Ladies and gentlemen of the Jury you are excused for the morning. We will return this afternoon and begin hearing testimony from the witnesses. Please be back by two o'clock and we will proceed at that time. Thank you.

Appendix I

Sample Expert Witness Examination

SAMPLE EXPERT WITNESS EXAMINATION

(A recess was taken.)

THE COURT: Mr. Gross.

MR. GROSS: Your Honor, plaintiff calls Daniel Rowsky to the stand.

DANIEL ROWSKY,

having been first duly sworn, was examined
and testified as follows:

DIRECT EXAMINATION

BY MR. GROSS:

Q. Good morning, Mr. Rowsky.

A. Good morning.

Q. You are here to testify about damages in this case, is that correct?

A. That's correct.

Q. And you are assuming that the jury finds infringement, correct?

A. That's an assumption of mine in coming up with a damage calculation, that's correct.

Q. Let's start by hearing about your background. First of all, where are you from?

A. I grew up in Black Bear Lake, just south of Local City.

Q. Do you have a family?

A. Yes, I have a wife and four boys.

Q. Where do you live now?

A. In Pine Lakes, north of Local City.

Q. Mr. Rowsky, why don't you tell us what your present job is?

A. I am the president of a company called Money Advisors, LLC.

Q. What does that do?

A. It's a company of six people in total that provides financial consulting and advice to individuals, companies and lawyers, oftentimes in disputes like this, and then provides expert testimony on damage calculations.

Q. Mr. Rowsky, could you tell the jury about your educational and professional background?

A. Yes. I went to high school in Black Bear Lake. Then I went to college at Local University and obtained an accounting degree. I then worked for a number of years in public accounting. My first job was at Peat Moss, which is a CPA firm in Local City.

Then I went to work for a local company called RXY Capital, which was a wholly owned subsidiary of RXY Corporation. I worked there for eight and a half years. The last three years I was there I was the corporate controller. I was going to law school at night while I was working there. I completed my law degree in 1990 and then went to work for Big Accounting Firm, which is also a CPA firm located in Local City.

I worked there from April of '90 until August of '97, and I was the managing director of their litigation consulting practice for the last three years. And then my partner and I left in August of '97 to form the company called Money Advisors.

Q. Could you tell the jury a little bit about what you did when you were at Big Accounting Firm between 1990 and 1997?

A. Yes. I started in the litigation consulting practice there as a manager, and I would work on projects like this. I would meet with lawyers or meet with companies and determine what their facts were, what the case was about, and then either help determine what the damages were for a company or help determine what a rebuttal of damages might be.

In addition to that, the practice area that I worked in also did mergers and acquisitions type work. So we would do valuations of companies on behalf of companies that were looking to buy divisions or buy smaller companies and do due diligence investigations, that kind of thing.

Q. Mr. Rowsky, do you have a CPA?

A. I am a CPA, that's correct.

Q. And you have a CMA?

A. That's correct.

Q. What's a CMA?

A. A CMA is a certificate in management accounting. While I was at RXY Capital, it was viewed as a positive thing to study for, sit and take a test, which is a two and a half day test for determining your skill and expertise in performing management accounting functions—internal reporting, taxes, decision analysis, that kind of thing. So I studied for, sat for and passed that exam in 1983.

Q. Mr. Rowsky, can you tell the jury what experience you have in performing lost profit and price erosion damages calculations in patent infringement cases such as this one?

A. Sure. There are a number of different ways that damages can be calculated in projects, whether they are intellectual property or not. One way is an out-of-pocket loss, which is common. Another way is lost profits, which is also common, determining what sales were lost and then what were the profits lost from them.

Then there is a variety of other means. Calculating damages could be a pricing type claim. It could be the loss of value of a company's stock, a variety of different ways. Specifically in an intellectual property case, lost profits is very common because a machine or a device that has a patent which is allegedly being infringed takes sales away from a company who holds the patent.

Q. While you were at Big Accounting Firm, were there other people within the firm who also did a similar type of work?

A. Yes. When I joined the group in '90, I was the fourth person in that group. And the group would fluctuate from '90 through '97 between that four up to approximately twelve people.

Q. Were there also people outside of the local office who did this type of work at the firm?

A. Yes. There's actually about six hundred people across the U.S. involved at Big Accounting Firm that would be performing the activities similar to what I just described.

Q. Can you tell the jury over the last, let's just say, eight or nine years, have you had conversations with others who do this type of work either at the firm or other places?

A. Yes. At Big Accounting Firm, there would be regular meetings of litigation practitioners and mergers and acquisitions practitioners, probably for the most part twice a year to get together and talk about different approaches, different processes, different cases that have been determined and just good practices for investigating and for evaluating and calculating out-of-pocket claims, lost profit claims, damage claims.

Q. Have you also talked with others in this field who don't necessarily work at the firm over the last several years?

A. Yes, I have.

Q. Have you attended seminars from time to time that cover topics on these types of issues?

A. Yes. And I have also been a presenter at a number of legal seminars as a damage claim expert.

Q. So do you have a general understanding of the type of information that's relied on in these types of investigations?

A. Oh, yes, I do.

Q. Did you use that type of information in this investigation?

A. Yes, I did.

Q. Was that the type of information that's reasonably relied upon?

A. Yes.

Q. Let's turn to this case. Were you hired by Law Firm in September of 1997 to perform an analysis of damages?

A. Yes, I was.

Q. Why don't you tell the jury what you were asked to do, what was your task and then tell us what type of information you gathered as you began performing this task?

A. Well, I was initially given information about the case, about the plaintiff, Hayseeder, and about the defendant, Machine Systems, information background in terms of what the companies were like, how long they'd been in business, what their products and size was, what the complaint and the answer indicated.

I was given access to all of the documents that were produced in discovery, but I would focus in on principally the financial documents, documents that relate to the company's sales, pricing, the quantity of units sold, the costs, customers, price lists, dealers.

I'd look at tax returns, product brochures, that kind of information, to get a good understanding of the products we're talking about, the selling price, the margin or the cost and the margin and the number of units sold, specifically by the defendant, Machine Systems.

Q. Mr. Rowsky, do you have some exhibits in front of you beginning with Plaintiff's Exhibit 25 to your right?

A. Yes, I do.

Q. We're not going to go through all of those. Is that a collection of exhibits that were prepared that relate to your report?

A. Yes. At least these are some of them.

Q. Sure. Now, Mr. Rowsky, did you file, or did you write an initial report in this case?

A. Yes. I prepared a preliminary report in October of '97.

Q. And did you then issue a final report?

A. That's correct.

Q. When was that?

A. That was in April of this year.

Q. And can you tell the jury what kind of information you had when you formed your initial report versus your final report?

A. When I prepared my report in October of '97, discovery was under way, but it was not complete. And so the information I had about the number of sales, the number of units that had been sold by Machine Systems was for a short time period. I believe it started in October or November of '95, and it went through an interim time period.

Q. Then what happened when you got to the final report?

A. In fact, after I issued that report, I had asked for more information, which came in between the time I issued the October report and sometime early in April. Then I was provided more information that was helpful to me in terms of determining the number of units sold, the type of units, the revenue value or the sales value of those units. And the information that was provided I believe was up through April 16th of this year.

Q. Mr. Rowsky, based on your investigation and your general experience, have you formed an opinion as to the amount of damages that the plaintiff has incurred in this case?

A. Yes, I have.

Q. Is that set forth in Plaintiff's Exhibit 25, which is already admitted into evidence?

A. Yes, it is.

Q. I'll put this up on the ELMO. Can you tell us, first of all, what's this? What's Exhibit 25?

A. This is a document that was included as an exhibit to my April report, and I have titled it "The Damage Claim Summary." And it breaks down the damage claim.

The damage claim that I have determined in this case is $1,549,271. And that is for sales of Machine Systems through April 16th of 1998. And it's broken into two parts. One part is the lost profits to Hayseeder on the lost sales of machines, and then a price erosion claim or a reduced selling price that Hayseeder was forced to provide as a result of Machine Systems' pricing actions.

Q. I want to make sure something is very clear. Did you do any investigation as to whether the defendant infringed plaintiff's patent?

A. No, I did not.

Q. So for purposes of your opinion on damages, just to be clear, you are assuming that the jury finds that the defendant has infringed plaintiff's patent, correct?

A. That's correct. I am not an expert on patent infringement or patents and just accepted that the defendant has infringed the patent that's at issue in this case.

Q. So if we change the assumption, if the assumption was the defendant was not infringing, then the damages would be zero, correct?

A. Yes.

Q. Now, I notice that your first category is lost profits. Why don't you tell us what are lost profits, what's the methodology and how did you get to that number? I have Plaintiff's Exhibit 26. Would it assist you if I put that up there?

A. Yes.

Q. The jury is going to have this back in the jury room. This is Plaintiff's Exhibit 26.

A. Yes.

Q. Go ahead, Mr. Rowsky.

A. This exhibit was also in my April report. And this is a step-by-step approach to coming up with the amount of dollars that are included in the lost profits claim.

The first step is determine how many of the Machine Systems' units that were infringing were sold that were appropriate for inclusion in the damage claim. So I looked at the information that had been provided by Machine Systems, and they had provided a listing, many pages, of the machines that they had sold by serial number and by date and by customer.

I went through that list and determined which of the machines that had been sold were—there were some serial numbers that were on that list that weren't sold. They went to shows for show purposes. They went for demonstration models. So those models I did not count because they were weren't actually sales even though they were listed.

Then I identified the different types of sales they had. Some of the machines were sold to their dealers, which would mean a dealer price. Some of the machines were sold to end using customers, which would be a different price. Then they have different models. They have models that are sold to the sod industry for sod applications and models that are sold for gravel applications to the gravel industry.

Q. We've heard about the sod industry?

A. Yes.

Q. What does the number "529" represent?

A. It represents the number of machines that Machine Systems sold to the sod industry from the earliest point, I believe November of '95, through April 16, 1998 that were actually sold to either end users, customers or to their dealers.

Q. Mr. Rowsky, did you count any of the machines that were sold to the gravel or sand industries?

A. No. Those were excluded. They were not included.

Q. Why was that?

A. Because I understand Hayseeder and Machine Systems to be primary competitors in the sod industry. So that's where I focused my damage claim evaluation, where they'd be principal competitors.

Q. So we understand that Machine Systems sold 529 to this sod industry, correct?

A. That's correct.

Q. You heard opposing counsel talk about your numbers being in general agreement?

A. This number of 529 is broken down on another exhibit that I included in my report by year. I heard yesterday you mentioned some of those numbers, and he seemed to believe that that calculation or the amount by year of units was correct.

Q. So if we know they sold 529 units, can you tell us what are lost profits? What does that mean?

A. Well, the lost profits is the end result of the process that I go through. But it's the actual profits that Hayseeder lost by not being able to sell those machines because someone else was selling an infringing machine to customers, end users and perhaps dealers that Hayseeder would have sold but for Machine Systems' unit sales.

Q. You are testifying in your analysis these would be sales that Hayseeder could have made.

A. Actually, as I go through this, not a hundred percent of those. My calculation does not indicate that they would have sold all of those, but 90 percent of them.

Q. Mr. Rowsky, why don't you just take us down this chart and explain what this shows.

A. As I mentioned, I determined of these units sold which ones were sold to dealers and which were sold to customers. Using Hayseeder's pricing, I plugged in end user customer pricing for those sold to end users and dealer pricing for those sold to dealers and determined the sales value or revenue value of those units. And that is as I've labeled here, the total revenues would be $1,937,114.

Q. How did you come up with the next item?

A. I understand that Hayseeder and Machine Systems are primary competitors, but I also understand that there may be other people in the marketplace selling similar units or selling units to those applications, not many units, not many competitors, but I did want to give some indication that there were some other people out in the marketplace perhaps competing with them, perhaps selling units. So I factored it down by using a 90 percent, meaning not every single unit that Machine Systems sold Hayseeder would have sold, but nine out of ten units Hayseeder would have sold because of their relative market share of 90–95 percent.

Q. Let's go down to Hayseeder's lost sales. How do you figure that?

A. After determining what the total revenues were on the 529 machines and then multiplying that by the 90 percent market share, you arrive at Hayseeder's lost sales of $1,743,403.

Q. Keep going.

* * *

Q. On this chart that we prepared for trial, was there a mix-up on the names on one of these two?

A. Yes. As I was looking at this in preparation for testimony, I noticed that the model names were not correct. On 1998, if you look, there are five models listed. All of the amounts are correct, but the model name down on the bottom, you'll see there are two Model 3s. And the bottom one should be Model 3X. That was inadvertently omitted from the schedule.

Q. Okay.

A. There were similar model corrections for 1997 as well.

Q. And did that affect the substance of your opinion?

A. No. The actual amounts and the quantities of units and the dollar amounts and pricing is all correct, but the reference to the correct model was incorrect.

Q. No further questions.

Appendix J

Sample Closing Argument #1

SAMPLE CLOSING ARGUMENT #1

THE COURT: Thank you. Mr. Gross.

MR. GROSS: Thank you, your honor.

I want to start out by thanking all seven of you for sitting in on this trial. It's not easy to sit in on a trial because you can't ask any questions and you really don't know what's going on because you haven't talked to the witnesses before they came, and all of you listened carefully and I think really showed that you're going to give a fair result, and that's all the Culpeppers want is a fair result.

I also want to say something about everybody in the courtroom. You may be thinking I'm going to stand up and talk about the evil empire and the evil defendant, but I'm not going to do that. I have nothing against the defendant, and neither do the Culpeppers.

This isn't a case where everybody hates each other. It isn't one of those cases. It's simply a case where the Judge is going to give you some instructions, you're going to read those rules, and then based on the evidence you're going to decide whether we've proven our case with the evidence, all right? So we're not looking for sympathy, oh, my goodness, these poor homeowners, let's write out a check. I have tried as hard as anybody can try to have witnesses come in and testify to what I'm proving and to have documents come in to show what I'm proving. In other words, I want to prove my case to you. That's why we want to win damages, not because we want any sympathy.

Well, let's start out by talking about evidence, and I want to focus solely on evidence. Mr. Grimsrud, when he just gave his closing argument, said a lot of things that have almost nothing to do with evidence. There was no evidence about the property value of the Culpepper home. Do I care? No. But my point is you have to talk about evidence, what witnesses said and what documents came in. I mean there was no evidence that Home Builder Company didn't know about the warranty approval by Warranty Company. I mean there was no witness from Home Builder Company who said, "You know, I never knew that. That's interesting to know. Oh, my goodness. You're kidding. Oh, wow, that's fascinating." No one said that. There's no evidence that Home Builder Company didn't know that.

You have to rely, when you go back in the jury room, on what people said on the witness stand under oath, and there is a good reason for that because I could tell you all kinds of things to try to get—to win the case; but if you haven't heard it from a witness, you know, what's—how is that—how is that any good? So let's stick with the evidence. What did I say at the start of this case? I said at the start of this case that this is a case where the Home Builder Company actually admitted that there is a major structural defect in the home. Remember when I said that? That was one of the big lines that came out of my mouth. And then I said they actually accepted responsibility, and then I said they did nothing. And it was my job to prove that with evidence and testimony, and that's what I did.

Let's talk about whether Home Builder Company admitted that there was a major structural defect. First of all, very curious, did you notice there wasn't a single Home Builder Company witness who said there wasn't a major structural defect? In other words, Bob Smith didn't take the stand and say, "Well, you know, we were—we didn't believe it was a major structural defect all the time. We thought it was the deck that caused the problems in the house" or "Well, let me tell you, those damages are cosmetic" or "It's not affecting the load-bearing portion of the home." He never said that. Smith said, "I visited the home," and it's Exhibit 45—Exhibit 45 is the submission to Warranty Company in the spring of 1996. Smith took that exhibit, and he walked through the Culpeppers' home, and he verified all of the structural damage to the home, so there is no dispute. The Home Builder Company fact witness, Mr. Smith, the former warranty manager, signed off on that submission to Warranty Company. He said it on the witness stand. Mrs. Culpepper said it. There's no disagreement about memory. So in that sense Home Builder Company through a witness at trial was acknowledging that there was a major structural defect, that there was this damage to the home that's in that submission.

And Jim Randall took the stand, and did you notice that not even once did Mr. Randall say, "Well, you know, I've been to the home—" he said he visited the home. He didn't say, "and, you know, these damages are just cosmetic" or, "You know, it's pretty clear that it's the deck that caused the problems in the house. That was obvious to me." He's been in the construction industry for twenty years, all right? So if one—one person's going to be able to make some observations, it's going to be Mr. Randall, but he didn't say that.

So there is no witness from Home Builder Company who is disputing what the Culpeppers said, and I find that fascinating, that a multi-million-dollar company that builds thousands of homes, largest home builder in the state, knows what it's talking about, they don't bring a witness to contest anything the Culpeppers have said about their home, and that's what I mean when I say the Home Builder Company acknowledged that there was a major structural defect that they had admitted.

And there's more. There is a letter from Mr. Wong that was sent in the summer in which he said "we believe there are structural issues." "Based on your engineering report, we believe there are structural issues." He used the word "we." He was the authorized attorney. Remember I asked Mr. Smith and Mr. Randall, Mr. Wong is he the authorized attorney? Sure, he was the person in charge of telling the Culpeppers what their—what Home Builder Company believed. Mr. Wong was meeting with Jim Randall. He was meeting with Bob Smith. And he said we believe, based on your engineer's report, that there probably are structural issues. That's called an admission. They're admitting it, that there are structural issues.

But there's something even more significant. And again, this is evidence, proof that you will have back in the jury room based on testimony about Home Builder Company admitting there is a construction defect. Remember at the beginning of the case when I said that our engineering expert, Sandy Moss, is one of Home Builder Company's experts, too. I tried to prove that to you, and I want to tell you now how I proved it to you with evidence. Mr. Moss took the stand and said he's been hired by Home Builder Company. He's been—received money from Home Builder Company in the past. He had his secretary check his records. He's worked with Home Builder Company six times since 1996, three times where he's paid by Home Builder Company, three times where he's working with Home Builder Company. In addition, he is approved by Home Builder Company. Home Builder Company approves his hiring by the Culpeppers. They say, "Yes, we approve." This is evidence and testimony from Mrs. Culpepper, Bob Smith. It's all undisputed. Why did they approve him, by the way? They approved Sandy Moss because he's a fantastic engineer, he's very objective, and he's very truthful, and he calls it as he sees them, and he's been doing that for twenty years—thirty years. You saw him testify.

Real quick question, if someone had a problem with their home and they were trying to determine whether it's a major structural defect or whether it's a deck or whether it's water, whatever it is, who would they call? They would call Sandy Moss, and that's because he's a trustworthy, objective engineer.

Home Builder Company approved his hiring. They even agreed to pay for his services. In that sense they're hiring Sandy Moss. If you're paying for the guy, obviously you're signing off. You wouldn't pay for someone you didn't find trustworthy.

But there's something that is such incredible confirmation that Home Builder Company admitted there is a major structural defect, and I don't know if you caught it because, you know, when you have a four-day trial there is testimony flying all over the place, so I just want to take one second on this one.

We sue Home Builder Company in January of 2000. Do you remember what Mr. Carter said? He said the parties were in an adversarial relationship. Guess what? He's right. When you get served with a lawsuit, that's kind of a signal that there's an adversarial relationship going on. That's just the first hint that maybe you've got a problem, right? If you're a corporation and homeowners sue you for damages, they say you broke your word, they say there's a major construction defect, at that point in time you're thinking, okay, I've got a problem, we're in an adversarial relationship.

And what does Home Builder Company do? Well, we know it has no basis for defending the suit. That's all admitted. But they eventually hire this trial expert, Dr. Green, and we all know that he's a trial expert. That's what forensic means. He does trial testimony. He's been in over two hundred lawsuits. He's only here for the trial, never worked with Home

Builder Company before, advertises in *Claims Magazine*. I mean he's just a trial expert. We know that. Doesn't mean he's a bad guy. He certainly earns a good living, but he's a trial expert, only here for this trial this week, no other reason. We all know that.

But what's fascinating is he comes out in April and he says it's obvious that it's the deck, clear as can be there's no major structural defect. Dr. Green is hired as a trial expert for Home Builder Company, and he says it's as obvious as can be, and he tells everybody on that side of the fence what the story is. And what does Home Builder Company do in the fall of 2000? We're now nine months into this lawsuit. Dr. Green has already told everybody his calculations, his report, everything. Who does Jim Randall, the corporate designee of Home Builder Company, and Bob Smith, the warranty manager—who do they call to consult about whether some local decks are causing damage to homes, whether it's a major structural defect in those local homes? They don't call their trial expert, Dr. Green. Instead, they call our expert, Sandy Moss. Do you remember Sandy Moss testified, he said, yes, there were some decks in the area, and Jim Randall and Bob Smith called me to look into the problem for them. Well, there's only one reason they called him, and that's because they trust his opinion. And they obviously could have called Dr. Green. They didn't because he's only a trial expert.

Can you imagine the situation in some sort of product case, you know, product defect, say you want to sue somebody and the company signs off on an expert, signs off on his conclusions and actually hires him during the lawsuit because they trust his opinion?

And that's pretty simple. We all know there is a major structural defect, and we all know Home Builder Company knows that. That's why they call Sandy Moss when they need help.

There are a few more reasons. Do you remember when I asked Bob Smith, I said, "If you even suspect there's an alternative cause, like a deck or something like that, what do you do?"

And he testified under oath that they immediately tell the homeowners. Remember I said, you know, "In your practice and policy when there is a serious issue and you think there might be alternative explanation, don't you tell the homeowners?"

He says, "Right away," and that's because that's the fair thing to do, absolutely, you always do that.

Home Builder Company never even suggested to the Culpeppers that there was an alternative theory, that it wasn't a major construction defect. They never did that.

Now, there is one other thing, and there is no easy way to talk about this because it's—it was kind of a dramatic moment I thought. I'm probably the only one, but it's worth talking about. I put Jim Randall on the stand, and I asked him "Are you the corporate designee?"

And he said yes.

I said, "Are you authorized to be here?"

He said yes.

"Okay. Do you understand you're talking to the jury?"

"Yes."

"Do you understand you're about to give Home Builder Company's position?"

"Sure."

Okay. I mean I was really careful. I know I tend to ask 12 questions on the same thing, but I was very careful to get it clear to Mr. Randall that I want to know Home Builder Company's official position once and for all. And I asked him, I said, "with respect to the warranty under the State Statute—" I used the phrase "State Statute," and I said, "As we sit here today in front of this jury," he's up there on the stand, I said, "I'm correct that it's the position of Home Builder Company as we sit here today that this—" remember I pointed to zero "—that this is the amount of money that Home Builder Company will honor under its warranty?"

And do you remember what his answer was? His answer was "I would say no." That was not the position. He wasn't about to tell you that it's Home Builder Company's position that there is no major structural defect and, therefore, the Culpeppers get zero under the warranty.

Now, in what other case does a corporate designee, given the official position of the corporation, say, "Okay, we will honor the statutory warranty. I'm not saying we're not going to honor the warranty and that the Culpeppers get zero." I'm not sure what more I could have done to prove that Home Builder Company admitted there was a major structural defect. With all the witnesses and all the evidence I think that's pretty clear.

And so now we go to the next point, and that is Home Builder Company accepts responsibility for reasonable repair, and this is a separate issue. This is this promissory estoppel claim. Smith agreed to pay for the engineering fees and to work with the Culpeppers. Mr. Wong sent a voice mail to the Culpeppers. He sent the letters. And you know what? Read the letters. You can interpret the letters.

Here is the question. It's one very simple question. Did Home Builder Company make a deal? Okay. That's it. That's it. In fact, I'm going to go with their lawyer, Mr. Grimsrud. Let's

314

make that the test. I think that's the test. We'll call it the deal test. If you have a deal, you know it's firm and definite, you know you can rely on it, you know you're working together, you know you got a deal. We've heard that phrase "A deal's a deal," and you've heard the phrase "You're not backing out of the deal, are you?" And that's how we live our life. That's what a promise is. If somebody makes a firm and definite promise, you got to say to yourself, okay, we got a deal. Listen to the Judge's instructions, and you hear about whether there is a promise, whether it's firm and definite, whether there was reliance. That's another way of saying do we have a deal.

August 16, 3 P.M., this is in Exhibit 23, you will be having this, it's submitted into evidence, point 31 of Mrs. Culpepper's chronology that she gave to Home Builder Company, every single point that had happened. This is the package Home Builder Company didn't respond to. I want to read you a quote out of this packet. This is evidence admitted into trial.

The note refers to Mr. Wong talking on a voice mail: "I'm sending you a letter back. I don't want you to get the wrong idea that we're backing out of the deal, but your August 5 letter makes it sound as if you have a blank check for remediation, and obviously we could never do that. What we want to do is get the engineering report. Let us see it. Let us talk about it and let's go from there because obviously if you have structural problems, and we think you do from things you have submitted and stuff, but we want to see an engineering report to confirm that, there shouldn't be any problem that Home Builder Company will cover it." That's the deal, okay?

The deal had nothing to do with Warranty Company. The deal wasn't, "Sorry, we can't do anything. Submit your claim to Warranty Company. I'll talk to you later." Mr. Carter suggested that. Only one problem. You have to have evidence. In other words, you have to say, "And the witnesses said this was the deal" or "the documents show this was the deal." That's what I meant about evidence. We can all say what we want in closing to be persuasive, but it has to be based on evidence. And what I just read to you is admitted evidence in this trial of a deal. And you know what? Everyone and their mother and father knows that Home Builder Company made a deal with the Culpeppers in the summer through their authorized representative, Mr. Wong, and through Bob Smith. And the deal was as simple as can be. It was guess what, you don't have a blank check. You don't do the over-priced repair that Mr. Moss was talking about, which they didn't do. Remember he talked about the blank check repair? You're not getting the blank check, but we will pay the reasonable cost of the repair. One caveat, we want to see the engineering report and evaluate it, make sure there's structural issues.

Undisputed fact, Bob Smith reviewed both engineering reports and approved them. He said that under oath on the stand. Not a single witness was ever presented who said, from Home Builder Company, "We didn't have a deal," who said, "Well, let me tell you my understanding," "Well, actually, what I said was this." Nothing. Home Builder Company chose not to put any witnesses on the stand to dispute what the Culpeppers said. So we have an undisputed fact that there was a deal created, and Home Builder Company knows that.

Now there is a little—there is a section in a promise claim about injustice. One question, should you enforce this promise, you as the members of the jury enforce this promise against Home Builder Company and require them to pay for the repair—and by the way, the Judge will tell you this, but on the promise claim—well, I'll come back to damages, but make sure you subtract the Warranty Company payment. The Culpeppers have already got the Warranty Company money. They don't want the Warranty Company money from you. If you give them the Warranty Company money, I'll have more problems, so we don't want the Warranty Company money, and I'll talk about that in a minute.

Let's talk about Exhibit 23. On October 4, 2000, the Culpeppers sent a packet to the head of Home Builder Company, and they said you're backing out of a deal. And you can cross-examine Mrs. Culpepper all you want. She had some concerns in August, but she was still comfortable there was a deal. It's not as if the Culpeppers thought, oh, yeah, Home Builder Company has just decided we are completely breaking off all communications. You can read the chronology, read the letters. There is no question there is a deal.

But anyway, look at this: October 4, 2000, the Culpeppers send a plea for help to the head of the company, and now let me tell you more evidence that I showed you to prove my case. I asked Bob Smith "If this was given to you, what would you do?"

He said, "I would respond."

Remember when I said, "In your wildest dreams—" I either said "In your wildest dreams" or "In a million years would you ever not respond?"

And he said no.

And I said, "That's because that wouldn't be fair?"

He said, "That's right. That wouldn't be right."

I said, "Exactly. You'd never consciously fail to respond to this?"

He said, "Of course, I would never do that."

Whose side, by the way, is Bob Smith on in this case in terms of evidence and testimony? Who did he testify in favor of in terms of whether there was a deal, whether we should work things out, whether Home Builder Company should pay for the costs of the repair. And God bless him, because he is now working with a company that is getting business from Home Builder Company, but he stood up there and told the truth.

But you know what? Jim Randall, sitting right here, the corporate designee, took the stand, and I said, "Mr. Randall, would you respond promptly to something like this if you were given it?" Now, that's not an easy question when you're the corporate designee sitting through this lawsuit. And guess what he said? "I would respond promptly, of course I would."

And again, I'm proving my case with evidence and witnesses. The president said he gave this package to John Morris, and he said, "Handle it." John Morris gave the package to Bob Smith, and Bob Smith gave it to the attorney, Mr. Wong, but they never responded to the Culpeppers. And I've proven to you through evidence, through witnesses, through testimony that that was really, really bad.

And when Mr. Grimsrud was trying to talk to you about there's some Warranty Company thing and, oh, the Culpeppers broke their promise—the only problem with that is there is no evidence, and in a trial you got to have testimony, you got to put someone on the stand and talk about your Warranty Company theory, and you got to explain why that is. You can't just stand up and say it. So I've proven to you there was a deal, and I've proven to you they backed out of it and that was really wrong and that they should have responded to this, and we all know that. We all know that next time Home Builder Company gets a package they're going to pick up the phone and call the homeowners. They're not going to not call and then two years later defend themselves in a trial by suggesting that the homeowners did something wrong. Everybody in this courtroom knows that.

So, I'm sorry, Home Builder Company, you have to pay for the reasonable cost of repair because you promised to, and the reasonable costs of repair, I will tell you, is what they have spent on the repair minus the payment by Warranty Company, and that's our promise claim.

Now, I want to talk for a few minutes about Dr. Green. When you come to the issue of major structural defect, the answer is yes. And the reason the answer is yes is for all the reasons I've given, but I'm going to ask you to do this, simply rely on Sandy Moss. If you think Sandy Moss perjured himself, if you think he's not reliable and trustworthy, then don't find a major structural defect. But if you think he tried to explain as carefully as he can why there is a major structural defect, then find there is a major structural defect.

And by the way, we didn't need to bring Sandy Moss here. We could have just said Home Builder Company's admitted it, because, you know, when you get in an argument you say to somebody, "Well, hold on. Don't start telling me all this stuff. You just admitted it five minutes ago," right? I mean sometimes that happens in our life. Well, Home Builder Company admitted there was a major structural defect in about five hundred different ways, as I've proven to you. But still, we still put Sandy Moss on the stand, and he explained that to you. Who would someone rely on, Sandy Moss or Dr. Green, their house was having a problem? Who would Home Builder Company rely on, and who would the Culpeppers rely on and who would everyone in this courtroom rely on?

Dr. Green is a professional trial expert from *Claims Magazine*. He didn't do a report. I mean he didn't do a report. He didn't do any drafts. It's been his practice since 1980 to throw out drafts. That's fine, but all that says is the only time the Culpeppers heard his theory was at trial. I think that's strange. I mean when Sandy Moss does a report and sends it to Home Builder Company and they say it looks—they say it looks good, when our damage expert does a report, their damage expert even did a report, well, one thing Dr. Green should have done is a report to do peer review so people can look at it. He didn't do that. He did talk about peer review as involving Mr. Carter and his law firm, but that's not really peer review. I mean that's helping the opinion. Peer review means objective, independent review.

Now what I want to do is I want to talk to you for a couple minutes about damages for our major construction defect claim.

* * *

So that's our position on damages, but I want to return to Dr. Green for a moment. We showed Dr. Green a foundation crack. A deck can't cause a foundation crack. He admitted that. We showed him a picture. Remember the blown-up picture? Dr. Green didn't analyze the actual deck. Do you remember he said he did it off the plans and then he agreed that plans can be wrong? And in fact, he got some things wrong. Remember he thought that it had been twisted in with deck screws, that if you went—if you walked around the deck, it was all deck screws. That was actually wrong. It was nails. And he admitted he wasn't really sure where the bolts were.

What Dr. Green was doing is what every trial expert does, and that's build a theory, kind of build an argument. And that's fine, but that's academic. If you're going to prove that the deck is causing damage to the home, you have to have evidence and testimony. And if your trial exhibits actually don't conform to the deck, then your whole theory does—it doesn't matter. You have to prove it. They didn't prove it.

All right. So why are we here? We're not here because Mrs. Culpepper made edits to a soil report. You're probably wondering, you know, why did Gross—why did he introduce Mrs. Culpepper's edits of the soil report on those fancy exhibits? Was that some sort of trial trick? No. It's because I wanted to show you at the end of the case that all the exhibits that Home Builder Company has are trial exhibits. In other words, they're just for the trial. You know, they are the fancy trial exhibit kind for Dr. Green.

They didn't offer a single note from Home Builder Company. They talk about Mrs. Culpepper being meticulous. This is a multi-million-dollar company, builds homes all around the country. It took no notes? Does that make any sense? It took no notes in the Culpepper matter. Nope, never took a note, no internal memos. Does that make sense to you? No internal reports, nothing? And they are criticizing Mrs. Culpepper because she made some edits to a soil report? Can a company really say that, that we took no notes, that we have no evidence?

* * *

But when a homeowner, a mother with two children makes some edits to a soil engineering report and saves the drafts, don't tell me she did something wrong because she didn't. And when she gives you the drafts and says, "Do what you want," what's the point? Why do we spend hours and hours this week talking about the edits? It's not to show that she's a bad person or she did something wrong. It's not to show Sandy Moss is unprofessional. We all know he is professional. Home Builder Company acknowledges that. It's just irrelevant.

And does that have anything to do with damages, by the way? No. I think there is one reason, one reason that Home Builder Company has taken the position of attacking those soil reports, and that's because they contain a dirty little secret, and Sandy Moss explained this to you. Do you remember when he said that when you look at the soil borings, which Home Builder Company didn't want to do, you notice that there is a problem with the pad. In other words, when they built the home, they made a mistake. They kind of screwed up on the pad. Well, Home Builder Company did not want to know if there was a problem with the pad. It didn't want to know if there was a problem with the fill. It just wanted to pay for the repair. Why would Home Builder Company say, "Don't do soil borings. They are unnecessary"? They would say that for one reason, because they believe there is a major structural defect and they don't need to know why. Because they have agreed to pay for the repairs and so they don't care what's going on, so why do soil borings? So Home Builder Company didn't want the soil borings done. The Culpeppers did them because Sandy Moss said you should, they are part of the repair. And what they found was that Home Builder Company had made a mistake in building the home.

* * *

Another thing I found fascinating was Dr. Green didn't suggest otherwise. You've got your trial expert on the stand. Okay, Dr. Green, did they screw up on the pad? Did they screw up on the fill? They didn't even ask him. That's why Home Builder Company took the offensive on the soil borings, because it wanted you to not see that they had made a mistake because in a construction defect case, even though we just have to show actual damage to the load-bearing portion, which there obviously is, it's kind of nice if you know why. You kind of like to say, you know, I'm still curious as to what went wrong in the construction, even though we don't have to prove that. There's no instruction from the Judge we have to prove what went wrong, but it's kind of nice to know. Home Builder

Company didn't want you to know that, but you do, and it's under oath. And guess what? It's undisputed, undisputed.

Home Builder Company had a choice. I tried to prove to you this trial as clearly as I could that it had acknowledged there was a structural defect, that it had accepted responsibility and that it did nothing and that that was really, really, really, really, really, really wrong. It should not have done that.

The choice was do the repair. The Culpeppers, testified under oath that what they would have preferred is if in the spring of 2000, Home Builder Company would have just done the repair. Was this a big scheme to make money? Which do you think the Culpeppers would rather have had, Home Builder Company just completely handle the repair; they hire their people; Bob Smith runs everything; they just say, "We will just take care of it"; Culpeppers don't even know what they are doing, okay—you know how that happens sometimes, you know, the company just takes care of it. I've got a—you know, you've got a boiler problem, I've got a, you know, basement water problem and they just say, "You know what, sir, ma'am, we will take care of it."

That's what they wanted, okay? If you asked them which would you rather have, Home Builder Company just handling the repair and your home is going to drop in value, okay, you might not get everything you want, they'd say I'd much rather have that. And what if I said, "Well, hold on. You might get damages two years from now, after litigation, after you sit through a full-week trial, after you get cross-examined." They'd say no, thank you, no, I don't want that. I seriously don't want that. This is the lesser of what they want, and that's clear. And again, I've proved that. I put them—I had them look you in the eyes and tell you that.

But guess what? Home Builder Company chose not to do the repair, and in America you can do that. But if you choose not to do the repair, then you should pay for it. Home Builder Company was going to pay for it, and they assured them they would pay for it. We all know that, by the way. Lawyers can write whatever they want in letters. If you read the letters, listen to the testimony, read the chronology, they had a deal. I mean there is no question they had a deal based on evidence.

But you know what? If you agree to pay for repairs and then you stop and do nothing and you do what everyone says is one of the most unfair things in the world, which is not to even respond, and then you get sued and you have no basis for denying it but you deny it anyway and you hire a trial expert and you play hardball and you go for it and you do it and you fight and you lose, well, guess what? You made a choice. The choice you made was to breach the warranty. That's fine. You can do that; but if you choose to breach the warranty, then pay full damages. You got to make—you got to compensate them fully.

Home Builder Company made the choice. The Culpeppers didn't make the choice. The Culpeppers sent that package to Home Builder Company and begged Home Builder

Company to call them, begged Home Builder Company to call them. Home Builder Company didn't call them. They admit that was the worst thing they ever could have done. Under oath witnesses said, "I would never do that to homeowners." But they did it. And if you do that, if you consciously breach a warranty, then you pay full damages, not excessive, but full damages.

And you know what? A good lesson, the lesson is do the repair. Do the repair. I promise you that's the lesson. I promise you the next time Jim Randall even gets wind of something like this, Home Builder Company will do the repair. Or if you promise to do the repair and pay for it, they will pay for it. I promise you that. But if you choose to play hardball, you choose to go to trial, you choose to say no major structural defect, everything is cosmetic, but you don't bring any witnesses and you don't bring any evidence and it's basically undisputed that you've acknowledged the problem and agreed to the repair, then you're going to pay, and you're going to pay full damages based on what the members of the community who have lived their whole lives dealing with people in all kinds of different ways decide what's fair. Okay, Home Builder Company? That's the lesson.

And that's not Jim Randall's fault. He had nothing to do with this in the fall. I'm saying that on the record with a transcript. It's not Bob Smith's fault. He never would have done this. He said that. He had no idea this was happening. And it's not the president of the company's fault. He gave it to T. J. Budd. And it's not Mr. Wong's fault. Read his voice mails. He sounds like the nicest man in the world. Read his letters. They are the most polite letters you could read, "I have patience. You have patience." Bob Smith testified the Culpeppers had patience. Bob Smith had patience. Everyone had patience.

There's one human being who is responsible for this decision. His name is T. J. Budd. He got the engineering invoice, didn't want to pay it. He got the package from the president, was told to handle it. He was the one talking to Mr. Wong. It wasn't Jim Randall. The buck stops there. T. J. Budd is the head of the local division. Guess what, Mr. Budd? If you decide to play hardball, then you're going to pay for the breach of warranty.

That's your lesson. Next time don't play hardball.

Thank you, Your Honor.

THE COURT: Thank you very much.

PTM

Appendix K

Sample Closing Argument #2

SAMPLE CLOSING ARGUMENT #2

MR. GROSS: May it please the Court, members of the jury, parties and defense counsel. I want to begin by extending my professional courtesy to counsel for the defendants. You probably notice we get along quite well and we're good friends. We have enjoyed the trial, although it has been a very hard battle as you can tell and we each really want to win for our clients. But I do want to say I enjoy trials when each side's counsel is treating each other with respect and trying to make this an enjoyable experience for the jury. So I appreciate that.

I would also like to take just a moment, as I traditionally do, to thank the members of the jury for paying attention. I've sat on a jury. I know what it's like. You have witnesses out in the hall. You don't what they're going to say. You can't ask questions. You don't know why some people are asking questions. Everything is thrown together. It's extremely frustrating. You add sod feeders to the equation and it's a long week. So I want to thank you for paying such good attention.

What I am going to do today is I am going to talk to you about one thing and one thing alone, evidence. Because you know what? There is only one way to win a trial. Evidence. If you don't have it, you lose. If I don't have it, I lose. If they don't have it, they're in trouble. If I prove my case and they don't have much in evidence, it's over. The process of a trial has been around in America for a long, long time and it works really well. Real simple rules. Give an opening statement, talk about what you are going to prove, prove it through evidence and then explain to the jury how you proved it. It's a great process and a great system. What I will do now, about as carefully as I can, is show you through evidence the plaintiff has proved it's case. And evidence is what wins cases.

It is true there are grave, serious consequences to this lawsuit. This is very important. Hayseeder is a local company that views this lawsuit as very, very important. And the defendant views this lawsuit as very, very important. That makes your job that much tougher and that's true. But believe me that's on both sides. And you can tell that. You saw the witnesses. You listened. You saw the pride that Mr. Hamm had in his company that he founded, that he worked for years to build up and that he now sees revenues going flat because he thinks there is an infringer. So it's very serious, that's true, on both sides.

All right. Let's talk about whether we proved in our opening statement what we said we were going to show. The first thing my partner Mr. Liebman talked about was that Mark Hamm had a great invention. He said he was going to have Mark Hamm on the stand. Mark Hamm is here in the courtroom. He is going to talk about his invention. He is going to show it to you. Well, we did that.

By the way, have we proven that our invention is a great invention? We don't have to use the word pioneering. Have we proven it's a great invention? Yes, we have.

Let's talk about evidence. Plaintiff's Exhibit 7 is an article from Sod Review, kept in a frame because there is a lot of pride in this article, dated August of 1990, almost eight years ago. And when you go back to the jury room, if you want to, you can look at Plaintiff's Exhibit 7 and that will tell you about how Mark Hamm's sod feeder revolutionized the sod industry in sod machines.

Remember how he talked about this? His sod feeder, I mean, took the market by storm. He sold a million dollars in sales within the first year. He sold five to $6 million after a few years. I mean he took over the market because he had a fantastic invention.

Now he explained to you what some of the outstanding features were of his product. Remember how he talked about the size of the product and how it fit perfectly in the sod industry, how it was a friction feeder with a deck angle and how that worked in the sod industry. It was very effective.

How he came up with a gate member and the O-ring and how in the sod industry that had been extremely effective. And he went on and on and on. We proved to you that there were outstanding features to his invention.

We also proved that Hayseeder became successful and it is a successful company that sells only feeders. This is what Hayseeder does. That's its entire business. You heard defendant talk about how they had systems to do various things, they're in various markets trying all kinds of things. That's fine. This is our company. That's why this lawsuit is important. Feeders are the whole thing that Hayseeder does.

Now, what happened here? Machine Systems wanted some of Hayseeder's profits. I think that's clear. I think we proved that. That Machine Systems saw what Hayseeder was doing and said, we want some of that. And in America it's a great thing when a competitor says I want to compete. That is what makes our country great. But the United States Constitution, and judge will instruct you as well, says you can't infringe a patent. You just can't. Obviously, you can sell something for a lower price, but if you are infringing a patent, then you have to pay damages. Mr. Scurry didn't suggest otherwise. So if you find infringement, we will get to damages and then we will talk about willfulness.

You are going to get a verdict form. The first question on the form, Do you find that plaintiff has shown by a preponderance of the evidence that the defendants have infringed Claim 1? We want you to check yes. And now I will try to show you through evidence why the answer to question one is yes. We have proven it's more likely than not that our patent was infringed.

First of all you remember Mr. Scurry in his opening statement, he said, Hayseeder is stuck with the claims. And Mr. Akers agreed. But who else is stuck with the claims? The defendant. Now, what is the claim. Claim 1 is that Plaintiff's Exhibit 1, column 7, line 48.

You will actually go back and you can turn to column 7 at line 48 and you will see Claim 1. You will also see it at Exhibit 43 and Defendant's Exhibit 27. And these are blowups of those two exhibits.

What do you do? As Mr. Akers and Mr. Milbrett, Mr. Scurry and the judge will tell you, you apply the claim, the claim to the accused device right here. All right. That's what you do. When you are trying to figure out whether there is an infringement that's the first step. Apply the claim. You don't apply the pictures in the patent. You don't say all right, I'm looking at this page, let's apply the picture. The judge will instruct you you don't do that. You heard overwhelming testimony by the end of this week, you understand you don't apply the picture, you apply the claim.

And you don't apply Hayseeder's device. The judge is going to talk to you about what's called the commercial embodiment. He is going to say you should not compare Hayseeder's device to Plaintiff's device. So for infringement you don't say, I am going to look at the Hayseeder device. I will look at the device that they're infringing. The judge is going to tell you you do not do that. All the witnesses also said that: Mr. Akers, Milbrett and Foudy. But it can be confusing, that's why I'm talking about it.

So this is the device. You apply the claims to that device. You know this by now: Infringement. Why is there infringement? You start with one question. What parts of Claim 1 literally cover this device. All right? Mr. Milbrett and Mr. Akers have talked about that. Why do we care about what parts of the device the claim literally covers? We want to know what the parties disagree about. Is this a really big agreement where there is all kinds of words people are fighting about or is it a situation where the defendants have barely escaped a few of the words?

Well, let's look. We have plaintiff's chart. You will have this back there. It says the device. Device is covered by every single word in this claim, except for the ones highlighted. A second surface means having a coefficient of friction, which is higher than the first surface means. And we know what that means, second surface means down here is higher than a little bit up here, the first surface means.

Mr. Akers, the expert for defendant, in his professional opinion, and he testified to this, said, yes, yes, yes. He agreed with Mr. Milbrett, our expert. And then he said no, and he explained that the Hayseeder device does not include a variable coefficient of friction. It has a uniform coefficient of friction. Therefore, the second surface would not have one higher than the first surface.

What do we have? We have two experts who completely agree. Mr. Akers, the defendant's expert, said yes, that was pretty much right. They agree on how it literally applies. That makes this case a simple case for you, because the first question is, all right, what do they disagree about?

Then the next question is, all right, what change did defendant do? What's the missing element that barely avoids literal infringement? By the way, this is Milbrett and Akers. Each point I make, I'm going to tell you that evidence supports, and it's almost always evidence on both sides, this isn't one of those Akers doesn't get things. I mean their expert got it and he explained it to you. It was very clear.

Why the missing element here avoids infringement. It's as simple as this: Claim 1 says you have to have a higher coefficient of friction down here where the sod comes through than the surface up here. And the judge will instruct you that the two surfaces are down here and a surface up here. That's Claim 1. That device has a surface that's the same. It's rough down here and rough up here. It's the same. That's it. Okay? No other change matters.

Did you notice that in his closing argument Mr. Scurry didn't show you defendant's big chart, which started coming out at the beginning of the trial. You know why he didn't? Because Mr. Milbrett and Mr. Akers agree that almost everything on this chart, this is an exhibit you will have, Exhibit 189, is irrelevant to this first issue of what's the missing point.

It doesn't matter if you have a curved guide plate. That doesn't matter because the claim doesn't talk about a curved guide plate. You remember Mr. Akers, he said, irrelevant, irrelevant, irrelevant. The only thing he said was relevant was that the O-ring have the same coefficient of friction. Well, guess what that means? That means this exhibit goes bye-bye. It's no longer relevant. By the way, look at what they're doing. Interesting. Machine Systems gate member. Hayseeder gate member. By gate member they mean that gate member. This isn't claim language. Mr. Akers explained you don't do this. This is not right. But since Mr. Scurry didn't talk about this exhibit, I'm not going too spend much time on it.

The next question is, all right, guys, you have this one thing. You have a uniform surface. You have an insubstantial change. Have you shown a substantial difference or is it an insubstantial difference? Mr. Milbrett, our expert, explained to you, this is not a big change. Remember when he went through friction he talked about the concepts, you got low friction up here, you have high friction at the second sheet. You have low friction down here. What happens is the sod pieces come down and stop here and go through. There are two ways to do it. You can have the different coefficient of friction so you have a slippery surface up here and these sod pieces will come down or you can work at the angle of the gate member. You work at the angle of the gate member and the sod pieces still come down substantially the same way. Interchangeable. Well known in the art. What did Mr. Milbrett say—you know, he explained all the basis that he needed to. What did Mr. Akers say? I showed him this. I said, Mr. Akers, you agree there is one way you do it where you change the coefficient of friction? *Yes.* And one way you change the angle or the downward force? Yes. This was known in the art. Sure. Well, that means that they're substantially the same way.

You don't need a Ph.D. to understand that. It's in the patents. The patents talk about that you can change the angle, you can go downward with the force, that you can change the coefficient of friction.

Now, what was critical, I asked Mr. Akers this. I said, Mr. Akers, this is the one change that matters, right? He said yes. Then I said this to Mr. Akers. Mr. Akers, was the idea of having a gate member with a uniform coefficient of friction was that well known by the people in the art? Yes. What about having a variable coefficient of friction? Yes. So was it a big change from one to the other? No. This is Michael Akers, their expert saying that this one change was nothing. It was not a big deal. It's not a big deal to take a gate member and change the surface, and that's the only thing they did to get out of literal infringement. And that's the only thing that matters and that's why this case is so simple. That's why this case is so straightforward because all the confusion is coming from that side. This is straightforward stuff.

What does it literally cover? What's the change? Is that well known? Is that easy? No witness testified and I mean no witness testified that this itself is a substantial change. Dr. Foudy did not say, well, we have a gate member and you move around the coefficient of friction and uniform coefficient of friction and that's a really big change. He didn't say that. No witness said that. That's all you have to focus on is Akers' chart.

And then he was asked, all right, is that substantially different? Is that a very big change that somebody in the art wouldn't have understood or is that not a big change? It's obviously not a big change.

We all know that by the end of this trial, because there has been no dispute about that chart. By the way, why do I keep going to the chart? Because I am trying to prove my case with evidence and it's always good if both sides agree. That's why when we came to this trial we blew up defendants' chart and we have been using it the entire trial with all the witnesses, because if everybody agrees then you don't have much work to do. And here Mr. Akers, their expert, agrees there is only one reason and it is not a big deal. He testified under the oath. It wasn't because I was asking trick questions. He was testifying under oath and he was telling the truth. That's the only question.

Now, Tom Milbrett, our expert, tried to explain to you as carefully as he could why there was infringement under the doctrine of equivalents. Why should you trust Mr. Milbrett? Well, he has been a patent attorney for almost forty years. He is past president of the Intellectual Property Association. He has written thousands of patents. He has read thousands of patents. He has sod feeder patents. But more importantly he has been practicing for forty years. All right? He has been looking clients in the eye and saying, sorry, you infringed. Or, well, I don't think you infringed. He has been doing that for over forty years and he is really proud of that. He is extremely proud to be here this week and he is proud of his opinion. But guess what? This is the first time ever in his entire career that he has come to a courtroom and testified to a jury that a device is the equivalent of a claim.

Do you think Mr. Milbrett is a hired gun? Do you think he is someone who says, yeah, I will help you win your case. Yes, let's do some illusion. Let's do some smoke and mirrors. It's fun. I love this stuff. Is that Tom Milbrett? I put it all in your hands. They obviously infringe. Tom Milbrett knows what he is talking about. If he waits forty years to take the stand and explain this to someone, they infringe. Believe Mr. Milbrett. It doesn't matter what you do, this fact alone ends it. Answer question one, yes.

Now we get to damages. If they infringe we get to damages. Well you saw how the trial began. We're talking about geez, there are a lot of competitors. Defendant will be saying well, you know, there are a lot of competitors out there. Fluid market. They're kind of fighting us on whether they're stealing our sales because we were trying to say, Mark Hamm was talking about how Hayseeder had about 85–90 percent of the market and Machine Systems was taking the sales and eroding the prices. But after a couple days it was so clear that these guys were primary competitors. I mean the marketing materials say, why is the competition complaining about us. Who is the competition? Hayseeder. They're sending rebuttal letters at each other. They're talking about the competition. It's always Hayseeder. Every witness under oath, who is your primary competitor? Hayseeder. Hayseeder. When they did their patents it was about Hayseeder pricing. Hayseeder is mentioned everywhere.

So by the time Mr. Rowsky took the stand, who is a CPA and CMA, BA and all these initials, and he has been doing this for fifteen years. He takes the stand on damages and what do they do? They don't ask him any questions. Why is that? Because we proved they're the primary competitor and they're taking sales.

Now notice by the way that their sales were pretty low in 1996, but when they got sued in early 1997, they kept right on going. In fact, they tripled their sales of this device. Remember, they do a lot of different things and they sell in different markets. This case only involves one market, sod markets in terms of damages. We are not alleging that they're the primary competitor of us in other industries. We're trying to be conservative. We're trying to base it on evidence that we know we can prove and we know we can prove that in this sod industry they're primary competitors. The gravel industry, another story. Sand industry, another story. Systems? We don't do systems. All this other fancy stuff, we don't do that. Were we careful? Did we show good judgment in seeking only damages for a market that we knew they were taking our sales? I believe we did. The evidence shows it. They didn't cross-examine Mr. Rowsky.

By the way, what's the amount of damages? You saw the number $1.5 million. I am going to tell you what the amount of damages are and I am going to say you are absolutely required to give this amount and that is: what you think is fair. Okay? That's the right amount of damages.

* * *

Now let's talk about willfulness very briefly. In opening statement Mr. Scurry said their inventor, Overbeck, did not want to infringe or copy Hamm. That's what he said. What did we prove to you. And my partner Mr. Liebman said—this in his opening statement. He said Chastain installed and trained on the Hayseeder in 1991. Chastain had Hayseeder in mind. Remember I asked Mr. Chastain that? Plaintiff's Exhibit 48, the disclosure document that was filed. Take a look at it for a second. It just mentions Hayseeder and no other company. And then it talks about the patented process that they're trying to work. No other company, Chastain admits, except Hayseeder. Then you go to the calendar entries and you will see. They're all reviewing Hayseeder sod feeders. We all know after a few days testimony that these guys were sitting there with the Hayseeder device and copying it. We have proven that to you with several different witnesses and through Exhibit 48.

Mr. Overbeck had a Hayseeder in his apartment for two months. He was asked to copy a Hayseeder. He began development only after being asked to copy. Defendant admits to copying aspects. Mr. Chastain, finally after a few questions I said, you admit you copied some of it and he said yes.

No other machines in the sod industry were bottom friction feeders that had the size, frame, gate material, O-ring, deck angle. Remember when Mr. Chastain said I didn't copy and I said, can you tell me one other machine in the industry where you could have gotten this idea and he said, no I can't. Chastain took apart a Hayseeder machine in the last few years. Just look at the devices. Chastain says there is no other device that does these things we talked about, size, frame, and a big revolutionary technology.

The other thing, did you notice as the evidence started to get clear and convincing there was a switch, big change in the defendant's theory. Beginning of the case Chastain did not copy. And by the way, in opening statement Mr. Scurry didn't say they copied some of the device, but not all of it. He didn't say, oh, sure, they looked at the device and they copied aspects of it, but not all of it. He said they did not copy. We then proved through overwhelming evidence that these guys copied a machine. Then there was a change, which happens in trials all the time. Now the experts are saying, copying is a good thing. We started to hear from Dr. Foudy and Mr. Akers, look, we like copying. That improves the market. That's fine, but a total change from what they had been saying.

All right, another issue on willfulness, did they rely on a competent opinion. Exhibit 4 is the Venturini letter. It doesn't mention the doctrine of equivalents. Okay?

* * *

You may not have noticed a tiny little fact about Mr. Akers, their expert, because I am sure you were thinking to yourself, he seemed to testify for the plaintiff. Why does he keep saying all these things? Why is he saying there are other reasons? Why is he saying that the only reason is an insubstantial change? Why is Akers saying that?

Here's one reason for it. Do you remember when he said during his examination that, well, originally he thought there was what's called prosecution history estoppel, but he doesn't think that anymore? I said, your professional opinion is prosecution history estoppel and he said, no.

I said, what is prosecution history estoppel? Isn't that where you make certain arguments and then because you made certain arguments you can't bring a doctrine of equivalents claim and he said that's right. I said, Mr. Akers, do you still believe that and he said, no. What does that mean? That means that prior to today, prior to this trial he was of the view that there is prosecution history estoppel. What did I ask him? I said, okay, now that you had time to think about it, can you have an equivalent and he said, yes, you can have equivalence. That's what he said.

All right, a few more defenses that have been raised that they said they were going to prove. This is their lawyer Mr. Scurry. Let me say right now by the way, what I say Mr. Scurry said is not evidence. It has to be at your recollection. I think I have it right, but if there's anything wrong, it's your memory that will be guiding.

Here is the difference. We have an elliptical shaped football gate member. They have a round cylindrical shaped gate and to say that they're the same thing is to say that catching a softball is the same as catching a football. Again, you can't use a softball and a football example because you are just talking about stationary things. If you take a softball and throw it, that's not stationary. If you take a football and throw it, that's not stationary. Again, if I am just trying to drive a wedge, okay? Someone brings me a softball that has two surfaces or someone brings me a football that has one surface, it doesn't matter, is substantially the same way. The experts agree. So that's one problem with that point.

But there is a bigger problem. Claim 1 literally covers elliptical gate members. Milbrett, Akers, I believe Foudy even said that. Akers. Remember when I drew the shapes and I drew this shape. He said it's literally covered. You can't escape literal infringement by the shape of the gate member. What does that mean? Gross, what are you talking about? I am talking about this. Gate forming member. Gate forming member. Gate forming member means any shape, right? It doesn't say circular.

I said to Mr. Akers and I wanted to be really clear, because again why do I keep asking Akers? Because I want Milbrett and Akers to agree. If the experts on each side agree, your job is much easier. Does a gate forming member include this circle? Yes. Does a gate forming member include this circle? Yes. Does a gate member include a surface? Yes.

Mr. Akers, tell the jury what that is. An ellipse. That means we literally cover their elliptical shaped gate member. Don't be telling us how you got this great shape. We were smart, okay? Our patent counsel was smart because it's a very broad term, gate forming member. Could we have said circular gate forming member? Yes. It would be a completely different claim. In fact, if you look at the other claims, circular gate forming member. Is this a broader claim? Yes. Who said that? Akers.

So for Mr. Scurry to say here is the difference that's not Akers' difference. Akers' difference is just that he had a gate member with a different surface, that's all. Akers' difference is not a shape. You can look at the chart for two hours and you'll never see Akers say also they have an elliptical shaped member which escapes literal coverage. He never said that. He wouldn't be telling the truth and it wasn't a trick question.

So they're running out of defenses. They're showing you evidence out of context. They're showing you evidence that is irrelevant. They're showing you evidence that's refuted. But, again, you can do that but you don't win. If you show the wrong evidence, if you don't prove it, you don't win.

Mr. Liebman said every time you hear mention of defendant's patent, remember this, defendant's own expert did not rely upon that patent. It was not relevant. We proved that to you. I mean, Mr. Akers, he looked at some pictures. He had an associate read to him the history of their patent and he decided it was not going to be a basis for his written opinion. Remember he said that? And it wasn't a basis at his sworn deposition, okay? He didn't do a supplemental written report. It wasn't relevant to his core opinion. He thinks their patent is irrelevant like we do. Mr. Milbrett explained to you why it's irrelevant. It was granted for a different reason. It didn't apply Claim 1.

Mr. Scurry told you that there was an equivalence test and it's the same test required to be used by H. Grant Skaggs, the patent examiner. But Skaggs did not apply Claim 1 to the Machine Systems device. I asked Mr. Akers, did anyone from the Patent office, did he take this claim or she take this claim and apply it to that device? No. What about the equivalence? No. If there was any evidence in the record that that had occurred, then their patent would be relevant and I would be telling you. And if it showed it wasn't the equivalent, we would be telling you that, all right? We only want to win fair and square. We do not want to win through a trick. We want evidence to show why we win. But if they don't have evidence that's relevant, then they can't win. That's not fair.

There wasn't a Claim 1 in the file. I want you to go through their prosecution history, Exhibit 31. Look for Claim 1, it was not even in the file. They didn't even give this to the patent office. Is it fair to say that the examiner essentially applied Claim 1 to that device? No, it isn't. By the way, I asked Mr. Akers, I was very careful. I said, Mr. Akers, was the patent granted because of this change? He said, no it wasn't. Is there any evidence in Exhibit 31 that this change is why they got that patent? No. What's the only relevant change for you? This change. This is what gets them out. Is it fair for them to say, well, we got a patent, patent on an elliptical gate member. Does that matter if it said gate forming member includes an ellipse like Mr. Akers said? That doesn't matter. Mr. Akers said our claim covers an elliptical gate member. The patent examiner looked at the picture, the picture of a Hayseeder patent. A different patent than the '831 patent. So the picture isn't the claim because a picture has a circular gate member.

By the way Mr. Milbrett explained how they amended the claim to add a pivot so their patent was most likely granted because of a pivot, not because of an elliptical shape and if you go to Exhibit 31, you will never see any words like Mr. Skaggs that says that an elliptical shape gate member is the reason for patentability.

It is ironic by the way that their patent doesn't have that statement for reasons and yet they're telling you they know the reasons. And Mr. Akers has said they don't necessarily state all the reasons. You don't even want to imply it. Have they proven to you that their patent was granted for one reason? They don't even have a statement of allowance and there was an amendment about a pivot. They did an amendment in Exhibit 31. You can say you are going to prove something, but then prove it. Show evidence that it was granted for that reason and make it the relevant reason, okay? Make it the relevant reason. Don't say, hey, we have patent on an ellipse and then have Akers say the claim covers an ellipse.

How did we start off this case? Mr. Liebman showed you how we were going to prove infringement. We then proved it. How did they start off the case? From hearing their opening this was a case about a guy named H. Grant Skaggs, a United States patent examiner, as if he were going to testify at trial. Same human being, same umpire calling all the strikes. Same patent examiner. Same patent examiner. H. Grant Skaggs. Same primary patent examiner. H. Grant Skaggs. His actions speak louder than words. By the end of their opening you were ready to hear about H. Grant Skaggs. Did you notice in the closing argument of counsel not a single time did he say, same umpire calling balls and strikes. Same patent examiner. Same patent examiner. Same primary patent examiner. His actions speak louder than words. You know why that is? Because they did not prove that.

MR. SCURRY: Objection. There isn't anything that says we have to prove anything.

THE COURT: Objection overruled. The jury will hear the Court's instructions and review the evidence. You may proceed counsel.

MR. GROSS: We've covered why we proved our case. I am now addressing their defenses and I am showing that their defenses fall apart. We win because of the first fifteen minutes of what I said to you, that all the experts agree. These are their defenses.

That's right. They don't have to prove these, but if they don't, they don't have what's called a defense. If we prove our evidence, we win.

Rolla wrote the office action. Akers said it was false to say somebody else called the balls and strikes in the office action. He said defendant's case is irrelevant. And then we learn that our patent, was not part of the file, was not in the file and was six years before and 709,451 patents before their patent. I am going to ask you this question. Do you think Mr. Skaggs, 800,000 patents later, with no evidence in the record and with a patent not in the file, six years later was applying the claim of that patent? Did they prove that? The reason they didn't say this is because they didn't prove it and it actually turned out to be false. Who said that? Mr. Akers. When both sides experts agree the issue goes away, all right? Then there is no dispute. That's when we've shown infringement.

And when their defense evaporates through their witnesses and our witnesses, then they don't have a defense. That's why Question 1 is an easy yes. Is damages a more tough question? Yes. Depends on members of the community based on the evidence. Is willfulness tough? Yes. We proved it but it's tough. Infringement is not tough when everybody agrees.

Mr. Scurry talked about the inventors had a duty to submit any information. Guess what? He then claimed we didn't submit information. He cross-examined Mr. Milbrett and then I showed Mr. Akers, we actually did submit all our references. Mr. Hamm played by the rules. When he got his patent he gave a bunch of references. Did they submit any references when they went for their patent? No. Did they have a copy of the Hamm patent? Of course. They'd gotten an opinion from Venturini on it, and they didn't give it to the Patent Office. Is it fair for them to say that when they didn't give the patent to the Patent Office, you should find that H. Grant Skaggs knew about this patent which was six years and 800,000 patents before where somebody else is calling the balls and strikes and so therefore they don't infringe? No. That makes no sense.

Last point. Dr. Foudy, their other expert, is irrelevant. He didn't disclose a recent deposition, which I thought was strange. He had one line on a CV that mentions law agencies. It should have said law firms, it was misleading to say law agencies. We all know what law agencies are, right? They're law agencies. I mean they're not law firms, they're agencies, if you've heard of the Justice Department, you have heard of law agencies.

That doesn't make him a bad guy, but it means he was trying to give the impression that he doesn't do a lot of traditional businesses-fighting-each-other litigation. He actually does three court cases per year for twenty years. That's sixty. And look at his CV, Defendant's Exhibit 65, he enters every single thing he has ever done in his life except that he has done sixty cases.

Now he used the wrong test. He required a fourth-level mathematics. He required mathematical proof. There is no support of that in the prior art. Look through the prior art and see if at any time somebody does a complicated mathematical proof. Then he kept his own proof in his head. He never tried it before trial.

For all these reasons we believe the evidence is more than clear that they infringed, because everybody agrees, Dr. Foudy did not address that change. We are entitled to damages based on members of the community and we ask for a finding of willfulness.

Thank you, Your Honor.